NATURE, CHANGE,
AND AGENCY
IN ARISTOTLE'S *PHYSICS*

NATURE, CHANGE, AND AGENCY IN ARISTOTLE'S *PHYSICS*

A Philosophical Study

SARAH WATERLOW

CLARENDON PRESS · OXFORD
1982

Oxford University Press, Walton Street, Oxford OX2 6DP

London Glasgow New York Toronto
Delhi Bombay Calcutta Madras Karachi
Kuala Lumpur Singapore Hong Kong Tokyo
Nairobi Dar es Salaam Cape Town
Melbourne Auckland
and associates in
Beirut Berlin Ibadan Mexico City Nicosia

Published in the United States by
Oxford University Press, New York

British Library Cataloguing in Publication Data
Waterlow, Sarah
Nature, change and agency in Aristotle's Physics.
1. Aristotle. Physics   2. Change
I. Title
116   BD373
ISBN 0-19-824653-6

Library of Congress Cataloging in Publication Data
Waterlow, Sarah.
Nature, change, and agency in Aristotle's Physics.
Bibliography: p.
Includes index.
1. Science, Ancient.   2. Aristotle. Physics.
3. Change.   4. Philosophy of nature.   I. Title.
Q151.W37   509'.38   81-18772
ISBN 0-19-824653-6   AACR2

Set by Hope Services, Abingdon
and Printed in Great Britain at the
University Press, Oxford
by Eric Buckley
Printer to the University

To FREDERICK BROADIE

τροφῆς χάριν

Rome   1. ix. 80

Contents

I

Nature as Inner Principle of Change

(1) The physical doctrines of Aristotle are a disappointing chapter in the history of science . . . The science of the Renaissance period was obliged to shake off the fetters of his authority before it could return to the paths of progressive and fruitful research.

These remarks of Theodor Gomperz[1] voice a common verdict on Aristotle's philosophy of nature. It is not my purpose here to endorse this verdict, nor to challenge it, but to show how the typically Aristotelian doctrines on which it has been passed stem from one fundamental idea. This is the conception of a natural substance as characterized above all by an 'inner principle of change and stasis'. This notion of 'the nature of a thing' links Aristotle's metaphysic of substance to his physical system, and it determines almost every one of that system's distinctive positions. It is the object of the present work to support and illustrate this claim. It will be shown, for instance, how Aristotle's concept of natural substance issues in a theory of living things as irreducibly organic unities, and hence in the rejection of materialism in favour of teleology. The same concept will be seen to generate his doctrine of the simple bodies' 'natural movements' and 'natural places'. Not only Aristotle's cosmology but his chemistry too can be traced back to this principle, and on a more general level it shapes his entire approach to the topics of change and process. This in turn dictates his famous denial of change to agents of change; and from the same source, finally, come the culminating doctrines of eternal motion and an eternal unmoved mover.

The least initial deviation from the truth is multiplied later a thousand-fold . . . The reason is that a principle is great rather in power than in extent; hence that which was small at the start turns out a giant at the

---

[1] *The Greek Thinkers*, vol. IV, p. 108.

end. (*De Caelo* I.5, 271b8 ff., tr. J.L. Stocks)[2]

The words with which Aristotle prefaces his attack on the notion of infinite body could be aptly quoted back at him with reference, this time, to his own conception of natural substance. But whether or not this represents an 'initial deviation from the truth', I hope here to show that for good or ill in Aristotle's system it 'turns out a giant at the end'.

(2) Let us then turn to the passage where Aristotle introduces this concept, at the beginning of *Physics* II.1:

Of things that exist, some exist by nature and some through other causes. By nature there exist animals and their parts and plants and the simple bodies such as earth, fire, air and water. For these and similar things we say exist by nature. All these things manifestly differ from those not constituted by nature. For each of them has within itself a principle of change and stasis, some in respect of place, some in respect of growth and decline, some in respect of alteration. But a bed and a cloak and any similar kind of thing, so far as such a description holds of it, and to the extent that it exists through artifice, possesses no innate impulse of change. But so far as they happen to be made of stone or earth or mixtures of these, they possess such an impulse, and just to that extent. This suggests that nature is a principle and cause of change and stasis in the thing in which it primarily subsists, being in this thing of itself and not *per accidens*. (192b8-23)

Now, apart from nature, Aristotle recognizes two other types of cause: artifice, and 'the spontaneous' (or coincidence).[3] The latter, which we might well hesitate to count as a *cause* at all (for reasons of which Aristotle was aware), receives no attention in this opening passage. The reason is simple: whether or not 'the spontaneous' is rightly called a 'cause', it is a secondary concept, defined in terms of the concurrence of causally independent factors, which factors have their causes either in human intention or in the nature of a natural substance. Assuming that in the present passage Aristotle is loosely using 'artifice' to cover all the cases in which a new state of affairs is brought about through skill, we can say that he here makes an exhaustive dichotomy of the primary types

    [2] Where there is no acknowledgement to the contrary, translations from Aristotle are my own.

    [3] On this triple division of causes and its Platonic antecedents, see A. Mansion, *Introduction à la Physique Aristotélieienne*, pp. 94-7.

of cause. However, the products of skill that mainly focus his attention are *artefacts* in the ordinary sense, objects such as beds and clothes, rather than conditions such as the health of a naturally sickly person or skilled activities like dancing.

(3) That the products of nature and artifice form mutually exclusive classes is a datum of common sense which Aristotle does not question. He does not for instance speculate on possible reasons for regarding natural beings as artefacts of some supernatural agent like Plato's Demiurgus. This accords with Aristotle's general insistence, evident in the *Physics* as elsewhere, that every type of enquiry be conducted in terms of concepts and methods appropriate to its subject matter, and confine itself to the questions that fall within its scope. Even if nature could be looked upon as an artefact or system of artefacts (which Aristotle has good reason to hold that it cannot),[4] such a point of view would lie outside the province of natural science. For the super-artificer himself, his purpose, and the materials he may be supposed to have used, are all, *ex hypothesi*, factors outwith the world of nature. It is not therefore to be expected that either the scientist or the philosopher seeking to clarify the concepts essential to science, should do otherwise than take it for granted that water and earth, animals and plants, are not artefacts; it not being their business to question this on theological grounds, any more than it is their business to discuss the Eleatic Theory 'that Being is one and motionless' (*Physics* I.2, 184b25-185a3).

(4) Leaving aside then the metaphysical possibility that human artificers are themselves (divine) artefacts and therefore similar or at least analogous to the artefacts which they themselves construct, we can say that the artefacts of ordinary experience differ radically from natural objects both in their causes and in their power to cause other things. For artefacts are made by the skill of beings not artefacts like themselves, whereas natural beings come into existence only from other natural beings. Artefacts moreover are not in turn artificers, and nor do they need to be for further artefacts to

[4] Cf. *Metaphysics* A9, 991a20-3. Also *v.i.* Ch. II, paras (4) and (27), and n.23.

be produced; whereas natural beings generated by other natural beings must in turn possess the power to generate others, since apart from themselves there is no source from which further natural beings could continue to come into existence. And if the *production* of natural beings depends not on the activity of an agent or agents outside the order of nature, but only on other natural beings, the same must be true of the *changes* necessarily involved in production. A new substance comes into existence through processes of change in substances already existing, and unless these changes can be accounted for from within the world of nature, the new substance itself cannot be so accounted for either. Thus the world of nature, unlike the artificial environment, is self-contained as regards production and the changes necessary for production.

(5) It is plain then that natural substances collectively speaking contain within themselves a principle or principles of change. This follows from the self-sufficiency of the natural order to keep and have kept itself going. The concept of principles that are 'inner' in this collective sense is uncontroversial for all who believe in the very possibility of science, i.e. in the possibility of explaining (in some sense of 'explain') natural phenomena in terms of natural phenomena. However, Aristotle's inner principles are also supposed by him to be 'inner' in the stronger and by no means so obviously acceptable sense of 'intrinsic to each individual substance'. The notion of the self-sufficiency of nature as a whole appears quite compatible with the view that any change in any object results from the action of external factors happening to stand to that object in the appropriate spatial and temporal relations. On this view, the cause of change, in any given case, is as much external to the object changed as artificer to artefact. It is precisely this that Aristotle is denying when he speaks of an 'innate impulse' (ὅρμη ἔμφυτος) of change; for if the impulse is innate, present in the object from inception, then it and its results are not imparted by anything external.

(6) We now have to consider in detail what sense can be given

to this notion of 'innate impulse' of change. Aristotle apparently regards the phrase as requiring no special justification or analysis. On the common-sense level we no doubt often distinguish changes in which the changing object seems to change of itself from those where it appears inert and passive, itself contributing nothing to what happens. But this distinction remains unproblematic only so long as we ignore the fact that every change in the natural world depends to some extent on external conditions, even if only on the absence of obstructions. If every change is externally conditioned, then in what sense can any be said to come especially "from within" the object?

(7) In attempting an account of Aristotle's concept of change from an inner principle, we shall find it useful to consider two limiting notions: (a) that of change entirely beyond the power of external conditions to affect; (b) that of change entirely dependent on such conditions. I call these 'limiting' since each represents a conceptual extreme not coherently applicable to any change having place in a system of natural phenomena. A change fitting the first description would be *either* such as could occur under any external conditions whatever, *or else* caused by something which also had absolute control of the external conditions so as to ensure that they are always disposed in ways permitting the change. On either alternative, the change could be neither interrupted nor deflected. Its cause would be so to speak omnipotent so far as this change is concerned. But in that case the change is not part of a system of natural events. For either there are no external conditions of any causal relevance (which would be true only if it were itself identical with the sum of events in nature, or alternatively formed an entirely separate system on its own); or else the change is caused by some being with supernatural power to prevent natural obstructions.

(8) Suppose on the other hand an object with changes entirely shaped by external conditions: that is to say, an object which has no character or nature of its own either to determine or to limit what takes place in it: indeed, it is no more than a "place" of change, resembling the space of Plato's

Timaeus (and for that matter of Newtonian mechanics) in its total indifference as regards what can happen in it. (For Aristotle, not even space, or place, itself is like this, let alone substances.) If change were possible at all in a universe of such objects, then everything would change in the same way under the same conditions, since only the conditions would determine change. But why should there be change at all in such a universe? The objects as we have described them are of infinite potentiality. For there can be no property that any of them by its nature is excluded from possessing, since this would imply a limitation on the changes that they could undergo. In such a universe, then, an object can have any property logically compatible with its other properties at the time. Thus if a change occurs when certain conditions arise, it cannot be said to have occurred because, under these new conditions, the object *could* not remain in the state it was in before, as for instance we say that wax *cannot* stay hard if heated beyond a certain point. It is logically true that if wax when heated softens then heated wax cannot stay hard; but there is no logical necessity (nor, in such a world, necessity of any other kind) for heated wax to soften. So why should it? Moreover, objects lacking any character to determine their reactions to other beings can hardly be supposed to possess a character to determine the reactions of others to them. Therefore in such a universe nothing determines any specific change to happen that does happen, and there is nothing to explain why it should have happened.

(9) Aristotle proclaims his rejection of any such view of the actual world in *Physics* I.5:

We must first lay it down that no existent thing is such that any chance thing can act on or be acted on by any chance thing, nor does any chance thing come to be from any chance thing, unless one describes the situation in accidental terms. (188 a31–4)

By 'any chance thing' he means a thing such that its role in a given change situation might just as well have been filled by anything else. This is precisely what would be true of everything if nothing had any intrinsic character determining the changes it undergoes or produces. A given agent or patient can of course be described in terms denoting properties that are irrelevant ('accidental'), but there would not *be* an agent and patient acting and being acted upon unless they were also truly describable in terms of characteristics in which the causal relationship is grounded. Aristotle continues:

For how could what is white come from what is cultured, except in the sense that being cultured might be accidentally conjoined with being not-white or black? Instead, what is white comes from what is not white, and not from anything not white but from what is black or of an intermediate colour, and what is cultured comes from what is not cultured, but not from anything not cultured, but from the uncultured or some intermediate state. (a35–b3)

At first sight Aristotle seems to be making a purely logical point, namely that the coming into being of X presupposes the prior absence or non-being of X. Thus it is incorrect (although not necessarily false) to say that white comes into being from cultured, for being cultured does not mean or entail being non-white. If we are told that up to a certain moment something was cultured, and that after that it was white, we cannot infer that there was a change, since the statement is consistent with the presence of whiteness before the moment in question. However Aristotle is not only saying that the coming to be of white should be described in a way that makes it clear that the whiteness replaces its own prior absence. For white does not come from 'anything not white, but from what is black or of an intermediate colour'. Not everything of which 'not-white' holds true can give place to white: a geometrical point is not white but cannot come to be white. Thus the not-white from which white comes to be must be such that white *can* come to be from it; it must be an opposite or intermediate in the same range. And the range, we have seen, has a narrower field of application than the field within which 'not-white' could apply. Thus the patient or subject of the change to white is already more than a mere locus of change: it is *such as to* admit the range black–white: it has to this extent a character that marks off its kind from just everything else; and this differentiating characteristic is not the result of change, but its precondition.

(10) In paragraph (8) it was argued that the concept of an

object changing in ways entirely undetermined by a character of its own makes it nonsense to attempt to explain why any given change in it should occur. But one can also show that for Aristotle this concept would make nonsense of change itself, not merely of explanation. Some of his predecessors had found change to be so paradoxical that they preferred to turn away from the study of nature (which, he implies, they would otherwise have pursued) rather than accept the paradox. Aristotle remarks on the lack of sophistication which led them into the difficulty, but he in no way suggests that having once been gripped by it they were wrong to take it so seriously. From this we may assume that he regards it as a problem requiring to be solved before the concept of change can be accepted as sound and coherent. I shall now argue that his own solution depends on the very same conception of objects in nature as led him to say in the passage already quoted that not any chance thing acts on or is acted on by any chance thing.

(11) The first investigators into the truth and nature of things were so to say diverted on to a different path, being forced back through their naivety (ὑπὸ ἀπειρίας). They say that nothing that exists either comes into being or passes away, because it is necessary that what comes into being comes into being either out of being or out of not being, and yet from either of these it is impossible that it should be. For that which is does not come into being, since it already is, and nothing could come into being from not being, since there must be some underlying subject. (I.8, 191a24–31)[5]

The last remark, 'there must be some underlying subject', is Aristotle's comment in *propria persona*, rather than a description of the difficulty as it presented itself to the earlier thinkers. The expression 'underlying subject' is his, not theirs, and the clause in which it occurs does not, as might first appear, pose one side of the ancient dilemma; on the contrary, it carries Aristotle's own solution.[6] Yet the phrase is not entirely out of place in this brief account of the paradox,

---

[5] Cf. *Physics* I.4, 187a26–9, 32–5; 8, 191b31–3.

[6] On this example of Aristotle's 'reading his own doctrine into earlier systems', see H. Cherniss, *Aristotle's Criticism of Presocratic Philosophy*, pp. 53 ff.; F. Solmsen, *Aristotle's System of the Physical World*, pp. 81–2. On the general tendency see Cherniss, op. cit., pp. 348, 354–5.

because it reflects a conceptual requirement to which the earlier thinkers were no less sensitive than Aristotle himself, although unlike him they could not see how it was to be reconciled with the fact of *change*. In expounding the problem we must begin by recasting the requirement that there be 'some underlying subject' in imprecise terms that will capture some of the original puzzlement. It was a nebulous thought that generated the difficulty, and once its vague bearings are distinguished and accurately articulated, the logical mystery of change vanishes, or so Aristotle believes. On the one hand, let us then say, if X comes into being, X could not have existed before, since X would then be nothing new in the world, and would not have *come* to be. But on the other hand it is impossible to accept that the X which comes into being was not somehow rooted in what went before: but in what? If we say: in things other than X, this leaves us no better off than if we had said: in nothing at all. For things other than X, whatever they are, are themselves, they are not X, and so for them to be themselves and to exist there is no need for X. If there was a time when there were only things other than X, then X was no more present among them than it would have been present in a state of affairs in which nothing at all was the case. So if X comes into being but is at the same time rooted in what went before, it cannot have been rooted in nothing, nor in what was other than itself; so the only remaining possibility is in *itself*: but not in its own prior non-existence (for if this made sense, so would either of the two rejected possibilities); therefore in itself as previously existing. Thus it must have been before coming to be, and therefore did not come to be.

(12) From the very first, Aristotle tells us, this dilemma shaped attempts to philosophize about change and becoming. He himself, as his own approach shows, saw the paradox as defining a necessary adequacy-condition for any theory of change: whatever else a theory might offer, it must at least solve or dissolve the paradox. It is no accident, then, that many of the forerunners who refused to draw the Eleatic conclusion that change and becoming are impossible, should have built their theories round the concept of opposites.

(Even Parmenides described the "illusion" of becoming in terms of opposite poles.) For this concept seems to solve the problem. Let us consider how it might appear to do this. There are at least three conceptual advantages in equating X's coming into being with X's coming into being from the opposite of X, say A. Firstly, this permits us to say that before X came into being, there was not X, but its opposite. Secondly, *what* existed prior to X's coming into being, namely A, can be positively described as 'A', not merely as something other than X, or as the absence of X, or as not-X. Thirdly, the positive description 'A' necessarily implies a reference to X, the opposite. For an opposite must necessarily be one of a pair; without one there could not be the other; thus A, even though it is not-X and is other than X, does require that X should exist in order to be A and exist itself. We ourselves are too acutely aware of the difference between logical and causal relations to find this convincing; but such would be the considerations that led those earlier thinkers to see contrariety or opposition as providing a middle way between the impossible alternatives whereby X must either come to be from what is already X, or from what is not-X and other than X and therefore devoid of any connection with X.

(13) Yet that very relationship between opposites that seems to undercut the dilemma also permits its reformulation in stronger terms than ever. If opposites of necessity exclude *each other*, so that each in itself seems to point to the other, they also *exclude* each other. One cannot be present when the other is, and from this point of view each depends on the other's *not* existing and continuing not to exist. How then can opposition begin to explain coming *into* existence? How can X come into existence from what is not only not X, but so alien to it that its own continuation even depends on there being no X? No reality can be so internally incoherent as to tend, of its own nature, towards its own non-existence; yet (as Aristotle points out in connection with the Platonists' account of change, *Physics* I.9, 192a19–22) this is exactly what coming to be would entail if opposite were generated

out of opposite.[7] If the thinkers who were content to analyse coming to be in terms of opposites did not see this, it may partly have been because of the ambiguity of 'out of' (ἐκ). The distinction of meaning which concerns us here is between (a) the sense in which what X comes to be 'out of' continues present in X when X has come to be; and (b) that in which what X comes to be 'out of' is superseded when X has come to be. Let us call the first sense *constitutive*, the second *non-constitutive*. Further distinctions are possible within these senses, at any rate within the latter. The first corresponds to Aristotle's material cause, the second covers both the efficient cause and the opposite or contrary from which a change proceeds. Both the contrary and the efficient cause cease as such to exist when X has come to be and as such they are not present in X. In *Metaphysics* A 4, 985a10 ff., Aristotle comments on the weakness of his predecessors' grasp of the difference between material and efficient cause: that is, between the constitutive and one of the non-constitutive senses of 'out of'. But if these could be confused, so could the constitutive with the other non-constitutive sense, that which applies to the opposite superseded in change. Hence it may not have seemed so obvious that the coming to be of opposite X out of opposite A means the destruction of A in favour of X. A may seem still to be present as a constituent of X, so that despite the opposition there is continuity of existence.[8] Better still if we can think of A itself as having come to be from an earlier X; for A then seems to have that X as *its* constituent, so it is no surprise if a new X comes to be from A: what more suitable material for the second X than something already made of the first?

(14) But this semblance of intelligibility vanishes on a clearer view of the ambiguities of 'out of'. There is then no ignoring the mutual exclusiveness of opposites, nor the impotence of this relation to solve unaided the original paradox. The only escape, Aristotle maintains (I.8, 191a23-4), is through his

---

[7] W.D. Ross, *Aristotle's Physics*, p. 23; Mansion, p. 276.
[8] Cf. *Physics* I.4, 187a31 ff.

own analysis of becoming.[9] This is more properly termed an analysis of the language of becoming,[10] since the evidence to which he appeals consists in 'what is said' ('φαμέν', 189b32; 'φῶμεν', 190a4-5; 'λέγεται', 5-6; 'λέγομεν', 9). He means in effect to show that the conception revealed in ordinary modes of speech coherently satisfies both sides of the ancient dilemma. It is doubtful whether Aristotle would ever have raised the question whether or how we can know that the thought-structures expressed in our language reflect corresponding structures in reality. But it is fairly certain that even if he had framed this question, it would not have seemed to him the concern of the philosopher of science, whose task is simply to clarify as science requires the conceptual data of which we are all already dimly possessed (cf. *Physics* I.1, 184a16-b14).

(15) Aristotle's analysis begins as follows (I.7, 189b32-190b 21): sentences of the form '— becomes —' are of three types. In two of them what occurs on either side of the verb is a simple term; thus:

(i) (A/The) man becomes cultured.

(ii) (A/The) uncultured becomes cultured.

In the third type what occurs on each side is a complex term:

(iii) (A/The) uncultured man becomes (a) cultured man.

---

[9] The reduction of all change to locomotion of particles might seem to offer another way out, since it is clear that in locomotion no new *thing* (i.e. subject of change) comes to be. Moreover the mathematical continuity of abstract motion entails a sense in which a new arrangement B of particles can never be said to supersede any single specifiable different arrangement A, since between any two there was another. Thus B comes to be neither 'from' itself nor 'from' any condition *definitely not* itself, and so the paradox can perhaps be avoided. (This point was suggested by remarks of Prof. G.E.L. Owen.) But for Aristotle the reduction to locomotion is ruled out: *v.i.* Ch. II, paras (35) ff. and Ch. III, para. (8).

[10] Cf. W. Wieland, 'Das Problem des Principienforschung und die aristotelische Physic', *Kant-Studien* LII, 1960-1, pp. 206 ff. especially pp. 212-13 and 216-19 (the translated article is Ch. 8 in *Articles on Aristotle*, vol. I, edd. Barnes, Schofield, and Sorabji). See also B. Jones, 'Aristotle's Introduction of Matter', *Philosophical Review* LXXXIII, 1974, pp. 474 ff. On the general approach see G.E.L. Owen, 'τιθέναι τὰ φαινόμενα', *Aristote et les Problèmes de la Méthode*, ed. S. Mansion, reprinted in *Aristotle*, ed. Moravcsik, pp. 167 ff.

These sentences are obviously descriptions of one and the same fact. This is a vital premiss of Aristotle's argument, although he does not enunciate it. Now sentence (ii) displays the fact that becoming involves replacement: the uncultured that becomes cultured cannot still be uncultured; nor can it already have been cultured: this is ruled out by the mutual exclusion of contraries. Sentence (iii) displays the fact that becoming involves an element that is present both before and after. The complex term 'uncultured man' represents a whole which is replaced by the whole corresponding to 'cultured man'. But these two wholes each have an element corresponding to 'man'. And man in one whole is not to be thought of as replaced by man in the other, since 'man' and 'man' are neither contradictories not contraries. Sentence (i), on the other hand, displays neither replacement not continuance. The terms on each side are not contraries, nor are they the same or the same in part. Yet the fact described by (i) is truly described by (ii) and (iii). We may draw two conclusions: (a) Becoming always involves each of the two aspects severally displayed by sentences of types (ii) and (iii), even though this may not always be apparent (as when the description is given by a sentence of type (i)). (b) The replacement aspect must be compatible with the continuance aspect, since the same fact can be described from either point of view.

(16) Let us sum up the position reached so far in Aristotle's own words:

These distinctions drawn [sc. between sentences (i), (ii) and (iii)] , one can see that in all cases of becoming, if we examine them in the way suggested, there must always be something that underlies, viz. that which becomes, and although this is numerically one it is not one in form. (By 'one in form (εἴδει)' I mean the same as 'one in formula (λόγῳ)'.) For it is not the same to be (a) man and to be uncultured. And one of these remains while the other does not remain. That which is not an opposite (viz. the man) remains, whereas the not-cultured and the uncultured does not remain, nor does that which is a combination of them both, i.e. the uncultured man. (190a13–21)

Let us say that just as a sentence such as (i) above represents a *fact*, so the expressions occurring on the right- and left-hand sides of the verb in (i) represent *components* of this fact. Then just as sentences (ii) and (iii) represent the same

fact as (i), but under different descriptions, so the left-hand
and the right-hand sides of (ii) and (iii) represent the same
components as the corresponding sides of (i), but under
different descriptions. Thus although 'uncultured' does not
"remain" (i.e. it cannot coherently be added to the right-hand
formula in any of the sentences), another description, 'man',
of the same component does "remain". Thus the same thing
(component) remains under one description though not
under the other. By similar reasoning, from the fact that
'man' remains it does not follow that another description,
e.g. 'uncultured', also remains.

(17) This analysis is the basis for Aristotle's solution of the
traditional paradox of becoming. It is not in itself the solution, nor does he think that it is, as his order of presentation
makes plain. After reaching the position just outlined and
showing how it applies to various kinds of becoming illustrated by a variety of examples (I.7, 190a31–191a3), he then
turns to the paradox and makes further distinctions in order
to answer it (I.8, 191a23–b27).[11] As the Wicksteed-Cornford
translation says, 'At this critical point of Aristotle's exposition, the text, as we have it, is elliptical almost to the point
of unintelligibility'.[12] I shall therefore presently offer a para-
phrase. But it will help too if we first consider (not that Aristotle explicitly does this) how the above analysis cannot as
it stands provide a solution. Now the analysis does succeed in
showing how the same fact of becoming, and the same components of that fact, are and must be describable in different
ways which between them reveal both the replacement and
the continuity involved. No doubt vagueness concerning the

---

[11] However the answer is partly anticipated at I.7, 190b17–27. Cf. W. Charlton, *Aristotle's Physics I, and II*, pp. 46–7.

[12] Loeb text *Aristotle, The Physics*, vol. I, p. 83. Small wonder if Aristotle is 'clumsy' here (the charge of Charlton, p. 80). Without technical vocabulary he must (*a*) make the distinction between what in the text I call appropriate and in-appropriate descriptions; (*b*) differentiate between grammatical subject and com-plement of 'γίγνεσθαι' (either of which may be meant by 'τὸ γιγνόμενον'); (*c*) manage the different senses of 'ἐκ' (*v.s.* para. (13)); (*d*) (in my view, although not according to all interpretations) shift the scope of 'κατὰ συμβεβηκός' from subject to complement of 'γίγνεται' (*v.i.* n. 13).

distinction between difference of *description* and difference of *things described* contributed to the early thinkers' perplexity about becoming (and every other topic too, one would suppose). But even if they had fully grasped that distinction, they could still have put the paradox, as follows: We accept that sentences (i), (ii), and (iii) describe the same fact. But what a survey of these sentences shows is that this fact cannot be fully described without absurdity. Take sentence (iii), '(A/The) uncultured man becomes (a) cultured man'. From this one can derive (ii): '(A/The) uncultured becomes cultured'. And one can also derive another (iv): '(A/ The) man becomes (something that is a) man'. Now (ii) and (iv) each represent one side of the original dilemma whereby something either comes to be from its own opposite, which we saw to be unintelligible, or from what it already is, which is self-contradictory. All that Aristotle has done so far is to show that the paradox is by no means a recherché one which reveals itself only to those who abandon ordinary speech for some esoteric terminology. On the contrary, ordinary discourse shows it up in all its force; and while the ordinariness may explain why the man in the street is untroubled, since he naturally feels at home in his modes of thinking, it cannot mitigate the objective problem; if anything, the paradox is all the more unnerving now it is found to lie at the heart of our untutored responses to the world. The philosopher who sees this will not stop at wondering how *change* is possible: for the incoherence of a notion so central to the human picture of the world casts doubt on all our claims to knowledge. Who could confidently assert even the Eleatic alternative once he has realized the extent to which we are constituted by nature to utter meaningless statements without suspicion of their meaninglessness? Who having seen this can be sure that he can acquire knowledge of anything?

(18) Thus in upholding the reality of change and becoming, Aristotle is also defending our title to consider ourselves potential knowers, rather than beings incapable of registering reality except through meaningless responses to an unintelligible environment. But how does he escape this last formulation of the paradox? His answer (and here I paraphase) is

this. Different sentences may describe the same state of affairs; different terms may stand for the same thing. The sentences may all be true, and the terms may all be true *of* their referent. The sentences and terms are all meaningful, although the meanings differ. But this does not entail that meaningful and true descriptions of the same state of affairs are all equally appropriate, or that all equally reveal the structure of the fact. It may be true to say that the physician builds a house, or that the architect gives orders to the physician, but the fact described would be better portrayed by 'The builder builds a house' etc., even though the other statements are not false if the builder happens also to be a medical man. Seeming paradoxes result if we assume that every description is equally appropriate. Thus the sentence 'The patient dictates a programme for his medical adviser' may be true, but taken as the proper description it is paradoxical, since it seems to contradict what (by the very meaning of 'medical adviser' etc.) we take to be the normal and rational state of affairs. The difficulty disappears once we see that its truth derives from that of certain unparadoxical sentences, viz. (*a*) 'The architect dictates a programme to the builder'; (*b*) 'The builder is also the medical expert'; (*c*) 'The architect is one of the medical expert's patients'.

(19) To continue: There are appropriate and inappropriate descriptions of becoming. This is because the left-hand and right-hand sides of a 'becomes' sentence can be filled by appropriate and inappropriate descriptions. (By 'appropriate and inappropriate descriptions' here, I mean descriptions which are appropriate or not for the position assigned them in the '— becomes —' matrix.) Now the term appropriate for the left-hand side is the one which in sentences of types (iii) and (iv) above appears on both sides. The term appropriate for the right-hand side is the one which appears on the right in sentences such as (ii) and (iii), replacing a contrary or contradictory term on the left. Thus the appropriate sentence for describing becoming is of the form of (i): '(A/The) man becomes cultured'. Paradox results if we (*a*) assume that all sentences give equally appropriate descriptions, while (*b*) implicitly acknowledging two principles already hinted at in

the above remarks. These two principles are firstly, that that which "does" the becoming, i.e. which corresponds to the grammatical subject, and whose description appears on the left, *remains*; and secondly, that that which the latter becomes (corresponding to the grammatical complement), whose description appears on the right, *replaces* something previously present. If these principles are let loose on the assumption that all descriptions are equally appropriate, we get the following absurdities: (*a*) Since '(A/The) uncultured becomes cultured' is (by the assumption) appropriate, it follows that the process results in something both cultured and uncultured (since by the first principle what appears on the left in an appropriate description also remains). We then are forced to reason that what is supposed to remain does not do so in fact, since opposites would be true together; or else that opposites somehow are true together, perhaps because one manages to persist as the "matter" of the other. (*b*) Since '(A/The) man becomes (something that is a) man' is (by the assumption) appropriate, it follows that what does the becoming was both a man and not (something that was) a man before the change, since by the second principle what is mentioned on the right in an appropriate description replaces its own opposite or contradictory. We have then to conclude either that nothing can really be replaced in becoming, since the presumed replacee (not-man) can only have been there to *be* replaced if the same being was both man and not-man; or else that there *is* replacement and the same being *was* both man and not-man.

(20) Such are the troubles kept at bay by Aristotle's conclusion that on the appropriate description ('κυρίως'), that which comes into being does not come to be out of not being: and that which is does not come to be out of being (I.8, 191a34–b27). As I read the passage,[13] Aristotle is here using

---

[13] Fortunately commentators agree on the main drift although not on details of interpretation. On top of the general obscurity there is a textual doubt at 191b20–1, although choice of reading here seems not to affect the main point of the argument. The interpretation I have chosen to expound in para. (20) assumes (*pace* Mansion, p. 76) that 'ἐκ' has the same (constitutive) meaning in both halves of Aristotle's reply: (i) 'ἡμεῖς δὲ καὶ αὐτοί φαμεν γίγνεσθαι μηθὲν ἁπλῶς ἐκ μὴ ὄντος . . . (ii) ὡσαύτως δὲ οὐδ' ἐξ ὄντος οὐδὲ τὸ ὂν γίγνεσθαι' (191b13 ff.; 'ἁπλῶς'

'out of' in the constitutive sense (*v.s.* para. (13)). The product of coming to be, say the cultured man, is a complex "made out of" (= whose continuing constituent is) a man (as a statue is made out of bronze). In this sense of 'out of', that out of which is what I spoke of as "doing" the becoming (*v.s.* para. (19)), or as corresponding to the grammatical subject. So Aristotle is saying that what does the becoming should properly be described as what it was, is, and will be before, through, and after the change, i.e. as 'man', although it would not be false to describe it as not being what it will become, i.e. as 'not cultured'. And he is also saying that what does the becoming should properly be described as becoming what (as yet) it is not (cultured), although it would not be false to say that it comes to be what it is (a man; since what it comes to be *is* a certain sort of man — a cultured one). The wielders of the paradox obtained their weaponry by seizing on these not-false descriptions and treating them as *best* descriptions.

(21) We must ask: Has Aristotle any ground for his preference of descriptions of type (i), 'A/The man becomes cultured', aside from the fact that once these are accepted as uniquely appropriate, the paradox cannot be sustained? If not, is he not begging the question in his own favour? Adherents of the paradox, if they were alert, could flatly deny the superiority of type-(i) descriptions; they might hold that types (ii) and (iv) are not merely as good but better, since they, unlike (i), do not allow you to overlook the paradox, which after all is still there! But does Aristotle need to give a further reason for preferring type (i), once he has shown that the 'phenomena' make sense if it is preferred, not otherwise?[14] If anybody needs to have it proved to him that it

---

or an equivalent should be supplied in (ii)). This entails that in the corresponding 'κατὰ συμβεβηκός' clauses the scope of 'κατὰ συμβεβηκός' shifts from the grammatical subject (in (i)) to the complement (in (ii)) of 'γίγνεται'. At 191b20-1 I would keep the MSS reading; the oddity of the example makes this the *lectio difficilior* as compared with Laas' emendation, and the latter yields a poor sense for the argument: witness the struggles of Ross, who adopts it (op. cit., pp. 495-6), and Charlton (op. cit., pp. 80-1; Charlton however seems less convinced of the MSS' wrongness).

[14] Cf. *Eth. Nic.* VII.1, 1145b6-7, referred to by Owen, 'Τιθέναι τὰ φαινόμενα' Moravcsik, p. 173.

makes most sense (whether in conceptual analysis or in science) to choose the account which itself makes most sense of the data, then his plight is not that of the early puzzlers whom Aristotle describes as students of nature *manqués*, 'forced back' by the paradox of becoming. A *hindrance* exists only for those who desire some goal, and they, once a path is cleared, do not require to be further persuaded of the rationality of following it.

(22) Yet Aristotle is speaking not only to would-be scientists waiting to be reassured that the language of becoming is logically coherent. His most attentive listeners have always included those whose principal concern has been to understand the very possibility of becoming itself. For them the discussion has only just started. What Aristotle has shown so far, on our exposition, is that whether or not becoming and change are possible in themselves, the concepts cannot be condemned on the ground that they generate inconsistencies. But it is one thing to have it proved that a concept breaks no logical rules, another to have it explained what must be the case if that concept has real application. No doubt in this instance we cannot help believing that it does; but then the question is: what must be the case for the world to be in this respect as we cannot help believing it? To give this question more of an edge, let us now focus on a problem which the argument so far has left completely unanswered.

(23) Granted that "something remains" on the above analysis, how does this meet the paradox, when the paradox centres precisely on the fact that something is supposed to come into being that was not in being before? For apart from whatever can be shown to remain, there must be something new too, or we should not be dealing with *becoming*. But if there was a problem in the first place, how can there not be one still — not, perhaps, about everything that earlier seemed so puzzling, but at least about the nuclear requirement that in becoming there should occur *something* whose presence replaces its own absence. And if this needs no solution, whether by comparing sentences of ordinary discourse or by some other means, then why was there a difficulty in the first place?

(24) The point may be put as follows. Aristotle's explicit analysis is devoted to showing how something can be *coherently said* to remain the same through becoming in a way that yet makes room for change. But this surely leaves unexplained how anything *can* become cultured from uncultured, or how a man *can* "become" anything but what he always was, a man. The difficulty is this. If the uncultured becomes cultured, then why should we not say that what 'cultured' stands for has come into being, not having existed before? If there is no difficulty about this, then why was it so important to show that anything remained throughout? And how does it help to point out that what 'man' stands for remains throughout? This only means that there is no immediate difficulty with respect to 'man', since 'man' in this context does not represent anything that is supposed to appear where it previously was not. But it does not mean that there is no difficulty with respect to the new appearance of what does newly appear, namely whatever corresponds to 'cultured'. Now Aristotle would doubtless say that he has already given an answer, in stating in I.7, 190a15-17 and b24-5 that the man and the cultured are the same in number (the same individual) although not in formula. Therefore, he would say, it is false that what 'cultured' stands for suddenly appears in existence, since it stands for what 'man' also stands for, and this, it is agreed, was there all along. Now this answer could be made more sophisticated (e.g. by recasting in terms of the modern sense/reference distinction), but it seems to take care of the question. But it does not as it stands provide the rationale of the question's being taken care of in this way.

(25) Aristotle has not, in other words, explained why it is not legitimate to think of 'cultured' as referring to a new existent or thing. If it were, then 'uncultured' presumably would refer to a past existent. The uncultured would be a thing that no longer exists, the cultured would have started to exist. The cultured man who comes to be according to sentences of type (iii) would be a conjunction of two existents: a man, present all along, newly joined by a *cultured* appearing where previously it was not. The becoming of the cultured, then, is

really out of nothing, for what 'cultured' applies to is not identical with anything that existed before 'cultured' acquired a hold on the world. If the man is conceived of as a distinct thing from the cultured, the fact that the man pre-existed does not soften the *ex nihilo* arrival of the latter. But once the problem is set out in this way, it answers itself (as doubtless Aristotle expected it to). We have to regard 'cultured' as true now of something that pre-existed, otherwise the cultured is indeed a thing which comes from nothing. 'Cultured' therefore has to be true now of something, X, of which something else was also true (since otherwise X would have had no character, hence have been nothing at all, before 'cultured' became true of it). Presumably, 'uncultured' was true of X before 'cultured' was. But that which 'cultured' is now true of, and which existed before, cannot simply be identified as that of which 'uncultured' was previously true. For that too would mean that 'cultured' came to hold of something in itself characterless, which existed through the replacement of 'uncultured' by 'cultured' but without fulfilling any one description of its own during this change-over. The X, then, to which 'cultured' now applies must be describable by some such term as 'man', which was true of it even when 'uncultured' was true.

(26) But now if the difficulty seems to have evaporated of the cultured coming into being where previously it was not, this is because the cultured is no longer regarded as a distinct existent from the man. But still, when 'cultured' comes to apply, *something* new happens, only not the emergence of a new thing. We have to say that what 'cultured' imports when it starts to apply is not nothing at all, but not a thing either: in other words, it is a property of a thing, whether quality, quantity, relation, or whatever, so long as its category is not that of *things* or substances. And the difference that is now being driven home between things, and properties in other categories, is that the new appearance of the latter where previously they were lacking is not the paradox of 'something out of nothing' that it would be if such properties were things in their own right. Thus the distinction between things and properties furnishes us with an answer against those who

accuse becoming of entailing '*ex nihilo*'. We can now say that in every change there is a genuine some*thing*, which does not come to be in that change (so that for it the problem does not arise), and in every change there is also what is not really some *thing* at all, so that although *it* does come to be where previously it was not, the problem does not apply to it either.

(27) We have seen that the subject X underlying first the absence then the presence of culture must be characterizable; otherwise it could as well be nothing at all. Aristotle's analysis of the ordinary language 'becoming' sentences bore out this metaphysical point, since he proved on this level that something remains by pointing to the recurrence of the same *general* term 'man' on either side of the verb in (iii). But it is not enough to say that X must be characterizable by a general term. The term must import some characteristic C whose instances are substantial individuals *qua* instances of C. By contrast, a quality such as culture is exemplified by individuals already so constituted by the instantiation in them of some other characteristic. If it were not so, becoming cultured would *ipso facto* absurdly imply the coming to be of a new substance whose essence would be culture. Let us call the former type of characteristic 'substance-constitutive', meaning that the individual characterized is thereby constituted a substance of the sort that it is. It is now clear that the possibility of change and becoming depends upon the metaphysical distinction between things and properties that are not things, and hence also on the distinction between substance-constitutive characteristics and others. And these distinctions will have to be treated as absolute, unless we concede (as Aristotle emphatically would not) that from some points of view becoming is metaphysically possible, from others not, and that none of these viewpoints is objectively superior to the others.[15]

(28) Does our experience or our language, or both, enable us to give content to this distinction between the two types of characteristics by identifying specific instances as falling on one side or the other? If not, then although change may still

---

[15] See Appendix to Ch. I for a discussion of the special problem of generation.

be possible, it will not be something of which we can have specific knowledge. We shall be entitled to describe *successions* of phenomena, but not *changes* with a subject that remains. Specific substances too will be unknowable as such if they are characterized only by properties whose substance-constitutive power we are unable to recognize. Thus, since Aristotle is concerned with human knowledge of becoming, his theory now depends upon the possibility of our actually distinguishing among knowable characteristics the substance-constitutive ones from the rest. We must in other words be able, as he believes that he is, to fill in the doctrine of the categories by giving correct examples, and especially examples in the category of Substance. So now the question is whether there is any principle on which such a division may be made.[16] If not, his account of becoming remains a mere schema, such that we could never say for certain what (if anything) in the empirical world counts as an actual case. Two possible candidates for a principle of division suggest themselves. One concerns the temporal durations of characteristics, the other their causal properties.

(29) The relative lengths of time during which characteristics are instantiated in any given situation clearly plays some part in our allotting to one characteristic (or set of them) the status of substance-constitutive. After all, 'man' in the original example was distinguished as to its function from 'uncultured' and 'cultured' by reference to the fact that the former does, the latter do not, continue to hold on each side of the change (and through it too, if it takes time). But equally clearly, *remaining instantiated for longer* (in a given situation) supplies at most a necessary condition for substance-constitutivity. Not every continuing characteristic has or could have this status. (Suppose for instance that the man who became cultured was all the time in Athens.) There must be some difference other than degree of duration between the substance-constitutive property and the other

---

[16] The problem is not merely to find a formal principle, but to see whether anything about the content of a general term tells us that it expresses a substance-constitutive characteristic or not (and hence whether or not it fits the formal principle, supposing a satisfactory one to have been found).

properties present in a given case: for Aristotle, a non-substantial property could not conceivably get to be in the category of Substance merely by continuing to apply for longer. Moreover the difference must be one that applies in the same way to all cases; that is to say, for Aristotle, a substance-constitutive property is such whenever it occurs. Although the concept of substance has been developed in close connection with that of *subject of a given change*, being a particular substance, and being a substance of a given kind, is not relative to a given change-situation. If the man in the original example is as such a substance, then he is so in all changes, and all men are so in all changes. Thus substance-constitutivity cannot be equated with longer duration, for a property whose presence is relatively permanent in one instance may be relatively impermanent in another.

(30) 'All men by nature desire to know.' The opening remark of the *Metaphysics* throws some light on the question of what more adequate type of principle might be found to support the distinction between substance-constitutive characteristics and others. For whereas all predicates that apply to the subject of change throughout the change are equally true, they are by no means on a par as regards the information they convey. This being so, it is reasonable to suppose that *when* someone reports a change in order to pass information, he will naturally represent the subject by a more rather than less informative description unless there is some definite reason against. So far this is merely a descriptive generalization concerning human linguistic behaviour. Suppose, however, that we recast the observation in the normative mode, and maintain that the seeking and acquiring of knowledge are the highest human activities (or: the highest whose results can be expressed in language). Now we have a basis for also maintaining that the more informative description is that in terms of which the subject ought, most properly, to be described. If, moreover, among information-rich descriptions there are some which convey knowledge of an especially esteemed kind (for example concerning the object's impersonal relations to other objects, as opposed to its emotional effect on the speaker himself), then descriptions of

this type will for this reason too be assigned priority by whoever values such knowledge. It is, perhaps, not difficult to
see how such a normative attitude could present itself to its
holder in the form of a metaphysical doctrine of *substance-
constitutive* characteristics, or essences.

(31) Thus if something equally truly describable as 'a human
being', 'a pale object', 'something in Athens', 'something
weighing ten stone', is said to become (say) hot, Aristotle's
preference for describing this subject primarily as 'a human
being' can be justified as follows: that description tacitly
connects the subject, thus described, to the predicated
change in a way in which none of the others do. The sense
in which this is true will be thoroughly obscured if (like
Hume) we approach the matter believing that a "connection",
to deserve the name, must either be necessary or rationally
intelligible or both. By these standards, 'human' no more
provides a connection than the other expressions. The point
is, rather, that for a language user of normal experience, the
first description on the list provides some indication, however
sketchy and incomplete, concerning various possible circumstances under which, and processes by which, the change is
likely to have taken place, as well as concerning possible conditions for reversing it; whereas the other descriptions, again
for someone of normal experience, in themselves provide no
such information. The description of something as 'white',
'cylindrical', 'ten stone in weight', or 'in Athens' excludes no
possibilities whatever concerning its modes and conditions
of change. These gaps in information only begin to be filled
if we are also told something else about the thing: whether
it is a block of limestone, an animal, a roll of linen, etc. It is
to be noted that this way of distinguishing substance-constitutive characteristics does not (at any rate on this initial
level) depend on any conception of causation as involving
empirically unknowable powers. We are speaking of causal
relations as they figure in ordinary experience, and whether
or not they are to be explained by reference to powers, we
are concerned here only with their manifestation in regularities. Different particulars to which 'man' truly applies
behave in more or less the same ways under the same

conditions, whereas things to which 'white' and 'triangular' truly apply will behave utterly differently under the same conditions, according to what *else* is true of the white or triangular object in each case.

(32) The remarks of the preceding paragraph do not as they stand offer an unexceptionable criterion for picking out terms for substance-constitutive characteristics. They indicate the area in which such a criterion (if possible at all) might be found. The area is that of descriptions the use of any one of which, in reference to a particular subject, would furnish someone of ordinary experience with some information, however rough, *concerning the causal process by which a given change comes about in the subject so described.* (It is to be noted that the class of these descriptions is narrower than that of causal terms in general, since there are many terms, e.g. 'magnetic', 'poisonous', which denote kinds of changes that their subjects are likely to produce in other beings, and give no information about changes in the subjects themselves.) It cannot be claimed that any description meeting the condition just mentioned is automatically a term for a substance-constitutive characteristic. This conclusion could be drawn only if it had first been shown that no description representing what we should naturally regard as an *acquired* characteristic (i.e. belonging, when it belongs, to an already constituted substance) could meet the above condition. But this seems unlikely to be true. Therefore the class of substance-constitutive descriptions is only a *sub*-class of those mentioned, and it is not clear what the differentia of this sub-class would be.

(33) But enough, I hope, has been said to show that there is in ordinary usage some basis for distinguishing substance-constitutive characteristics from *per accidens* ones. The structure of ordinary thought therefore not only justifies Aristotle's analysis of change as requiring a continuing subject, but also provides an anchor for the metaphysical distinction between types of characteristic on which the analysis depends. The argument undertaken in paragraph (10) is now complete. There it was claimed that the idea of a universe of

things lacking intrinsic change-determining characteristics not only entails that change is inexplicable, but makes nonsense of the notion of change itself. This claim has now been shown to follow from the premiss common both to Aristotle and his predecessors, that change makes sense only if something remains. The latter vague notion was articulated by means of the concept of an 'underlying subject', and this in turn was found to depend on the distinction between substances and attributes, and therefore on the distinction between substance-constitutive characteristics and others. We have now seen that the former type of characteristic is marked off by its *causal* content, the causality being of change and stasis in the substance thus characterized. In this way the main topic of *Physics* I is related to that of II, where the subject of discussion is the nature of a thing defined as its 'inner principle of change'. Aristotle himself underlines the connection when he says near the beginning of II.1: 'Nature then is what we have said. All things have a nature that have such a principle, and these things are all substances. For each is a subject, and a nature is always in a subject.' (192b 32-4). Subjects of change are *such as to* behave as they do. Thus the behaviour is never a function of external conditions alone. All change then is at least partially determined by the subject itself, and in this sense there must be inner principles of change if there is change at all.

(34) But we now have to consider another and less obviously justifiable sense in which Aristotle holds a thing's nature to be an inner principle of change. To elucidate this let us revert to the initial comparison of *Physics II*: that of nature with artifice. A natural substance differs from an artefact in that the latter does not have an inner principle of change and stasis: it is developed and then manipulated by another being, artificer or user. But the contrast is not simply between natural substances and artefacts, for it points to another difference: between natural substances and *artificers*. The artificer, unlike the natural substance, brings about (*qua* artificer) change in something other than himself. Now in both contrasts the difference of nature from art impresses Aristotle precisely because in his view (as his subsequent

discussion will show) the two are otherwise so much alike. As artificer stands to the artificially induced change, so natural substance stands to natural change, *except that* in the former case the source and the subject of change are different, save *per accidens*, while in the latter they are necessarily the same. In putting the matter thus I may seem to underestimate the fundamental difference, but I mean only to display this against the background of equally fundamental analogy. Now following the analogy, we find that a natural substance gives rise to change from "within" itself not merely in the sense that *it*, being the kind of thing that it is, helps to determine the changes occurring in it, so that under the same conditions it would change in a different way from a substance of some other kind. For the craftsman (as we ordinarily view such a one) is causally *autonomous* as regards his craftsmanly activities, in the following sense: *he* dictates the shape and pattern of the changes he brings about and the objects or new situations thereby produced. He adapts his activity to the particular circumstances, but the way in which they are allowed to influence the pattern of production is determined by his objective. They play no part in shaping the overall form of change, only being harnessed to realize a form already determined. *What kind* of change takes place depends on the craftsman and his purpose, and the external conditions are relevant only insofar as they make possible change of that kind.[17]

(35) In parallel with this, the nature of a natural substance, as Aristotle conceives it, does not simply make *some* causal contribution to the character of its changes (which was shown to be a necessary consequence of the very notion of 'subject of change') but in the primary and central types of case it wholly determines the pattern. If we may extend from substances to changes Aristotle's own distinction between *what* something is and the *fact that* it is, we can say that a natural substance is causally independent of external conditions as regards determination of the whatness of change, although dependent as regards the actual occurrence at a

---

[17] Cf. A.P.D. Mourelatos, 'Aristotle's "Powers" and Modern Empiricism', *Ratio* IX, 1967, pp. 97 ff.

given time and place. Just so, the character of a particular substance is not a function of its surroundings, although it totally depends on their favour for the fact that being what it is, it exists. Now on this view of natural change, not all changes in a natural substance are determined as to their character from within, any more than every change that might occur in the sculptor's stone is dictated by his purpose. If rain happens to drench it, any effect of this on the stone lies outside his intended effect, and may interrupt or hinder the change he is in process of producing. Similarly with a natural substance. Given that the growth of a sapling is the change of which its nature is the inner principle, if the sapling burns down, this is no part of the behaviour that it was its nature to display. We may be tempted to deny this on the ground that the conditions under which it peacefully grew are of one sort, while those under which it burns are quite different, and we should not expect it necessarily to behave in the same way when circumstances have radically altered. Aristotle would not disagree; but nor would he draw what to us is the obvious conclusion that the object's nature fits it for both types of change, and that under different circumstances the same woody character is differently but equally displayed in various reactions. For Aristotle, this would be as absurd as arguing that since the builder would not expect a roof necessarily to withstand hurricane conditions, his purpose in building is as much, though differently, expressed in its blowing off as its staying on.

(36) We may sum up the last point as follows. If the nature of a natural substance is exhibited in the changes whose character it autonomously determines, then in these changes the only role left to the external conditions is that of permitting the change or not hindering it. It follows that if the conditions do hinder it, the resulting situation, whether it is a new change or a quiescent state, does not exhibit the substantial nature. Although the new situation may come about through natural processes as opposed to human interference, it is no more *natural to the substance concerned* than if it were the product of artifice. It is 'by nature' without being

natural to its subject: as Aristotle says, it is 'enforced'.[18]

(37) There is no doubt that ordinary experience affords plenty of examples that seemingly illustrate this conception of nature as an autonomous inner principle. Many if not most of the objects which attract our unreflective attention regularly exhibit patterns of change against a physical background which itself shows no corresponding isomorphic configuration, either dynamic or static. A stone falls, an animal jumps, a plant blossoms under conditions in which perhaps no observable external change at all occurs, or none that keeps in phase with the phenomena mentioned. Water may follow the line of its banks, but equally often it simply falls — *through* the air but not channelled by it. What more understandable for a virtual pioneer in natural philosophy than to assume that the natures of things can be read off from such changes alone, and to consign all other reactions to the category of the 'incidental', as reflecting nothing intrinsic in the objects that suffer them, but only the tendency of an interfering force? What more natural than to adopt (or fail to shake off) the ever-alluring analogy with the human purposeful agent? But a notion with plausible illustrations is not necessarily a coherent concept capable of actual instantiation, and we may well doubt the sense, as well as the scientific usefulness, of a view which obliges us to identify the changes natural to a given object with a mere *sub-class* of those occurring in it through perfectly natural causes. Aristotle himself would dismiss as fanciful the attribution of intention and deliberation to plants and animals; but is not the attribution of autonomous natures in the sense explained a similar mistake: one, moreover, that loses its rationale once we cease to regard all natural substances as purposeful agents?

(38) But the two mistakes (if such they both are) occur on very different levels. Aristotle saw as clearly as anyone that

---

[18] Cf. D.D. Heath, 'On some Misconceptions of Aristotle's Doctrine on Causation and τὸ αὐτόματον', *Journal of Philology* VII, 1897, p. 111: 'Aristotle's system . . . slurred over the consideration of natural *inter-action*, very commonly ranking it as something antagonistic to the natural order, βίαιον; and . . . tended to reduce the course of Nature to a series of self-developments of almost independent organisms.'

to interpret animal and plant behaviour as deliberate explains nothing that could not be well explained without it; whereas to deny natures and natural changes would for him be tantamount to denying the very possibility of all explanation. This concept is his starting point for any philosophy of the natural world, and so it is that at II.1, 193a1-9 he writes:

What nature is has been stated . . . But that nature exists it would be ludicrous to try to prove. For it is evident that there are in the world many such things, i.e. things endowed with natures in the sense explained. And to prove what is evident by means of what is not evident betrays an inability to discriminate between what is and is not in itself knowable. It is obvious that a person can be in this state: someone blind from birth might reason concerning colours. What this amounts to is that such people can only be arguing about words, without any meaning in mind.

Aristotle does not of course mean that a normally constituted human being perceives natures as he perceives colour. This might be the case with *change*, but a nature is a *principle* of change, and our recognition of principles comes from reflection upon experience: if they were sensory givens they could not function as principles. We start with 'confused things, which to us are initially more obvious and clear', whereas 'the elements and principles become known later from these upon analysis'. (I.1, 184a21-3). The comparison with the blind man makes the point that people can try to reason while lacking any conception of what they think they are reasoning about, and this lack of understanding shows itself in the very attempt: whether the subject matter is such that it can only be grasped through the senses, or whether (like the fact that there are natures) it provides the necessary starting point for any relevant investigation. The philosopher of nature must presuppose the reality of the physical world, the existence of change, and finally the actual part played by natures, in Aristotle's sense of 'inner principles of change'.

(39) Unfortunately Aristotle draws no distinction here between the ludicrous activity of proving the unprovable, and the far from ludicrous one of moving to an articulated understanding of it. He himself engages in this second activity when in *Physics* I.2 he argues against the Eleatic denial of

plurality, or in *Metaphysics* Γ shows how even the denial of the Law of Non-Contradiction involves at the same time its acceptance. But so far as the existence of natures is concerned, he proceeds as if the case is indeed like that of colours for a sighted person: such a one not only knows of their existence without proof, but cannot even conceive that he could question it. The reason for this may be dialectical: unlike plurality and the Law of Non-Contradiction, no one had ever challenged (except by implication, as a consequence of these two challenges) the Aristotelian concept of 'nature' and its applicability to the real world. And the reason for that is surely that Aristotle himself was the first to make this concept clear. Now in his arguments against Parmenides, and in part of his argument concerning contradiction, Aristotle relies on his own doctrine of substance and the categories as an unassailable point of departure. We shall now see that this also underlies the Aristotelian theory of natures as inner principles of change.

(40) Four assumptions make up the grounds of the theory. The first is that there are substances in the sense explained in the *Categories*. Secondly, we discover what it is for something to be a natural substance of a given kind by observing the regular behaviour of such substances. There is no other path to knowledge of the natures of things. Thirdly, there are irreducibly different kinds or species of substance. Fourthly, a substantial essence is unitary, and ought ideally to be conveyed in definition by a unitary specifying formula. From these premisses it follows that a substance of a given sort must exhibit its nature, or what it is, through change specific to that sort and also in some sense unitary. If observable changes in natural objects cannot be construed as specific and unitary, this would show, so far as empirical evidence can decide such a question, that the Aristotelian concept of substance lacks application in the physical world. Now the main problem turns on the type of unity that a change must display so as to be seen as expressing a substance. From our previous discussion it is clear that for Aristotle unity of change means in effect change in accordance with a single pattern, whether the pattern is immediately discernible to

the senses, like the typical lines of ascent and descent of "simple" substances such as fire and earth, or whether it can only be made out by repeated experience and the marshalling of many observations, like the complex and far more abstract pattern of a living creature's life-cycle. It is this conception of the unity of a substance-expressing change that leads him to hold that any change which diverges from some single typical tendency in a given direction represents nothing but interference: interference, moreover, not merely with the natural change itself, but with our one source of knowledge about the substantial nature concerned.

(41) Such a view has momentous consequences for scientific practice. It is notorious that 'with very few exceptions, the Ancient Greeks throughout a period of eight hundred years made no attempt at systematic experimentation'. So writes Professor Sambursky.[19] No doubt there were many contributing causes, sociological, psychological, ethical, religious.[20] But to these we may add the metaphysical notion of nature as an inner principle of change — for if Aristotle first articulated this concept, he did not create it *ex nihilo*; it had its roots in earlier philosophy, if not also in common sense. Once it is assumed that a natural substance manifests its nature through some single typifying pattern of change to which external circumstances contribute nothing but the opportunity of realization, two things follow. Firstly, posing and answering questions of the form 'How will it behave under such and such (positively specified) conditions?' adds nothing to a scientific understanding of the substance. To see this we need only divide the conditions of its existence into those kinds which favour the occurrence of the innerly determined typifying change, and those which suppress or interfere with it. Favouring conditions do not reveal the character of the substance; they only enable *it* to reveal *itself* in autonomous behaviour. Their positive description is not important, since their function is only to provide an arena. Thus, given that typifying behaviour T occurs in a substance S under

---

[19] *The Physical World of the Greeks*, p. 2.
[20] Ibid., Ch. X.

conditions C, it is incorrect to say that S is such as to exhibit T under conditions C. For according to the assumption, S is such as to exhibit T *simpliciter*. Conditions C are those under which this typifying change is not prevented and therefore occurs; but from this it does not follow that S is typified by exhibiting T-under-C. Now consider the conditions which prevent the occurrence of T. These are evidently powerless to reveal the character of S, since they preclude the only kind of behaviour in which this character shows itself. This point is more narrowly relevant to the question of experimental method, since it centres on the artificial control of conditions. It is Aristotle's view that substance-typifying changes are as a rule successfully realized in the natural environment. Most of the conditions in which most individual natural substances find themselves are such as to permit their self-characterizing behaviour, or at least most of the time. It is therefore senseless to place a substance under artificial conditions for better observation. This cannot enable us to identify the typifying behaviour in a given case; nor, if we believe that we have identified it, can it help us to study it better. For if the substance still exhibits the behaviour in question this teaches us no more about its nature than we could have learned through observing it in the natural context. But the artificial conditions are more likely than not to obstruct the typifying behaviour, and in that case we learn nothing at all about the substantial nature, since this could only have been revealed through changes other than those which are taking place. Experiment, in short, opens up no new access to the facts, and may succeed only in suppressing them. It follows that the only rational attitude for the scientist is that which Sambursky calls 'submissiveness' to the world of nature; for natural substances best "tell us" what they are when we as spectators leave them to themselves to operate under their own direction.[21]

(42) But it is surely a crude mistake to think that an object's unitary nature is manifested only in behaviour of a *single* observable pattern. Surely it is more scientific and intellectually

---

[21] See Sambursky, pp. 234-5, for an excellent statement of the conclusion, although without the metaphysical premises.

satisfying to construe the empirical data on the assumption that an underlying unity runs through all the object's be-havings, whether in usual, unusual, natural, or artificial surroundings. Seen thus, all its actions and reactions equally tell us what it is; all are equally natural *to it*; none is a di-vergence or interruption except from the subjective stand-point of some human purpose, as when we say that a machine has broken down, well knowing that it is of a nature to react to current conditions in the way that unfits it for use. For the same laws by which it worked also make it stop working, so that in this sense what it does and how it is is always the same, i.e. an expression of the same set of laws, the differ-ences being due to shifts in values of the *same* variables identically related. Our faith in this attitude has been justi-fied by the actual success of sciences such as mechanics and molecular chemistry. To understand Aristotle's blindness to the very possibility of such an approach, let us briefly con-sider certain aspects of these two sciences.

(43) In mechanics, it has often been pointed out, there is no place for the concept of specifically different substances. All bodies can be shown to behave at all times in accordance with the same set of laws, because the laws depend on the properties of body as such. These properties, moreover, according to Aristotle's categorial scheme, fall into cate-gories other than that of Substance: mass, velocity, position, duration, etc. The same individual Aristotelian substance could alter in respect of all these without impairment to its substantial nature. Thus mechanics studies, through their effects, the "natures" of these properties in their determina-tions and combinations. Hence in a mechanist account of an object's behaviour, none of that behaviour can appear as issuing from a specific *substantial* nature. Thus if the fall of a stone and the rise of vapour are explained mechanically, we can no longer say that these motions typify these sub-stances (earth and air) as such. But if the stone's substantial nature does not determine what seems its most obviously characteristic behaviour, we are in a poor position to claim that it determines *any* of the stone's behaviour. Thus sub-stantial natures as such must be set aside as metaphysically

"inert" and hence unknowable; since how could we hope to know of them if not through their self-expressing actions?

(44) With chemistry the situation is rather different. It is true that Aristotle's refusal to follow Plato's mathematicizing lead in the study of nature cuts him off from the basic concepts of physics and chemistry alike. Many writers have dwelt on this point, and I have nothing to add to their expositions. However, chemistry unlike mechanics does deal with specifically different substances (elements and compounds). Now the unity of the chemical behaviour of any one of these is confirmed by the conceptual unity of the molecular and atomic theory. The theory postulates for each type of substance a structure which is the starting point for explaining observed interactions with other types, in accordance with a few principles. Thus in chemistry as we know it, the structuredness of chemical matter is regarded as a necessary given, although it is an empirical question what particular structures should be assigned to given types of substance so as best to explain the phenomena. Now Aristotle by contrast with Plato does not regard structure in the natural world as inexplicable from within the natural world itself, being merely the product and sign of some metaphysical interface between physical existence and a transnatural order. But at the same time Aristotle does not take structure as *given* in any individual case: rather, it is what the individual natural substance by natural processes *achieves*. This means that in Aristotle the conception of empirically knowable structure is supplemented by another notion of order, that of the progression of a natural substance to full development of its structure. The progression is described and explained by reference to the structure, as tending towards it; and it cannot also be explained by reference to other already existing empirical structures. That would be to substitute the notion of structure as given for the notion of structure as achieved. Aristotle in common with Plato assigns to empirically knowable structure an empirically unknowable source, but with a difference: Plato's is the form beyond the world, while Aristotle's is the power of the natural substance to attain structure. This power is in the physical world, being

centred in a particular natural substance, but it cannot be identified in its own right with any actual set of empirically knowable structures or properties. Thus Aristotle like the modern chemist would account for an object's behaviour by reference to its structure — except that for Aristotle the structure is the terminus of change, not its precondition. In consequence, Aristotle cannot hold that the nature of a substance is impartially typified by all its changes under whatever conditions, for there is only one type of change that depends on the specific structure, namely that which results in the latter's full development. Aristotle is therefore forced by his own fundamental concepts to identify the behaviour that manifests substantial nature with a mere sub-class of all the behavings of which the substance in question is physically capable.[22]

(45) Thus Aristotle's notion of natures as inner autonomous shapers of change is not to be put down to a naive projection of the concept of conscious intentional activity. It is his metaphysic of substance that dictates the idea of nature, including just those features that so obviously invite comparison with artifice. We shall return to this comparison, since we have so far only touched on what for Aristotle, despite their resemblance, is the fundamental and decisive difference. First, however, let me state two corollaries of the position reached so far. In the first place, the distinction between changes that are natural in the sense explained and those which are not is as absolute as the distinction between the *per se* unity of a substantial form such as that represented by 'man', and the *per accidens* unity of a complex such as that represented by 'white man'. Secondly, natural change is ontologically and conceptually presupposed by change of all other types. All other changes result from the convergence of natural changes with factors in their environment. And in tracing back the causal history of any non-natural change, one will always reach a natural one from which the process

---

[22] Cf. Mourelatos, 'Aristotle's "Powers" etc.', pp. 102–3, who argues on rather different grounds from mine that Aristotle does not simply 'fail' to refer dispositional properties to micro-structural bases, but rejects *a priori* any such attempt at explanation.

started. Individual substances A and B come into contact, and A causes a counter-natural change in B. But either A came into contact through pursuing some natural change-pattern of its own, or it was brought by some other substance C. And if the latter, the change that brought A under the influence of C is either natural or not, and if the latter, the same argument can be repeated. But at some point we arrive at a natural change and an originating substance that changes "of itself", and what makes this certain is not any vague finitist distaste for infinite regression as such, but the following quite precise reason: if no change were natural, then substances would never as such express themselves through change. The concept of 'substance' would then contribute nothing at all to an account of the natural world, nor therefore to a metaphysics intended to subserve science.

(46) So far in this chapter we have examined two senses in which a thing's nature is an 'inner principle of change'. To attribute a nature in the first sense is to say that the thing in question has an intrinsic character that makes *some* contribution to determining the sorts of changes that take place in it. The relevant contrast here is with a featureless locus that lacks any character to limit the changes to which it is liable, so that any behaviour would be totally determined from without. No one would dispute Aristotle's rejection of this. The second sense is more dubious, although even here he is by no means obviously at odds with ordinary thought. In this sense, a substance, being of a certain nature, is *self-sufficient to determine the pattern* of its typical changes, the external conditions playing no part in shaping what happens, but only providing the stage on which the occurrence is possible. Here the contrast is with the substances of modern chemistry and the corporeal particles of classical mechanics, all of whose actions and reactions are co-determined by the character and properties of the objects themselves together with those of their environment. Now in both the above senses, the inner/outer contrast opposes determination of change by the substance itself to determination by external conditions or substances. We have now to consider a further sense in which Aristotle holds the nature of a thing to be an 'inner principle of change'.

(47) In this third sense, the implied contrast is between not determinants but *subjects* of change. It is from this point of view that Aristotle draws the distinction between nature and artifice which for him is no less vital than the analogy emphasized earlier. He writes:

Nature is a principle and cause of change and stasis in that in which it primarily inheres *per se*, i.e. not *per accidens*. I say 'not *per accidens*', because someone who was a physician might himself become the cause of his own recovery. But all the same, it is not insofar as he recovers that he has the art of medicine, since it has come about *per accidens* that the same man is both physician and recovers health. Thus the physician and the one who recovers are also sometimes found separately from one another. It is the same with all other things brought about by contrivance. None of them has the principle of the contriving in itself. In some cases the principle is in other things and external, as for instance with a house and anything else made by the hands, while in other cases it is in the things themselves, only not *per se*, since it is *per accidens* that the subjects in which they cause change are themselves. (II.1, 192b20–32)

So in natural change, the particular subject in which the change takes place is necessarily identical with the particular substance whose nature gives rise to it. In artifice, on the other hand, subject and source may be identical, but if so they only happen to be, as is proved by the fact that the same change in the subject could have come about at the hands of a different practitioner, and the practitioner who this time treats himself could have performed the operation on another.

(48) At first sight Aristotle seems to be saying that a natural substance is the source of an intransitive activity, while an artificer is the source of a transitive one. (I here use 'transitive'/'intransitive' to denote formal properties of activities, not grammatical properties of verbs. But I am using the terms in a sense analogous to the grammatical, not with the meaning they bear in the logic of relations.) However, the distinction between transitive and intransitive does not quite make Aristotle's point, since it fails to divide all natural from all artificial processes. In the first place, even where an artificer operates on an external object, his operating involves certain intransitive changes in himself: the surgeon and builder *move*

(intransitive) — and these movements are skilful — in order to produce their intended external effects. Even when the doctor treats himself, the motions involved in the treating can be distinguished from the change (recovery) brought about. Secondly, there are skilled activities such as singing and dancing which seem essentially intransitive: the dance is the performer's own movements organized to an artistically conceived pattern.

(49) These objections force us to realize that the contrast which Aristotle means is not primarily between natural and artificial activities, nor between changes, but between natural and artificial *forms* and their respective relations to the agent by whose activity they come to be realized. Thus the starting point of *Physics* II is not after all so philosophically innocent as might appear from its seemingly commonsensical contrast of nature with artifice. For he relies on an analysis, itself the product of philosophizing, of the concept of 'skilful activity' in terms of the notion of 'artificial form to be realized'. Exercise of skill may necessarily involve movements on the part of the agent, but these are only the means by which the intended form comes to be realized. That is, they are means to a further change in which the realizing of the projected form actually consists, e.g. the patient's return to health. Were it not for the agent's usually producing results of this form, we should not describe him as having the skill in question. The skill is defined by reference to the form. Aristotle's point then in the passage last quoted is that the artificial form, and the change which immediately results in it, could just as well take place in a subject other than the agent; so that if they do occur in him it is only *per accidens* so. As for intransitive skilled activities like singing and dancing, even here it is possible to distinguish the changes in which the realizing of the desired form *consists* from those necessary as means to these. It is true as a matter of fact that in these cases the agent realizes the form through changes in his own body, but this is not due to any necessary connection between the form and just this body, but to the unavailability of other suitably controllable subjects. It might be possible to affect the limbs or vocal chords of another person

so as to produce the song or dance through his body. It is true that the skill then manifested by the controlling agent would not be skill in *singing or dancing*, since *ex hypothesi* he does neither: what he so cleverly does would be better described as puppeteering or playing on a kind of instrument. But intransitive skilled activities are not really counter-examples to the distinction which Aristotle is making in 192b20-32. For although the activity properly described as 'dancing' may be necessarily intransitive, it consists in the realizing of a form which could in principle be realized in an external subject. But the form realized in natural change is necessarily realized in the same individual whose nature gives rise to the change.

(50) Thus the nature of a natural substance is uniquely related to one particular in a way not paralleled by the principle of artifice that defines an artificer. Both nature and artifice are embodied in particular agents, and in this respect Aristotle's anti-Platonism is impartial between the two kinds of cause. But they differ in that a particular exemplifier of skill (i.e. a particular artificer) stands to its effects as a Platonic 'one over many', whereas the opposite holds true of nature. The concept of a Platonic Form entails that any number of particulars can participate in it so as to exhibit the corresponding empirical property, and however numerous the participants the Form's capacity for being participated in is not exhausted. Similarly, the Aristotelian artificer can realize the same form in any number of particular subjects, and its realization in one in no way limits this agent's power to produce it again in others. Whereas the relation between the natural substance and the particular subject in which the natural form is to be realized is necessarily one-one, since 'they are necessarily the same individual.

(51) It is strange that after carefully distinguishing between nature and artifice in the way which we have just examined, Aristotle should shortly afterwards permit himself the remark that nature operates like a doctor doctoring himself (II.8, 199b30-2). Has he such faith in his own powers of exposition as to assume that this could cause no confusion once the

initial distinction was made? Or is it that he himself was earlier confused in supposing the distinction to be as clear and absolute as the opening passage of II.1 certainly suggests? Perhaps the temptation to use the self-doctoring analogy betrays the fact that we cannot after all conceive of the same individual as both source and subject of change except in cases where source and subject *might* have been different? In other words, does it perhaps make sense to identify them only when the identity statement is true *per accidens*? If this is so, it is incoherent to say that the natural substance as source of change is identical *per se* with the natural substance as subject. Instead we ought to refuse to describe the situation in terms of any kind of identity between source and subject. This does not mean that we should think of 'them' as distinct individuals. On the contrary, it means that there is one individual which cannot coherently be regarded as instantiating two distinct aspects in such a way that it then makes sense to assert the identity of itself under one with itself under the other. All that we can say, then, is that there is a change and an individual which changes, and that such change occurs regularly in individuals of this kind, circumstances permitting. To go further and attempt to distinguish a source and a subject within the ontological confines of the same individual can only cause confusion and pointless mystification.

(52) This criticism is damaging if justified, for it calls into question Aristotle's right to be talking of a thing's nature as a *principle* of change at all, even though it may not be clear either what it would mean to deny this. On the one hand we should hardly wish to rule against the legitimacy of saying that objects of a given kind change as they do *because* this is how things of that kind behave;[23] or that they do not simply *change* in this way, but are *such as to* do so. But on the other hand we might decide that the licence to use these expressions is too costly, if the price is a theory of sources that are somehow distinguishable from, but also identical with, their subjects. This is not just the crude reaction of someone unable to see how the same referent can be known

[23] Cf. Charlton, pp. 88–9.

and picked out via more than one sense (according to Frege's use of that term). For the problem here is compounded by the fact that one of the alleged senses, i.e. that corresponding to the source-aspect, is not empirically knowable (*v.s.* para. (44)). We see the morning star, and also, later, the evening star, but we never see the natural substance as giving rise to its change, only as changing.

(53) A full discussion of the issues here involved would take us far afield; for the present I shall confine myself to certain points directly relevant to Aristotle. I shall argue first that notwithstanding his use of the self-doctoring analogy, there is reason to doubt his liability to the objection mounted in paragraph (51). The gist of this objection was as follows: If the natural substance is properly described as source and subject of its own change, then this change is or involves a reflexive activity (such as self-medication). But a reflexive activity is transitive, and as such need not be reflexive: the patient could be other than the agent. It follows that we cannot contrast natural with artificial change on the ground that in the latter, the agent and patient may be different individuals, while in the former they must be the same. For if they *must* be the same, there is no genuine transitivity; nor, therefore, is there any genuinely reflexive element in the situation. And so it becomes meaningless to say that the same individual is both agent *and* patient, or both source and subject. Now as it stands this criticism does not touch the position which Aristotle presents in the *Physics* considered as a whole. In the first place, he does not in Book II or anywhere else say that the operation of a natural substance as such *is* a reflexive activity like curing oneself: he only compares it to the latter. But secondly, this is not because he never articulates the idea of a natural substance 'operating upon itself'. He does exactly this in Book VIII.4–5. Here he speaks of some natural substances as changing (transitive), and being changed by, *themselves*, and he also speaks of such substances as somehow comprising within themselves a somehow distinct changer (agent) and changed (patient): But he also makes it clear that *not all natural substances are or can be changers of themselves.*[24]

[24] Cf. Ch. V, paras (2) and (10).

This reflexive concept applies only to living things, perhaps only to animals, and not to the inanimate simple bodies, earth, fire, etc. Yet he also makes it clear in Book VIII that he retains the idea that a natural substance *as such* is both source and subject of its own natural change. This notion, then, continues to apply to all natural substances, including those to which the title of 'self-changers' is explicitly denied. Thus Aristotle regards a substance as *both source and subject without thereby regarding it as both agent and patient.* And this position entails that even if it is incoherent to assert that agent and patient are necessarily identical, it does not follow that the corresponding assertion concerning subject and source is incoherent too.

(54) In Chapter V I shall examine at length Aristotle's view of certain substances as both agents and patients of their natural changes. But the remarks just made indicate that we ought not to have to support this view (which is undoubtedly obscure) in order to make sense of the idea that natural substances *in general* are as such both subjects and sources. However, this does not prove that idea to be valid or meaningful in itself. A sceptic is entitled to ask how it is possible to make a distinction that applies even to the simple bodies between source-aspect and subject-aspect in one and the same substance. Why should he concede a distinction if it cannot be explained, and why then should he accept the terminology of 'nature as an inner principle'? Now this question can be asked on two different levels, on one of which we shall find no answer in Aristotle. This is so if what is being demanded is justification for holding that natural objects are *such as to* change in certain ways, as opposed to holding that they simply usually do so change, and for all we know, always. Aristotle would surely have regarded this question as lying outside the province of philosophy of nature, like the questions of people who wish to have it proved that change exists, or plurality. This is not to say that had he been faced with Hume, as he was with Parmenides, he would not have undertaken a counter-attack, even while making it clear that the philosopher of science as such is under no obligation to see

it successful before pursuing his own line of study.[25] But how Aristotle would have dealt with a Humean attempt to undermine (as he would have seen it) a basic (if not the most basic) presupposition of science, we cannot easily guess.

(55) However, the questioner may grant it meaningful and even necessary to say that things change as they usually or always do because they are *such as to* do so, while still wondering in what way a distinction can be drawn between the object as source and as subject of its changes. On this less radical level one might answer as follows.[26] Fire (e.g.) is such as to move towards and come to rest in the upper region, whenever not prevented. Accordingly it *does* so move when it can. It may cease to function as source or as subject of this change, but the ceasing in each case is different. If the fiery mass is kept down by force, it cannot function as the subject; similarly if it has already reached the upper region: it then has nowhere upwards to move. But it remains true that it is such as to move upwards when it can. On the other hand it could be treated so that it ceases to be such. The treatment would involve converting it into a different type of object, one such as to behave differently. These obvious remarks point to the following conclusion: either there is no difference between saying (*a*) that the fire is no longer in a position to move upwards, and (*b*) that it has ceased to be fire and such as to move upwards; or we must recognize a difference between the fact that something is (of the nature of) fire, and the fact that it is actually a subject of motion in accordance with that nature. Although I have taken an example from Aristotelian physics, this argument can be applied to what *we* should consider scientifically established facts. Sugar is such as to dissolve in water. This is true of the lump before it is immersed in water, i.e. before it is in a position to be subject of the change. So long as we find it necessary to distinguish between the fact that sugar is such as to dissolve, and the fact that some sugar is dissolving, we shall be regarding sugar as a subject and also a source of change.

[25] Cf. *Physics* I.2 185a17-20.
[26] Cf. P.T. Manicas, 'Aristotle, Dispositions and Occult Powers', *Review of Metaphysics* XVIII, 1964-5, pp. 678 ff.; and Mourelatos, 'Aristotle's "Powers"'.

Appendix to Chapter I

On the interpretation offered here of Aristotle's account of coming to be in *Physics* I.7-8, every becoming involves a subject which remains, and this subject is a substance. But it is arguable that this position holds only of non-substantial change. If this is true, Aristotle's scheme (as here understood) fails to cover (*a*) the generation of natural substances; and possibly (*b*) the production of artefacts. I say 'possibly', because in some passages he seems not to class artefacts as substances 'in the strictest sense': *v.i.* Ch. II, para (6). (His general view permits and may even require him to treat statues etc. as natural substances that have undergone change of quality, relations, etc.). The main problem lies with the coming to be of natural substances. The claim that this involves a substantial remaining subject faces two main difficulties:

(1) Aristotle's own statement of what the subject is in these cases suggests that it is not something that remains, for he says that in the case of living things, it is the 'seed' ('σπέρμα', 190b4-5); but a 'seed' is not as such still present in the product of the change (in the way in which man is present in the product *cultured man*).

(2) It has often been held (partly no doubt because of difficulty (1); cf. Charlton, p. 77) that the remaining subject of natural substantial coming to be is 'prime matter' in the scholastic sense; and this is not a substance.

Briefly, I would reply:

(*a*) So far as (2) is concerned, I agree with Charlton that there is no clear evidence that Aristotle introduces the concept of 'prime matter' (in the above sense) in *Physics* I (Charlton, 77 ff. and 129 ff.), although I would hesitate to accept Charlton's broader thesis that it never appears in Aristotle. (On *Physics* I, see also B. Jones, 'Aristotle's Introduction of Matter', *Philosophical Review* LXXXIII, 1974, pp. 474 ff.) Prime matter (or at any rate an in-itself-unknowable and inseparable subject) seems a necessary presupposition for one type of substantial coming to be, viz. the transmutation of simple bodies into one another described in *De Gen. et Corr.* and *De Caelo*. However, in *Physics* I.7-8 Aristotle does not appear to consider this type of case at all. His examples of generation are of plants and animals, where the new substance cannot be described as coming to be *through transformation from a different sort of substance* (*pace* Ross, *Aristotle's Physics*, p. 22), but only as *coming to be*.

(*b*) The theory of nature expounded in *Physics* II shows how Aristotle could coherently hold that organisms undergo a process which (i) is not a change in quality, quantity, etc., (or in any category other than

Substance), but (ii) has for its subject an identifiable describable substance. On this view, the subject-substance in generation is the same individual as the eventual mature creature. While development goes on, the subject-substance is identifiable and characterizable as a creature in process of developing the features typical of mature members of the species. This process cannot be classified as a change in any of the non-substance categories, for changes in these presuppose a subject whose nature is definable without reference to the end-state of the change. (What it is to be cultured does not enter into what it is to be a man.) On this account the fundamental difference between substantial and non-substantial coming to be is preserved without resort to a non-substantial unknowable and unidentifiable subject, (prime matter).

(c) However there seems to be a difficulty. The developing but undeveloped organism cannot be the *subject* of development, because the subject remains, and the undeveloped, *qua* undeveloped, does not. (This problem led Charlton to the conclusion that Aristotle does not believe in a remaining subject at all for generation. Since Aristotle makes it clear that there is a *subject* (the 'underlying thing') in *all* cases of becoming, Charlton has to maintain that by 'subject' Aristotle does not always mean 'that which remains through becoming'; which seems highly improbable. See Charlton, locc. citt.) But this would be a genuine problem only if there were no single substance-constitutive characteristic applying both to developing and to developed organism (giving the covering concept under which 'they' are the same individual). But there is: in both its phases the creature embodies the same nature in the sense of *principle* of life and change typical of members of its kind (see Ch. II, paras (19)–(20)).

(d) Ordinary organic-substance terms generally direct one's mind to the mature form. Thus although the subject of generation may truly be said to be all along a human being, it would be misleading to describe it as such; for then when we say that it develops into a human being we seem to say that it becomes what already it is. For this reason, I suggest, Aristotle in *Physics* I.7 prefers to call the subject a 'seed' (= 'embryo', not 'semen', in the case of animals; cf. *De Gen. An.* I.20, 728b32–4 and Jones, pp. 488 ff.), even though this locution risks making it seem that the subject disappears before the change is over, hence is not a remaining subject (but more like a contrary replaced). Unfortunately no handy terms are neutral as between developed and undeveloped; but Aristotle is used to ordinary vocabulary running dry when it comes to providing names for all the facts that his analyses enable him to distinguish; cf. *Physics* I.5, 188b10–11, *Eth. Nic.* II.7, 1107b1–2.

II

What Things Have Natures?

(1) Ordinary experience seems to afford plenty of examples of objects endowed with Aristotelian natures. This point was mentioned in the last chapter (para. (37)), with the proviso that the apparent examples can be accepted as genuine only if the general notions of 'nature' and 'natural change' are themselves coherent and viable. From now on this proviso will be taken for granted. But we still face a question which strikes at the foundations of Aristotle's natural philosophy as deeply as any previous doubts concerning the abstract soundness of its central notion. We have to consider the *extension* of the concept of nature as an inner principle of change and stasis. Even if we assume this concept to be in-stantiated, which if incoherent it could not be, we are not automatically entitled to the further assumption that what-ever seems an instantiation is one in fact. Now Aristotle himself says that all the things that exist by nature,

. . . animals and their parts, and the plants and the simple bodies such as earth, fire, air, and water — for these and the like we say exist by nature — all manifestly differ from things not constituted by nature, in that each possesses within itself a principle of change and stasis. (II.1, 192b9-14)

It is indeed a 'manifest difference'. But does Aristotle mean that the difference is real in all these cases, as well as clearly displayed; or might he mean that in all these cases there is a clear display of a difference that may or may not in every case be real? Even if he unhesitatingly means the former, we might expect him, here or elsewhere, to give some attention to the question of grounds for deciding which those things are that are to be assigned the status of natural *substances*. For that is the status implied by saying that a being has (in Aristotle's sense) a nature. And although it may be certain on metaphysical grounds that all change can be traced back

to natural substances whose nature it is to change 'of themselves', this does not tell us what things are natural substances.
It is when we turn an analytic eye on the objects of our
experience, bearing in mind the full meaning of 'nature',
that we may well begin to doubt whether Aristotle is justified in holding that all the objects listed above[1] are really
endowed with natures.

(2) The problem more specifically concerns Aristotle's right
to suppose that a complex physical object is endowed with
an Aristotelian nature. This may seem an extraordinary
question, since for him *organisms*, which even in their most
primitive forms are structured and complex, are the paradigms
of natural substance. Yet the enquiry has point in the light
of the following considerations. Such beings are composed
of physical parts, and the parts too may be complex. Experience shows that these beings and their parts are made up
of the apparently simple unorganized stuffs which Aristotle
calls the 'simple bodies', earth, fire, water, and air. For when
the more highly organized beings perish, they decompose
eventually into these apparently simple stuffs, and while
alive they take these stuffs into themselves by way of nutri-
tion. It is therefore not unreasonable to suppose that the
organic complexes and their structured parts *consist of* a
few universal basic materials differently arranged and modified. On this supposition, the complexity of the complex
being appears to involve both (*a*) physical and (*b*) logical
composition. For (*a*) the being has parts that are spatially
external to one another, and (*b*) these parts are, or are made
of, substances modified in various ways. These modifications
can scarcely be regarded as *per se* attributes of the substances
in question, for if this were the case, how could it also be the
case that the same few basic substances are capable of as
many different modifications as would be required to account
for the vast variety of complex entities? The fewer the basic
materials (and theoretical economy demands that few should
be postulated rather than many), the more indifferent each
in itself must be to which of a large range of possible

---

[1] As A. Mansion points out, pp. 57 and 118, the choice of these examples of
natural substance rests only on '*l'usage*'.

modifications is realized in it in any given case; for if the kinds of elements are few, their modifications and combinations must be many to account for the diversity of the natural world.

(3) From the point of view just summarized, it is difficult to see how a complex natural entity is not automatically on a logical par with a *per accidens* combination of mutually external circumstances. Such a set of circumstances may jointly cause a change, but they cannot on that account be regarded as collectively exhibiting a nature, precisely because their union is only *per accidens*. Now we call a complex object *an* object or thing presumably because it preserves its unity for a noticeable length of time. But apart from this, which seems an arbitrary distinction, what difference is there between such a 'thing' and what we would normally be inclined to call a *set* of circumstances? What difference, in other words, is there between a physically complex object that changes of itself, and a set of mutually external factors one of which externally determines a change in another of the set? Once we have taken into account *all* the factors that determine an externally determined change in a given object, why should we not regard these, together with the changing object itself, as forming a single (even if not necessarily a stable) entity which changes as a whole because part of it changes through external determination by other parts (just as a man, Aristotle says, may be said to move if a part of him moves: see *Physics* V.1, 224a23-6? *Ex hypothesi* this "single" changing entity changes "of itself", i.e. not through external determinants, because all the determinants have been included within it. Now if Aristotle would refuse, as he would, to attribute a nature in his sense[2] to such a set of mutually external factors, on the ground that it is not a unity of the proper type, what ground has he for attributing natures to complex objects such as organisms?

(4) There is another way of putting the same problem. Given that Aristotle regards e.g. organisms and their parts as having

---

[2] This is not to say that he would have denied that it exists 'by nature', '$\phi\acute{v}\sigma\epsilon\iota$'.

natures, although they are complex, with what right could he refuse to attribute nature to a self-moving artefact? We cannot dismiss this question on the grounds that self-moving artefacts would have been beyond his power to conceive, for evidently they were not:

> If every instrument could accomplish its own work, obeying or antici-pating the wills of others, like the statues of Daedalus, or the tripods of Hephaestus, which, says the poet, 'of their own accord entered the assembly of the Gods': if in like manner the shuttle would weave and the plectrum touch the lyre without a hand to guide them, chief work-men would not want servants, nor masters slaves. (*Politics* I.3, 1253 b 33-1254a 1, tr. B. Jowett.)

Of course, if only gods and their kin can make self-moving artefacts, the latter are as mythical as the former, and hardly need to be taken into account in a philosophical classification. But in *Physics* II.8, 199a12-15, Aristotle writes:

> If a house were one of the things that come into being by nature, it would come into being in the same way as it actually does through artifice. And if natural things came into being not only by nature but also by artifice, they would do so in the same way as they do by nature.

(By 'in the same way' he means 'in the same order of steps'.) It seems then that we cannot rule out the possibility that Aristotle might have had man-made automata in mind even while writing *Physics* II.1, and only chose inert artefacts to illustrate his initial distinction because (*a*) they are the obvious examples (for his audience) of artefacts, and (*b*) they obviously contain no principle of change (*qua* artefacts).

(5) Aristotle would certainly have regarded automata (even divinely made ones: Hephaestus was a craftsman) as *artefacts*, and therefore as radically different from natural substances. Now an artefact is a combination of simpler objects put to-gether in such a way that when each part behaves according to its nature, the whole system comes to be in a certain de-sired condition, or changes in a certain desired way. The parts are together *per accidens*, for if they were of their own natures thus combined, there would have been no need of artificial arrangement *ab extra*. If then we suppose that com-plex *natural* substances are *per accidens* combinations, it

follows that the distinction between complex natural substances and artefacts is not fundamental. It may be true that
all natural complexes have an inner principle of motion:
but then so do *some* artefacts (automata). And since self-
moving artefacts are constructed on essentially the same
principles as the inert ones more familiar to a pre-techno-
logical era, it follows that if complex natural substances are
comparable to automata, they are comparable to artefacts
in general. Of course the genetic process is empirically different in each case, but *what* comes into being in each case is
a system of essentially the same logical type, demanding in
the end the same type of explanation for its behaviour and
characteristics. In short, the distinction between complex
natural substances and artefacts is not fundamental unless a
certain assumption is true: viz. that expressions such as
'natural substance' and 'having a nature' are not appropriate
terms for just anything that changes from within, but only
for a special kind of thing, a *per se* unity, whose changes,
unlike those of a machine, cannot be wholly explained by
the changes of simpler components. Now for Aristotle, it
seems certain, the distinction between artefacts and natural
substances is indeed absolute, despite his awareness of the
possibility of automata. It follows that his entitlement to
apply the concept 'natural substances' to such things as
organisms rests entirely on his ability to show that these
are *per se* unities. This is the question with which I shall be
concerned in this chapter.

(6) The problem touches not only Aristotle's employment of
the concept 'nature', but also his ontology. If there is doubt
whether organisms (for instance) are *per se* unities, there is
doubt whether they are substances properly speaking. A *per
accidens* unity, e.g. that expressed by 'doctor' (= 'medical
man') may indeed be a subject of attributes, as when we say
'The doctor came and went', but *what* this subject is cannot
be expressed by a unitary formula, and there cannot in the
strict sense be definition of such a thing. In the previous
chapter we argued the intimate connection between the
concept of nature and that of substance, and in *Physics* II.1,
193 a9–10, we find Aristotle speaking of the 'nature and

substance' of natural beings as if these are alternative expressions.[3] Thus an attack upon the *per se* unity of a thing is an attack both on its claim to be endowed with a nature, and on its claim to the status of substance.[4] Now in *Metaphysics* Z 2, 1028b8-13, Aristotle gives a list of things held ('δοκεῖ') to be substances. This corresponds to the list of things having natures at the beginning of *Physics* II.1, except that in the *Metaphysics* passage he also includes the heaven and the heavenly bodies. But in the course of his elucidation of 'substance' in Z, he finds reason for rejecting some of the items in the 'ἔνδοξον', namely the parts of animals (and presumably of other living things) and the simple bodies (Z 16, 1040b5 ff.).[5] On this last point the *Metaphysics* doctrine differs from that of the *Physics*. For the equation in *Physics* II.1, 193a9-10 of 'being a substance' with 'having a nature (= inner principle of change)' entails a substantial status for the simple bodies. However, the point which mainly concerns us here is that in neither work does Aristotle hesitate to include such complex beings as whole organisms. Thus, for instance, in discussing 'becoming' in *Metaphysics* Z 7, he says: '. . . and what comes into being is a man, or a plant or the like, which things above all we say are substances'. (1032a18-19) And although there is no such explicit declaration in the *Physics*, this is clearly only because he regards it as unnecessary. But how is it that Aristotle is so certain? And who are 'we' in the above-quoted passage who 'say' with such certainty? As so often, it is not clear whether Aristotle means himself, or the consensus of philosophical opinion, or common sense, or all three. Common sense of course takes men, plants, etc. to be as genuinely real as anything can be, just as it takes tables to be solid, but equally of course it has no views either way on the question of their metaphysical status as substances.

---

[3] Cf. *Metaphysics* Δ 4, 1015a13-15. For the indefinability of *per accidens* unities, see Z 4, 1030a2 ff.

[4] These remarks together with para. (5) imply that artefacts are not substances, a position which may seem paradoxical given that they supply Aristotle's favourite illustrations for the form/matter distinction, which is of primary significance in connection with substances. Yet he himself denies substancehood to artefacts in *Metaph*. H 3, 1043b20-2. Cf. Charlton, pp. 75-6.

[5] See also Λ 3, 1070a18-20. Parts of animals do not count as substances because they have no 'separate existence' (*v.i.* para. (42)); the simple bodies because they are without structure, 'like a heap'.

(7) It is worth considering briefly why Aristotle *qua* meta-physician need commit himself on the question of which types of natural objects have substantial status. For this question appears to be an empirical one, insofar as it de-pends on deciding what phenomena are to be explained as combinations of constituents. The plausibility of the hypo-thesis that a given type of complex is to be thus explained rests with the empirical evidence.[6] It is difficult to see how Aristotle could have rejected this point out of hand. But once it is admitted to be an empirical question whether this or that sort of object is a substance, it is not clear how the metaphysician can continue to maintain his certainty that the concept of substance does apply to the natural world and plays an essential part in the conceptual framework of science. For if the question is empirical, the conclusion that any given type of object is a substance would always be sub-ject to revision from new evidence. Even the so-called simple bodies may turn out to be complexes of elements. The meta-physician might continue to maintain that there must be *per se* unities, since otherwise there would be nothing for *per accidens* combinations to be combinations of; but he could not identify any of the former for certain, nor therefore any of the latter. According to Aristotle's scheme, this entails that we should never know for certain which of our defi-nitions of things were in the strict sense definitions. But if, despite this, science can still keep going, then in what way is the concept of substance as *per se* unity necessary for science, and what function can it have in a philosophical account of how the scientist does or should operate? It is not clear that it has any value even as a regulative principle: on the con-trary, it might well be argued that science should proceed on the assumption that there are no ultimate unities in physical nature. And although this does not entail that none exist, what is the advantage, either to science or to metaphysics, of holding that they do? So far as the knowledge of nature is concerned, physical substances would be as otiose as Platonic Forms.

---

[6] Cf. A. Gotthelf, 'Aristotle's Conception of Final Causality', *Review of Metaphysics* XXX, 1976, p. 253: 'Philosophers of science today are in increasing agreement that the question of reduction is an empirical one . . .'.

(8) With these issues in mind we turn to the text. In *Physics* II.1, having stated what nature is, and that it would be absurd to try to prove its existence, Aristotle continues:

> Some hold that the nature and substance of natural beings is, in each case, the immediate constituent that is in itself unstructured,[7] so that e.g. the wood is the nature of a bed, the bronze of a statue. Antiphon says that this is indicated by the fact that if one were to plant a bed and the rotting wood got the power to send up a shoot, what came up would not be a bed, but wood: which shows that the arrangement in accordance with the rules of art is in it *per accidens*, whereas the substance is the wood, which also remains continuously present while subject to this arrangement (193 a9-17)

Aristotle has himself made the point that it is not the bed as such that has a nature, but the wood; his reason was that the bed is an artefact, the wood not. Antiphon's point as Aristotle presents it is rather different. It is that the wood is endowed with nature because the wood is *matter* as opposed to form, 'the immediate unstructured constituent'. For Aristotle continues:

> And if each of these things [sc. such as wood] stands in this same relation to something else, e.g. bronze and gold to water, bones and wood to earth, and so on, the latter is their nature and substance. For this reason some hold the nature of things to be fire, others earth, others air, others water, others some of these, and others all. For whatever thing any of these theorists takes to be of this sort, whether one thing or more than one, this or these he says are the whole of substance ($\tau\grave{\eta}\nu$ $\mathring{\alpha}\pi\alpha\sigma\alpha\nu$ $o\mathring{v}\sigma\acute{\iota}\alpha\nu$), and all other things are affections, states, and arrangements of these. Each of these moreover is eternal, since they do not pass away out of themselves, while all other things come into being and pass away time after time without end.[8] (193 a17-28)

(9) Aristotle does not dispute that complex physical objects are made of and can be broken down into a few simple stuffs (see e.g. *De Caelo* III.3 302a10-25). The fundamental difference between his position and the materialists' (to use a

---

[7] 'To $\pi\rho\hat{\omega}\tau o\nu$ $\grave{\epsilon}\nu\acute{\upsilon}\pi\acute{\alpha}\rho\chi o\nu$ $\grave{\epsilon}\nu$ $\grave{\epsilon}\kappa\acute{\alpha}\sigma\tau\omega,|\grave{\alpha}\rho\rho\acute{\upsilon}\theta\mu\iota\sigma\tau o\nu$ $\langle\mathring{o}\nu\rangle$ $\kappa\alpha\theta$' $\grave{\epsilon}\alpha\upsilon\tau\acute{o}$'. The context shows that Aristotle means stuffs such as wood, not the prime matter of the scholastics; cf. Ross, *Aristotle's Physics*, p. 502. It is doubtful whether 'prime matter' ever appears in the *Physics* (cf. Charlton, pp. 78-9 and 129-45). If it does occur in Book II, it is only in the most oblique fashion: see para. (16).

[8] Cf. *Metaph.* Δ 4, 1014b26-35. I take 'the whole of substance' to mean (i) that the simple bodies are all the substances that there are, and (ii) that they give substantiality or being to other things by constituting them.

convenient label) concerns the following question: given that
O is made of M_1, M_2, etc., does it follow that O has no
nature apart from the natures of M_1, M_2, etc.? Alternatively:
does it follow that O is nothing but M_1, M_2, etc., in certain
states and arrangements? An affirmative answer sums up the
materialist position presented in the passage above. According to this, not only artefacts fail to count as natural substances, but so do all natural objects composed of natural
substances. For the composite is only its constituents combined, hence it is no single substance with a unitary nature
in its own right. So if Aristotle is consistently to maintain
that men, plants, etc., are such single substances, his answer
to the question just posed must be negative. But before
turning to this, let us consider the materialist position in
more detail.

(10) The case as Aristotle presents it falls into two parts: (i)
where it is claimed that the nature of a thing is its *immediate*
matter (193 a9-17) and (ii) where it is claimed that the only
real substances or things with natures are the *elements* that
ultimately underlie all physical objects (ibid. 21-3).[9] The
second claim is reached from the first by analogical reasoning (ibid. 17-21): if what a structured thing is immediately
composed of is its nature, then whatever what composes it
is composed of must be the latter's nature, and so on until
we arrive at some stuff or stuffs that are not themselves
composed of anything. Now it is strange that Aristotle does
not notice that this analogical argument leads to a conclusion
quite contrary to the intended one. For if the nature of a
thing is the matter of which it is immediately composed, then
simple stuffs which are not themselves composed of anything
cannot be said to have a nature: in which case, how can they
be the nature and substance of everything else? It seems that
Aristotle has missed a point that favours his own position.
For he could have argued: if there are ultimate constituents,
then either they themselves have natures, or not. If not, then
the internal principle of change in a complex being cannot be
identified with the nature of any ultimate consitutent of it;
in which case there is room to argue that the complex being

[9] Cf. J. Burnet, *Early Greek Philosophy* (4th ed.), pp. 10-12, 363-4.

has, as a whole, its own nature, and therefore is a genuine substance. But if the ultimate elements do have natures, then having a nature does not necessarily depend on being composed of something; and in that case, there is room to argue that although a complex being *is* composed of simpler substances, its having a nature does not consist in its being thus composed, so that there is no ground for the claim that the nature it has is not really *its* nature, but that of some constituent or constituents.

(11) Thus there are particular reasons why the analogical argument fails as a link between parts (i) and (ii) of the materialist position, but in fact no argument could succeed. For given the synonymy of 'having a nature' with 'being a substance', it follows that if either part is true the other is false. If earth, fire, water, etc. are 'the whole of substance', then wood, being composed of these, is no more a natural *substance* in itself than the bed is.[10] The contradiction could be avoided by making 'substance', like 'matter', a relative term, or else by making it admit of degrees. Thus one could say that the wood is a substance relatively to the bed, or that it is more of a substance than the bed is, being fewer removes from ultimate (and non-relative) substances. If any materialist did hold both (i) and (ii) as a unified position, he would be compelled to admit that 'substance' can be said of wood only in a qualified sense. But there is some reason to think that (i) and (ii) actually represent distinct positions, each employing a different criterion of substancehood or nature. According to Aristotle, those who held that a thing's immediate matter is its substance or nature support the claim by pointing to cases in which the immediate matter can propagate or reproduce itself, while the thing as a whole (e.g. the bed) cannot. Thus they seem to be identifying the nature of a thing with whatever it is in it that gets itself reproduced without external contrivance. But if this is the criterion of nature or substancehood, then 'substance' in this connection is being used in an absolute sense: for the proposition that

[10] This appears to be the meaning of Empedocles fr. 8 Diels, quoted in *Metaph.* Δ 4, 1015a1-3, on which see W.D. Ross, *Aristotle's Metaphysics*, vol. I, pp. 297-8.

e.g. wood can reproduce itself is simply true, not true in relation to a particular conceptual context (like the proposition that wood is matter). Thus positions (i) and (ii) cannot be combined in the way suggested above. And in any case, the use of self-reproduction as a criterion for 'nature' fits badly with the view that the only real substances with natures are the primitive elements. For on this view, as Aristotle reports it (193a26-7), the elements are held to be eternal, hence neither propagated nor reproduced. Indeed, this supposed eternity appears to be the criterion followed in identifying these elements with 'the whole of substance': the presumption being that only the eternal is truly real, so that transient things are merely the latter's temporary modifications.

(12) Now the two materialist positions just distinguished have one feature in common: they both contradict Aristotle's own view that structured organic beings have, as such and in their own right, substancehood and nature. But they are sufficiently different to need to be argued against separately. It is therefore surprising, not to say disappointing, to find Aristotle treating them as a single position, or rather, as if the second were entirely merged in the first. For he opens his reply as follows:

So according to one way of looking at it, nature is said to be the immediate underlying matter in each of those things that have within themselves a principle of motion and change. But according to another way, nature is the shape and the definable form. (193a28-31)

He then goes on to argue (a) that it is right to regard form too as nature, and (b) that the form of a thing is its nature more than the immediate matter is (193b6-18). And this is the whole of his reply in *Physics* II.1 to the materialists. In other words, he here makes out no explicit case at all for the claim of form to be nature as against the claim of the *non*-immediately underlying matter, i.e. the more basic constituents. Nor, as we shall see, do his arguments in II.1 offer even an implicit defence against this, the second materialist position. Yet it is this that to the modern reader seems so clearly to present the real menace to Aristotelianism. In particular, it seems to make teleological explanation redundant or even meaningless. It is strange that in II.1 Aristotle appears unaware of the danger from this quarter. But by the end of Book II he has recognized, and, I shall argue, replied to it in full.

(13) Meanwhile, let us return to his more immediate concern in Chapter 1. He begins as follows his attack on the materialism that identifies nature with the immediate matter:

> Just as the word 'art' is applied to what is by art and an artefact, so the word 'nature' is applied to what is by nature and natural. In the former case, we should not say that anything is by art while it is only potentially a bed and does not yet have the form of a bed, and nor do we say that it is art. It is the same with things constituted by nature. For that which is potentially flesh or bone does not yet have its own nature [sc. as flesh, etc.] until it acquires the form specified in the definition, and nor is it by nature. Thus on the other account [sc. of what nature is], nature would be the shape and form of those things that have within themselves a principle of change, not separable from them except in formula. (The combination of these [i.e. the form with the matter], as for instance a man, is not a nature, but by nature.) Shape and form is nature rather than matter. For it is when a thing is actual rather than potential that its definition applies. (193a31–b8)[11]

(14) This argument is based on usage, and as with all such arguments it is not clear how linguistic premisses can establish a philosophical conclusion. But the present instance has defects of its own as well. It depends on a play on words, and on a question-begging use of the analogy between art and nature. In the first place, the remark 'that which is potentially flesh or bone does not yet have its own nature [sc. as flesh, etc.] until it acquires the form specified in the definition' may be taken two ways. On the one hand it states that something cannot be said to be a thing of a given kind unless it has the typifying characteristics of that kind, and that the typifying characteristics include the form, not merely the matter (that which is 'potentially' the thing in question). Here, 'nature' is being used to mean typifying characteristics, or what one would mention if asked to say *what* the thing

---

[11] Cf. *Metaph.* Δ 4, 1015a4–7.

is.[12] In this sense the remark is a virtual tautology; but in this sense too even artefacts might be said to have natures. Such 'natures' are not the prerogative of *per se* units or substances in the strict sense. They belong to anything whatever concerning which it is possible to state *what* it is. Thus to take an example of Aristotle's,[13] we say what a threshold is by saying that it is a piece of wood in a certain position; but this position occurs only *per accidens* in the wood considered as wood. However, 'nature' in the sense with which Aristotle is primarily concerned in *Physics* II.1 means 'inner principle of change'. On this other reading, the sentence just quoted asserts that an object's inner principle of change cannot be or be grounded in its component materials alone, and must therefore be (or at least depend upon) the form. But this is not only not a tautology, it is not self-evident either, being nothing other than the conclusion which Aristotle by this argument is in process of trying to prove.

(15) In the second place, he uses the analogy between nature and art to insinuate that the material of a structured natural object of type T is devoid of nature of its own so long as it has not yet acquired the specific form that makes it of type T. From this it would follow that nature (in either of the senses just distinguished) resides in form rather than in matter. If this seems plausible, it is because of the alleged parallel with art. As Aristotle points out, 'art' (in the sense of 'work of art'[14]) is properly applied to the product, not to the raw materials of an artefact. Since the materials become the product called 'art' by receiving an imposed artificial structure, there is good reason to hold that the product's 'art'-status depends upon the structure or form alone, since the materials necessarily acquire the one when they acquire the other, and vice versa. But a similar conclusion cannot be drawn for 'nature' unless it is as certain that the materials composing natural objects lack *natures* as that the materials of

---

[12] Cf. Mansion, pp. 102-3, and I. Düring, 'Aristotle on Ultimate Principles from "Nature and Reality"', *Aristotle and Plato in the Mid-Fourth Century*, edd. Düring and Owen.

[13] Cf. *Metaph.* H 2, 1043a7-8.

[14] Cf. Charlton, p. 90.

artefacts lack '*art*'. Now the raw material of an artefact by definition lacks 'art' in the sense of 'artificial structure'. It also lacks 'art' in the sense in which an artificer has it, i.e. the power to cause artificial change — necessarily so, since if the wood were able to turn itself into a bed, a bed would not *be* an artefact but a natural substance containing its own principle of growth. But the immediate matter of a structured natural substance does have a 'nature' in the sense of a definite character: it is flesh, etc. And so far Aristotle has said nothing to show that it does not have 'nature' in the sense too of 'inner principle of change'. And if it does, we have been given as yet no reason why we should not hold that the natural changes of a structured natural object of which flesh, etc. is the material are entirely due to, or indeed identical with, changes whose source is the nature of flesh as such. In any case, the art/nature analogy cuts two ways. Aristotle would hardly wish to deny that the materials of artefacts have natures (inner principles of change), since the materials of artefacts are natural substances. So, if natural structures are analogous, why not say that the materials of natural structures also have natures? And if this is conceded, the way is open (for all he has so far shown) to the further conclusion that the nature of a structured natural object is nothing but the nature of its material. Such is the lesson which Antiphon draws from the analogy between art and nature, and on the present showing he is as much entitled to his conclusion as Aristotle to his.

(16) We found fault with Aristotle's equivocation between two senses of 'nature', but the confusion also suggests an insight on his part which we have so far ignored. For although it is not the case that everything with a definable character possesses, as such, an internal principle of change, the converse does hold. Anything that has a nature in the second sense must be of a definite character. Since changes from within are expressions of what it is, there must be a positive answer to the question 'What is it?'. From this point of view, Aristotle's argument effectively answers a purely metaphysical 'materialism', such as would seek to identify the source of change with prime matter or the indefinite

('ἀόριστον')[15] particularizing element in a concrete thing, discernible only metaphysically from its 'whatness'.

(17) This position may be part of what Aristotle is opposing in II.1, 193 a31–b8. But if so, his presentation is far from clear. In the first place empirical cases such as that of the bed sprouting are irrelevant to the metaphysical point. Secondly, the distinction between immediate and remote matter employed at 193 a10 makes sense only as applied to empirically characterizable components at different levels of physical analysis. Thirdly, he does not maintain that matter contributes *nothing* to a thing's nature, only that the role of form is paramount. But the pure particularity of a thing cannot in any sense be or contribute to its nature. For the natures of things are, after all, what the natural scientist is supposed to study. This last point incorporates what for Aristotle would be the decisive objection against identifying the source of natural change with the metaphysical principle of particularity: for since the particularity of things lies beyond or below the scope of science (cf. *Metaphysics* B 6, 1003 a14), so, on this view, would the causes of change. So far then, the position which Aristotle has confronted may be viewed as a somewhat confused mixture of empirical and metaphysical materialisms. While he may be assumed to have an adequate answer to the latter, we have not yet seen an effective move against the former. In particular, the metaphysical thesis that the source of change must lie in the definite character of something tells neither for nor against the theory that the only true substances and natural sources of change are the basic (but empirical) elements, earth, fire, etc.

(18) Arguing still in II.1 that nature is form, Aristotle continues:

Moreover, man comes into being from man, although not bed from bed. This is their reason for saying that the wood, not the structure, is the nature: because if it grew what would come into being would not be a bed but wood. But if this is nature, the shape too is nature, since man comes into being from man. (193b8–12)[16]

---

[15] Cf. *Physics* III.2, 201b24–8.
[16] I have translated Ross's text, but the MSS 'εἰ δ'ἄρα τοῦτο τέχνη' yields an argument with the same import.

Here he is explicitly attempting to show what so far he has
not shown, that nature in the sense of the defining shape is
also the nature in the sense of principle of change. Growth
and reproduction are the changes that are significant for this
argument. Here Aristotle is accepting Antiphon's criterion for
'nature', i.e. that what has a nature is what reproduces itself,
but is also saying in effect that Antiphon's conclusion is
based on just one type of case, and not even a representative
one at that. As soon as we look past the bed example we find
ones where something of a given structure produces something else of that same structure. It is not clear whether by
'Man comes into being from man' Aristotle means growth of
an immature into a mature human, or the begetting of one
by the other, or both. But if Antiphon were right, man,
whose immediate matter is flesh, bones, etc., would only give
rise (in either sense) to flesh and bones not organized as a
man (or if so, only by accident). And there is no reason to
think that Antiphon is right even in some cases, since his
example is an *artefact*, which as such *has* no nature. Not
only is it false then to say that *its* nature lies in its matter,
but the example provides no ground for saying this of any
natural kind.

(19) Aristotle's objection to Antiphon, that man gives rise
to man, was based on a fact of experience. But Aristotle now
moves the discussion back on to the linguistic level, and
draws further support from 'what we say' (or rather, the
presumed etymology of 'what we say'), by means of the
following obscure dialectical argument:

Moreover, 'φύσις', in the sense in which the word is equivalent to
'genesis', means the process by which something arrives at its nature
(φύσις).[17] For it is not like 'curing', which denotes not the process
towards the art of curing, but towards health. For whereas curing
necessarily proceeds from but not to the art of curing, φύσις is not
related in this way to φύσις. Instead, the growing thing (τὸ φυόμενον)
passes from something into something, insofar as it grows. What,
then, is it growing to be? Not that from which, but that into which.
The shape, then, is the nature. (193b12–18)

[17] Cf. *Metaph.* Δ 4, 1014b16–17, with Ross's comm., vol. I, p. 296, and
Mansion, pp. 104–5.

This passage is confusing because Aristotle's point depends upon a contrast between nature or φύσις, and activities of artifice such as medicine; yet (as so often) he at the same time relies on features common to the two cases. In both, the process results in a shape, i.e. a structured state of affairs, whether this is the balance of qualities within the cured patient's body, or the mature form into which a natural substance develops. (In both cases too, although he makes no direct allusion to this point, the specific character of the process is defined by reference to the sort of shape achieved.) Now for the contrast. Firstly, the state in which the process of healing results is not medical art, i.e. the state of the healer that is source of the healing process. But the natural process of growth denoted by the word 'φύσις' (in the sense in which this means 'genesis') does result in a state that in turn gives rise to such processes, and this state is also called 'φύσις'. Evidently Aristotle is thinking of the fact that man generates man: i.e. that a full-grown man is a source of processes (in offspring) identical in kind to that by which he developed. Secondly, the agent that does the healing does not (*qua* healer) come to be in any new or more developed condition; whereas the natural entity that 'does the growing' *itself* passes into the developed state. Thus a kind of conceptual coincidence obtains between (*a*) the concept of the developed natural state and (*b*) the concept of the source of the process that gives rise to that state, for which there is no parallel in the case of curing. For in the first place, as we have just seen, the developed state in which the natural process results is a condition which is itself a source of such processes. And secondly, when we ask (as in the third to last sentence of the quoted passage) what the growing thing is, i.e. what sort of a growing thing it is, the answer is given by predicating *of that object* the same word as is used of it in the developed state. Thus we say that a tadpole is a (developing) frog, a child a (developing) human being, whereas we do not say that a doctor as such is a (coming to be) healthy person. Now the developing creature is not merely developing, but also still contains within itself the source of its (continued) develop-ment. For if by developing to some extent it somehow lost this principle of change, it could not be said to *be* still developing. Thus the developing creature has, firstly, φύσις in the sense of the process of growth, and secondly, φύσις in the sense of the inner source of this change. And the creature is also defined by the term denoting what it will develop into, which term, being definitive, gives its φύσις or nature in yet a third sense, the sense in which the nature of a thing is what somebody asks for who asks to be told *what it is*. Putting all this together, we may say (i) that both *qua* developing and *qua* developed, the natural substance is endowed with an inner principle of change; and (ii) that if 'C' is the predicate expressing the shape or form when fully developed, the creature both *qua* developing and *qua* developed is to be defined as a C. From this Aristotle concludes that nature in the sense of an inner principle of change *is* the developed form.

(20) Now it may be said that despite the close dependence just exhibited between nature as principle of change, and the developed structure, Aristotle exceeds his warrant in concluding that the former *is* the latter, since by the very terms of the argument, the latter is the *result* of the former, and is not always actually present at the same time. This indeed is perhaps the main difficulty surrounding the Aristotelian concept of 'form', which in a living thing at any rate is supposed somehow to comprise both efficient and final causes of the substance's natural behaviour. How can what something is to be, which it necessarily is not yet, *be* what brings about the present process towards what is to be? Writers sympathetic to Aristotelianism do not succeed in explaining this to those who are not. But however paradoxical the equation of final with efficient cause, consider the consequences of denying it, i.e. of refusing to identify nature as a principle of change or development with nature in the sense of fully developed structure. Suppose that we reject this, on the ground that the develop*ing* creature has one but lacks the other. It follows that when the creature attains developed form, it has a property which earlier it lacked. If this developed form is, as Aristotle always holds it to be, that in virtue of which the creature is a substance of the kind that it is, it follows that the still developing creature was not a substance of that kind.

Either it was of a different kind, or it was no substance at all. In either case, it is impossible that developing and developed should be the same individual substance at different phases of its history, for the same individual Aristotelian substance must, for as long as it exists, be of a single nature throughout all changes, including development. But if developing and developed are not the same individual, the developed never did develop, and there is no such thing as development. The alternative, for Aristotle equally absurd, would be to deny that the fully developed structure is an essential property of the creature which attains it. In that case, the developing creature lacked nothing in virtue of which the developed is the kind of substance that it is. But then what is the essential or substantial nature that was present throughout? The only likely candidate is the property of being a source of development (or developments) into such and such a type of structured object. This property is common to the developing and also to the developed (the latter being a potential parent of like offspring). This implies that being endowed with a source of development into mature structure C is of the essence of the object, even though having C itself is not of the essence; from which it follows that the substance might itself cease to be characterized by C (e.g. the structure of a mature human being) while retaining the essential power of giving rise to developments towards C: thus what is no longer a man (of human structure) could nonetheless generate man. To conclude: if a developing thing is a substance of the kind it is on account of the principle within it of development, and if a developed one is of the kind *it* is on account of its fully structured form, then these two natures, *natura naturans* and *natura naturata*, must be and all along have been in some sense identical, or else the same individual substance has different substantial essences.

(21) Having supported Aristotle thus far in his identification of nature (= principle of change) with form rather than matter, let us now see how effective this is against the materialist position, and in particular against the second of the materialist claims distinguished in (10) above. This was the

theory that the only real substances are the physical elements, while 'everything else' is only these elements in various 'affections, states and arrangements'. Now the concept of 'nature' which we have seen brought to the surface combines (*a*): 'nature' = 'a thing's typifying characteristics': with (*b*): 'nature' = 'what it is about a thing that gets reproduced in growth and generation': and these two with (*c*): 'nature' = 'the power of growth and generation'. But on the face of it, the construction of this concept neither entails nor presupposes the falsity of "elemental" materialism. For it seems perfectly consistent to hold (i) that a thing has a nature in the complex sense just explained, while also holding (ii) that this nature, both the power of reproduction and the typical characteristics reproduced, derives entirely from the ways in which the basic components of the organism are together in it. And the conjunction of (i) and (ii) again seems perfectly consistent with the view (iii) that the component elements are as they are in the organism merely in the natural course of their own natural behaviour and interactions. If (ii) and (iii) are true, then the nature of the organism can be fully accounted for, scientifically, in terms of its constituents. But in that case, the organism is not, *qua* having its nature, a *per se* unity, and any organic behaviour resulting from its nature derives ultimately from a *per accidens* combination of mutually external factors.

(22) That (i), (ii) and (iii) might all be true together is a possibility which in II.1 Aristotle seems to ignore. Certainly he is not troubled by it in this chapter. But, we might ask, why should he be? Having started with the comparatively simple notion of nature as inner principle of change, which covers homogeneous substances such as fire, earth, etc., he has now, by interweaving (*a*), (*b*) and (*c*) above, developed this so as to establish (as against Antiphon) the position that nature in organic cases is to be equated primarily with form rather than immediate matter. The resulting conception is coherent; it is supported by ordinary uses of 'nature' and allied words; and above all it can be applied on the basis of experience. What then is to be gained by additionally insisting that a natural substance is a *metaphysical unity* in a sense in which

this would entail that its nature is irreducible to those of more primitive constituent substances? Perhaps we ought not to be disappointed that in II.1 Aristotle offers no real opposition to the "elemental" materialists: perhaps indeed we should even applaud his quiet omission to take an *a priori* stand on what would nowadays be considered an empirical question (cf. para. (7)). Nor would this omission deprive him of the right to his initial equation of 'having a nature' and 'being a substance' (*v.s.* para. (6)): to retain it, he only needs to relax the concept of 'substance' so as to apply it (along with 'nature') without any presumption of unity in some possibly incoherent absolute sense. On these terms he would presumably reject the elementalist statement that fire, earth, etc. are 'the whole of substance', if by this is meant that these are the only things entitled to be called 'substances'; but he need not deny the other meaning that the words can bear (cf. para. (8), n. 8), i.e. that all things (including non-elementary substances) derive their natures from these.

(23) However inviting such a position, Aristotle makes it clear by the end of *Physics* II that it is not for him. This emerges beyond any doubt from his discussion of necessity in Chapter 9. He asks concerning necessity in nature:

Is the necessary necessary on a supposition, or absolutely? I ask this because on the current view of necessity in [natural] coming to be, it is as if one were to think that a house-wall had come into being by necessity because it is of the nature of heavy things to move downwards and of light things upwards, and therefore the stones and the foundations go at the bottom, the earth higher because it is light, and the wood at the top because it is lightest. But although it has not come into being without these, it is not *because* of them (except in the sense in which matter is a cause), but in order to enclose and protect. It is the same with everything else that has an end: it would not come into being without those things that possess the necessary nature, but these are not the cause, except in the sense in which matter is. The cause is the end: e.g. the question 'Because of what is a saw like this?' gets the answer 'So that such and such may result, and for the sake of such and such'. But this end cannot come about unless the saw is of iron. So it is necessarily iron if it is going to be a saw and to function as one. Thus what is necessary is so on a supposition, but the end product is not necessary. For the necessity is in the matter, whereas the end for the sake of which is in the formula. (199b34-200a15) . . . It is clear that there is necessity in the natural world only in the sense in which 'necessity' indicates matter and the changes of matter. The physicist must take account of both causes, the matter and that for the sake of which, but of the latter more than the former. For this is the cause of the matter, but the matter is not the cause of the end. The end is that for the sake of which, and the principle of a natural thing should be drawn from its definition and formula, as in the case of artificial products. Since a house is such and such a thing, these things must necessarily come about and be the case first, and since health is this, these things must necessarily come about and be the case first: so too, given that a man is this, then these, and if these, then those. (200a30–200b4)

These passages occur after the discussion (Chapter 8) in which Aristotle takes himself to have shown that the organization and behaviour of organisms and their organs can and ought to be accounted for teleologically. He now concludes that it is correct to say of an organism that it and its organs come about or are as they are by necessity *only to the extent that* the organism is made of certain materials which must necessarily be present and be disposed in various ways in order that there should be that organism. Only the matter and its states are necessary, and the necessary is only conditional. By thus confining necessity to the matter, Aristotle implies that the form, which is the end, is not only not necessary in the way in which the matter is (i.e. for a further end), but that it is not necessary at all, and therefore not a necessary consequence of the matter.[18]

(24) Aristotle's immediate purpose in limiting the role of necessity in nature is to uphold teleological explanation. But the passage just quoted also shows that he is committed still to regarding beings endowed with natures as *per se* unities. He has not lost hold of this metaphysical concept, even though our examination of II.1 led us to wonder whether it might not get quietly forgotten. For the condition for predicating *per se* unity of a complex natural being is identical with the condition for applying teleological explanation as Aristotle understands it. This condition is that the properties and behaviour of the complex being are not wholly explicable as the product of a *per accidens* combination of simpler

---

[18] M. Polanyi, 'Life's Irreducible Structure', *Topics in the Philosophy of Biology*, edd. Grene and Mendelsohn, pp. 128 ff. (originally in *Science* 160), calls the organism (or its form) 'the boundary condition', an expression well chosen to emphasize that the direction of necessitation is *from* form *to* constituents.

components and their respective behavings. Once such explanation is shown to fail, it follows (a) that the complex being is something other than a *per accidens* combination and (b) that in order to explain the being's characteristics and behaviour something other than its components must be invoked. (It should perhaps be remarked that (b) alone does not *entail* that the new explanatory concept will necessarily be teleological. For 'teleological explanation', as ordinarily understood by philosophers, including Aristotle, implies not merely that the explanation is *not mechanical*, but also, positively, that it invokes the notion of a good. In practice however, whoever accepts (b) will almost certainly regard (b) as proving the applicability of teleological explanation, since no other type of non-mechanical explanation seems to have been envisaged.)

(25) In the last paragraph, I spoke of teleological explanation 'as understood by Aristotle'. The point was to indicate the difference between him and those philosophers who hold that the same phenomenon can in principle be adequately explained both mechanically and teleologically.[19] Sometimes, too, it is suggested that while a teleological explanation may be satisfactory as long as the knowledge is lacking for an adequate mechanical one, such knowledge is in principle available and once it is achieved the teleological account should become a thing of the past, at least for the scientifically minded. It was useful as a heuristic device only, a metaphor that facilitated the construction of mechanistic hypotheses.[20] However, Aristotle's treatment of the artefact examples in II.9 shows that for him an explanation of complex

---

[19] For a discussion of this and related topics, cf. J.L. Mackie, *The Cement of the Universe*, pp. 276–84; for a tentative application to Aristotle, see Charlton, op. cit., p. 93. I have not taken account of the detailed study by R. Sorabji, in *Necessity, Cause and Blame, Perspectives on Aristotle's Theory* (esp. Part III), which appeared after the completion of this work.

[20] See e.g W. Wieland, *Die aristotelische Physik*, Ch. 16, (transl. as 'The Problem of Teleology' in *Articles on Aristotle*, vol. I, edd. Barnes, Schofield, and Sorabji), pp. 267–8: 'teleological explanation . . . is a concept which *make possible a more exact search for causes* simply by presenting itself as a *guideline* for the exploration of the particular'. (Author's italics.) For further references, see M. Grene, 'Aristotle and Modern Biology', *Topics in the Philosophy of Biology*, p. 7 (first appeared in *Journal of the History of Ideas* XXX). See also Gotthelf, pp. 252–3.

natural substances in terms only of the necessary behavings
of their component materials would be *inadequate*; inadequate, that is to say, *not* because such an explanation is as it
stands sufficient, yet is merely one of several types of sufficient explanation, so that on its own it does not exhaust the
possible accounts: but because the nature and behaviour of
the components are on their own insufficient to provide even
one satisfactory explanation.[21] In other words, for Aristotle
the concept of 'end' provides not an *additional explanation*,
nor one that can eventually be dispensed with, but the *only*
explanation of some*thing additional* (to the materials) in
the phenomenon to be explained.

(26) We must now face the question whether Aristotle has
any good ground for supposing the form of an organism (and
therefore also the principle that gives rise to the form considered as an empirically knowable structure) to be causally
extra to the matter. It is of course possible to distinguish
conceptually between the shape of a thing and what is shaped,
but this does not prove that what is thus shaped did not by
the laws of its own nature come to be in that shape. This distinction can be made even for some mass of inanimate matter,
say a lump of earth, yet Aristotle would certainly not attribute the shape in this case to a form that is somehow beyond
the matter (his matter–form distinction cannot be made at
all for the simple bodies: this is part of what he means by
'simple' in this connection). It might be objected that this
example makes no point, since bits of earth can be of any
shape, which shows that the particular shape is not of the
nature of a piece of earth as such; whereas what we are concerned with is organisms, which, within a given kind, have always the same morphology. But it could be answered that
this difference tells, if at all, on the side of the materialists,
since the very regularity with which an organic form recurs
suggests causal dependence: and what *is* there for it to depend upon if not the physical constituents? We may begin to
wonder whether Aristotle has not been enticed too far by
his analogy with artefacts. More often than not (even in

[21] Cf. Mansion, p. 340.

the *Physics*, but especially in the *Metaphysics*) he takes arte-facts as illustrations of the distinction between matter and form. And we may be forgiven for suspecting that they are not so much apt examples as the only coherent ones. For in an artefact, by definition, the form is causally extraneous to the matter, since that is why there was need of the arti-ficer. In them too the form is extraneous for the additional reason that the same artificial arrangement can in many cases be imposed upon diverse types of matter: there can be iron as well as wooden bedsteads. Whereas Aristotle makes it clear that in natural substances there is no such loose connection of form with proximate matter. 'What always happens neces-sarily happens': so that if there are never trees of iron this is surely because there could not be.[22] It is true that the im-possibility of there being a tree unless of a given type of material does not entail that such material must necessarily result in a tree. But the acknowledged dependence in one direction (no tree without woody material), which is not in general paralleled in the case of artefacts, suggests that he has not sufficiently investigated the possibility of dependence in the other direction too (no woody material of such and such a kind which is not necessarily in the form of a tree). The fact that this latter dependence does not hold in the case of artefacts cannot be used as evidence for its not holding in the case of natural substances. If natural substances differ from artefacts in respect of the former dependence, why not also in respect of the latter? And a similar argument could be based on another difference already examined in Chapter I, (50). A natural substance by contrast with an artefact not only requires a particular *type* of matter, but the principle which in any individual case brings the form to completion

---

[22] D.M. Balme, 'Aristotle's Biology was not Essentialist', *Archiv für Geschichte der Philosophie* 62, 1980, pp. 1 ff., takes *Metaph.* Z 11, 1036b 2-7, as showing that Aristotle believes in 'the possibility that . . . man, whose essence is rational soul, could conceivably be realised in matter other than flesh and bones.' But Aristotle says only (7-8): 'τοῦτο δοκεῖ μὲν ἐνδέχεσθαι, ἄδηλον δὲ πότε'. He is not only dis-cussing his own views, so 'δοκεῖ' may not refer to these; cf. 24-8, where he rejects the possibility in the case of 'man'. And 'τοῦτο' in 7 may refer to "separation" in general, rather than to this special case, so that the sentence would mean: 'Al-though it is not ruled out it is not clear in which cases ('πότε') it is possible', (the implication being that in some it is not).

is so intimately related to matter that it can only operate on *one particular* material object, viz. the body of the individual itself, and no other.

(27) If Aristotle simply ignored these disanalogies between natural objects and artefacts in order to maintain that matter in the former case cannot account for form, we might reasonably accuse him of falling unawares into the Platonism he is resolute to avoid. For if the form neither springs from the matter, nor is imposed by a maker within the natural world, where can it be "from" if not some transnatural realm, or the mind of a divine maker? In fact, however, Aristotle seems to see himself finding an adequate alternative to such Platonism[23] when he emphasizes precisely those aspects of natural substance that suggest the immanence of form. And these are precisely the respects in which we have just seen the analogy with artefacts break down. In short, our discussion so far has failed to show any way in which Aristotle could rebut the charge of taking up and putting down the analogy just as it happens to suit him. On the one hand, form in natural substance is regarded as causally extraneous to matter on the ground that natural substances are like artefacts; while on the other hand, natural substances must be held (on both *a priori* and empirical grounds) to differ from artefacts on precisely the points that enable us to say of an *artificial* form that it *is* causally extraneous to its matter. But if the analogy turns out to be useless to establish Aristotle's position (as set forth in II.9, and also in 3 and 7, where the final cause is presented as irreducible to any other kind of cause), the arguments of II.1 that we earlier reviewed are equally worthless. To point out that the structure of a thing, or that its developed state, primarily determines our concept of what sort of thing it is (and so of its 'nature' in one sense), is not to show that this structure and development is not explicable by the laws of the component materials. And whereas Antiphon's formulation of materialism may have fallen to the objection that man generates man, this does not disprove the deeper

[23] For his rejection of the Demiurge cf. *Metaph.* A 9, 991a20-3. See Wieland, *Die aristotelische Physik*, p. 273 and D.M. Balme, *Aristotle's De Part. An. I and De Gen. An. I*, pp. 94-5.

materialist thesis that being a man and a generator of men arises solely from the properties of more basic materials in certain arrangements. Now if the position of Aristotle in II.9 has any serious foundation in argument, the argument must have recognized and met this deeper thesis. So Aristotle himself realizes, for it is on this level that he reopens the issue of form as nature *versus* matter in Chapter 8, to which we must now turn.[24]

(28) Having stressed in Chapter 7 the theory of the four causes, Aristotle now sees the necessity of defending this against an attack which threatens to demolish not only the teleological explanation of natural phenomena but also any basis for maintaining that a complex natural substance is more than a *per accidens* conjunction of its elements.

Now we must explain, firstly, that nature is a final cause, and secondly the place of necessity in natural events. For everyone refers things to necessity as a cause, saying that since the hot and the cold etc. have such and such natures, such and such things exist and come to be, of necessity. For if they mention another cause, they only touch on it and let it go — Love and Strife in one theory, Mind in another. But there is a problem: what objection is there to holding that nature does not operate for an end, nor because it is better so, but instead is like the rain, which does not fall in order to make the corn grow, but of necessity? For what has been driven up must get cooled, and what is cooled turns into water and must come down: and it is an incidental result that the corn grows. Similarly, if someone's corn is spoiled on the threshing floor, the rain does not fall in order to spoil it, but this has happened incidentally. So what is the objection to saying that it is the same with the organic parts of natural substances: of necessity the

[24] The present account is at odds with D.J. Allan's remark, *The Philosophy of Aristotle*, p. 33; 'Since he does not assume the movement of inanimate matter to be governed by inflexible laws, he does not have to answer the question raised by modern exponents of vitalism and mechanism, i.e. whether these same laws can, without invoking new factors, be made to give a sufficient account of living organisms and their changes.' I accept the 'Since . . .' clause, but it does not justify the conclusion drawn. Prof. Allan here seems to confuse 'mechanism' (which in the context means 'biological reductionism') with 'rigid determinism'. 'Mechanism' has another unwanted modern association, with the concept of matter as inert. Thus the latter-day mechanist may in effect be denying the reality of what Aristotle calls 'inner principles of change'. But this is hardly at issue between Aristotle and the Presocratics attacked in II.8. For neither side is matter inert in the Newtonian sense (cf. D.M. Balme, 'Greek Science and Mechanism I and II', *Classical Quarterly* XXIII and XXV, 1939 and 1941). But there is still room for a reductionist controversy; see para. (42).

teeth come up with the front ones sharp and fit for tearing, and the molars flat and useful for grinding the food; since they do not come into being for the sake of that end, but happen to appear together? And similarly with all the other parts in which there appears to be an end. Thus in the cases in which all the parts came together as if it was for an end that they came to be, the organisms survived, being spontaneously composed in a suitable way. Whereas wherever this was not the case, they perished, and still perish, as Empedocles says of the man-faced oxenkind. This and any similar arguments might present a difficulty [*sc.* to the teleologist]. But it cannot be as they say. For these things and indeed all things that happen by nature either always come about in the way they do, or for the most part, whereas this is not true of any of the things that come about by chance or spontaneity. For we do not think it due to chance or coincidence if it rains often in the winter, although we do if this occurs in August; nor do we think it of heat-waves in August, though we would of heat-waves in the winter. If then it is agreed that 'by coincidence' and 'for an end' are the only alternatives, and if these things cannot be either by coincidence or by spontaneity,[25] they must be for an end. But all such things are by nature, as the holders of the theory themselves would agree. So 'being for an end' applies to things that come about and exist by nature. (198 b10-199 a8)

(29) Aristotle begins by preparing what seems an easy victory for himself. He attributes to his opponents a position that appears to be needlessly incoherent. He depicts them as holding that complex organically useful phenomena such as the set of teeth occur *both* by the necessary workings of the laws of their primitive components (the hot, the cold, etc., 198b13-14), *and* by coincidence ('συμπεσεῖν', 198b27, and 'ἀπὸ συμπτώματος', 199a1). Yet these, we might well object, are two very different positions, although both alike exclude Aristotelian teleology. It seems obvious too that whereas the first is reasonable and accords with the spirit of science, the second cannot be so described. Serious opponents of finalism would surely take their stand on necessity, and in general would neither need nor wish to assert coincidence. Yet it is only against the second that Aristotle directs his reply. The reply then seems based on an *ignoratio elenchi*, or at any rate on an *ignoratio* of the genuinely challenging core of the proposed theory, however confused its actual formulations by

---

[25] He is using 'by coincidence', 'by chance', and 'by spontaneity' as synonyms.

Empedocles and the others. But this objection to Aristotle betrays anachronistic misunderstanding. If we assume that 'necessity' (i.e. 'causal or natural necessity') and 'coincidence' offer necessarily different and even contrary accounts of the same phenomenon, this is because we are obsessed with the relatively modern problem of how to distinguish a causal or naturally necessary sequence of events from an accidental succession. For clearly the proposition that A caused B entails that B did not simply happen to happen after A. Thus we may think that no coherent theory could combine necessity with coincidence in the way in which Aristotle presents his opponents as doing. And since we are unlikely to believe that the only alternative theory to Aristotelian teleology is just such an incoherent amalgam of necessity and coincidence, we may well conclude that knowingly or not, Aristotle is misrepresenting the opposition.

(30) We shall see later whether this charge is a fair one. But first it must be said on Aristotle's side that he is not at all concerned with coincidence as a property of successions or sequences of events, or as implying absence of causality between earlier and later. He is not for instance saying that his adversaries suppose that the growth of the teeth is causally unconnected with any causal antecedents — a view which of course they did not hold. He is here using 'coincidence', and also 'by chance' (199a1) and 'by spontaneity' (198b30, 36), to refer (a) to a set of simultaneous phenomena each of which has an independent antecedent cause, and (b) to the (desirable) outcome of the concurrence. (This is the gist of his own analysis of chance and spontaneity in Chapters 5 and 6 of Book II.) In this sense, 'coincidence' is fully compatible even with universal causal determinism of later by earlier. For 'coincidence' means only that the result represents a convergence of mutually independent diachronic causal lines. Empedocles and the other physikoi are therefore portrayed by Aristotle as saying that organisms and their complex organic parts have come about through sets of independent causal processes involving separate material factors which behave and undergo transformation by the necessity of their own natures (cf. 198b12-14), and which merely *happen* to

occur together, since none occurs because any of the others do, or through the same cause.[26]

(31) Aristotle's statement of the theory he is opposing is not then logically incoherent, as at first it might have seemed; but even so he appears not to do his adversaries justice. This emerges from his reply, where he argues (a) that the phenomena to be explained cannot be regarded as happening by coincidence; and (b) that given that it is agreed ('δοκεῖ', 199a3) that they are either by coincidence or for an end, they must be for an end. Now Aristotle's reason for (a) is that we regard only exceptional phenomena as coincidental (in the sense explained), and that biologically useful conjunctions of organs and parts of organs are not exceptional. On this, he can appeal to the common-sense reaction to regularities of conjunction: if a conjunction regularly recurs, we take this as evidence of a common cause, which accounts not only for each conjunct severally, but also for their togetherness. And indeed the materialists can hardly have supposed that the teeth and other organs are 'together', forming an animal, through the entirely independent workings of separate causal lines. Why should Aristotle have imagined that they did think this, or that their position entailed it? The entailment does of course hold given Aristotle's premiss (b), but why should he have thought that anyone not already convinced of the need for teleology would accept (b)?[27] Granted that it is unreasonable not to suppose a common cause for phenomena regularly conjoined: but why should this cause necessarily consist in a common *end*? It might also be granted that if a regular conjunction regularly contributes to some good result, a satisfactory explanation of the regularity should make reference to that good. But the materialists are not logically committed to denying the relevance, in an explanation of the set of teeth, of the

[26] On this and the preceding paragraph cf. W.K.C. Guthrie, *History of Greek Philosophy*, vol. II, pp. 163-5 and 414-19.
[27] Cf. H. Cherniss, *Aristotle's Criticism of Presocratic Philosophy*, pp. 251-2. Cherniss attributes Aristotle's failure to recognize mechanical causation to a sheer inability to step outside his own conceptual system. Wieland, while more sympathetic, makes essentially the same point, *Die aristotelische Physik*, pp. 260-1.

fact that the *set* is useful (while its members would have been individually useless). Empedocles at any rate believed that he could do justice to our sense that such a denial would be unacceptable without resorting to a teleological account. Because such and such independent natural processes occurred, a particular fortunate conjunction came about, and being useful it (or rather the organism in which it occurred) survived, and reproduction together with the non-survival of non-viable conjunctions saw to it that conjunctions of this useful type became the regular thing. Aristotle's insistence that what happens regularly cannot be by coincidence seems crudely to miss the point of the Empedoclean account, which implicitly distinguishes between past and present infrequency, and between infrequency of types and of instances. The *types* of conjunction that are viable are few by comparison with all possible types, and also by comparison with all the types that have ever been actually instantiated. The *original instances* of viable types of conjunction were probably infrequent as compared with contemporaneous instances of non-viable types. But the *present instances* of the viable types are for obvious reasons vastly more frequent than *their* non-viable contemporaries. Thus in one way the set of teeth (and the animal it belongs to) is exceptional, in another sense not. There is no contradiction here, but a coherent (even if rather quaintly illustrated) theory, and one that does without teleology.

(32) If Aristotle fails to notice how the concepts of frequency and infrequency operate on different levels in this account, it may not surprise us that he commits what seems another obvious mistake: that of extending the concept of 'coincidence' as applied to the original coming together of elements in a viable combination, to their *remaining* combined, and also to the subsequent togetherness of similar components in the offspring. He argues as if in his adversaries' system coincidence, once introduced, carries on through all later stages. Just as the original conjoining was due to the mutually independent behaviour of different objects, so (he implies) the continuing existence of the resultant combination is due to nothing more: each constituent stays with the others by

being and behaving just as it would even if they were absent. On this view, the only kind of explanation for the combination's continuance will be a conjunction of explanations each showing how a given component came to be and still is where it is. This is the Empedoclean case as Aristotle construes it, and it looks like a straw man of his own making. Everyone would agree with Aristotle's rejection of this account, insofar as rejection implies belief in some connection between the various factors in the stable and self-reproducing compounds: a connection that calls for explanation in terms not reducible to a mere conjunction of independent causal stories. But Aristotle goes further: he assumes that the materialists could indicate no connection except a teleological one: the continuing union is for the sake of a useful whole. Yet to us it seems obvious that they could have grounded the combination in the natures of the factors themselves: these stay combined because they are such as to interact to form a stable system — which latter is the result but not an end for-the-sake-of-which. It results because the factors, once together, affect each other in such a way that they physically cohere; but it need not be supposed that when together they are as they are and behave as they do *in order to cohere*, any more than that when apart they behaved as they did in order to come together, or from any cause other than the necessity of their natures.

(33) No doubt the materialists' views on the detailed workings of combination in specific cases were nebulous almost to non-existence. Does Aristotle the philosopher then rest his refutation on nothing more than their inability to give convincing empirical content to an *a priori* position? Or is it that he takes 'Either by coincidence or for an end' to be some kind of conceptually necessary universal truth? Hardly this, since he himself does not treat the dichotomy as exhaustive.[28] He is willing to concede propositions such as 'what is driven up must get cooled, and what is cooled turns into water and must come down' (198b18–20), being well aware that these 'musts', in his opponents' mouths, do not

[28] Cf. Charlton, pp. 120–1.

signify his own (as yet unproposed) concept of 'necessary-for-a-given-end' (*v.s.* para. (23)), but the "brute" necessity that excludes finality. Nor on the other hand does he think that these elemental motions and transformations occur by coincidence: they come about through the intrinsic natures of the substances concerned (air or fire, and water), and (unlike the spoiling of the corn) they do not depend on the accidental occurrence of some special external circumstance (as that the corn happens to be laid out just where the rain falls). Such occurrences, then, he admits (or admits for the purpose of the argument)[29] are neither by coincidence nor for an end, but (as we should say) by laws of nature. But given this recognition of a *tertium quid* between 'by coincidence' and 'for an end', how can he be so certain that it does not apply to organic phenomena?

(34) Unfortunately Aristotle does not answer this question himself, nor even indicates having given it a moment's thought. This is because from his point of view, as I shall now argue, it hardly deserves serious consideration. First, it must be stressed that in this discussion Aristotle regards the onus of proof as lying with the materialists. This is clear from the fact that he has already (Chapters 3 and 7) propounded, without demonstration, his own doctrine of the four distinct types of cause. No doubt his confidence is partly a Platonic legacy. But that 'the teeth are for chewing' etc. would also have seemed (perhaps still seems) plain common sense. Furthermore, his own empirical investigations would have shown him that in at least one field of natural phenomena the systematic and detailed application of teleology results in hypotheses that are clearly statable, empirically verifiable, and very frequently also confirmed: whereas

---

[29] It seems that most writers take Aristotle's teleology to apply to all types of natural substance, including the simple bodies. See in particular Balme, 'Greek Science and Mechanism I', pp. 129 ff. This view is challenged by Charlton, p. xvii, and Gotthelf, p. 237, note 19. It is not clear how far there is real disagreement, since Aristotle did not always recognize the simple bodies as substances (*v.s.* para. (6) and note 5). Aristotle need not share the Empedoclean view that the descent of rain etc. is not for an end. He concentrates on the end-directedness of organisms because they are the most obvious examples, not necessarily because they are in his view the only ones.

materialism to date could claim no corresponding scientific success, nor did it suggest any definite method for achieving it.[30] Thus Aristotle does not see himself as obliged to argue against the abstract proposition that 'Nothing in nature happens for an end', but only against an actual proposal to this effect. The proposal was a reductionist thesis, as is clear from the second sentence of Chapter 8. Complex organic phenomena were claimed to come about by ("brute") necessity because reducible to simple phenomena which everyone would agree occur by necessity. It may be that there are coherent rejections of final causation which involve no reductionism. But Aristotle is not concerned to refute wholesale every possible denial of what to him is *prima facie* obvious; if he can deal with the problem in the form actually bequeathed him this is all that he needs to do.

(35) The simple phenomena on which the proposed reduction is based are 'the hot and the cold', and the physical subtances, fire, earth, etc., which are the primary bearers of these qualities. But for Aristotle the fundamental natures of such substances are expressed by motions in different directions. Apparently Empedocles for one did not disagree.[31] In *De Anima* II.4, 415b28–416a2, Aristotle says:

Empedocles is wrong in adding that growth in plants is to be explained as follows: the downward rooting by the natural tendency of earth to travel downwards, and the upward branching by the similar natural tendency of fire to travel upwards.

Aristotle has two objections to this explanation, the first being that it disregards the functions of the plant's parts: functionally, the roots correspond to the head of an animal (both contain the organs of ingestion). Presumably Empedocles would explain the growth of a head by the tendency of its main constituent element to travel upwards: thus phenomena which from the functional point of view demand the same type of explanation are for Empedocles instances

---

[30] Cf. Balme, 'Greek Science and Mechanism II', p. 28, Wieland, *Die aristotelische Physik,* pp. 267-8.

[31] Although his view, like that of Anaxagoras, is based on "like to like", not on "natural place". This difference from Aristotle does not affect the argument.

of opposite tendencies. To this, Empedocles might reply that it begs the question against him to insist that he be concerned with explanation in terms of function. But Aristotle's second objection meets him on his own terms:

> Further, we must ask what is the force that holds together the earth and the fire which tend to travel in contrary directions: if there is no counteracting force, they will be torn asunder . . . (416a6–8)

Clearly, if there *is* a counteracting force, it does not stem from the nature of any extra material element: for Aristotle, every element is necessarily characterized by locomotion in a specific direction; so that far from countering the "aliofugal" tendencies of earth and fire, anything else of the same type would simply add its own such tendency to the situation.

(36) Against this theoretical background, which Aristotle's opponents themselves do not reject, the materialist programme of reducing organic phenomena to the processes of their simple inanimate constituents must have appeared a hopeless fantasy to anyone who saw clearly the issues involved. Certainly there are no *mechanical* principles that could hold the components in a structured unity, and even the absurd suggestion that (in repeated instances) they are together because they *happen* to be together implies a physical impossibility. When it is the nature of a simple substance to move in a single simple direction, how could masses of even one such substance (let alone more than one) retain (if they could ever fall into) arrangements resembling even the most primitive organic structures? Even coincidence could not account for the phenomena, so that in saddling his adversaries with a coincidence-theory as their only alternative to teleology Aristotle actually allows them more than they deserve. Or are we perhaps overstating the case against them? Not, it seems, if we suppose that they suppose the simple elements to be present in the compound by way of mechanical synthesis. But we ought also to consider whether some notion of *chemical* combination might not serve them better.

(37) Aristotle distinguishes two types of combination,[32] (i) *synthesis*, which gives rise to a mere spatial aggregate of different objects (ears of wheat mixed with ears of barley); and (ii) *mixis*, in which the simple bodies combine to form a homogeneous substance with different properties from those of its components. This is his closest approach to our distinction between mechanical and chemical combination, but his concept of a 'mixtum' is nonetheless very different from our idea of a chemical compound. We conceive of a quantity of some chemical compound as consisting of qualitatively identical ionic agglomerates or molecules each of which is a structured system made up of "atomic" components, themselves in turn structured. An atom of a given substance (element) E is seen as a unit having just that structure or internal configuration that would enable it to combine (by electrical attraction) with atoms of other elements to form all the known compounds of E. There is a sense in which an atom of E in some compound cannot be described in exactly the same terms as an uncompounded atom of E. Thus, e.g., in the compound the outermost electrons of the E-atom relate not only to the nucleus of *this* atom, but also to the nucleus of another — hence the compound; whereas when E is uncompounded, its electrons relate only to its own nucleus. All the same there is an isomorphism between the compounded and the uncompounded E-atom, as between a one-inch square drawn on its own and a one-inch chequerboard square (which shares its sides with other squares), that makes it legitimate to say that the E-atom is *present in* the molecule or ionic agglomerate. (Moreover the nucleus and inner electronic shells of the atom are not affected by chemical change: which seems to entail that they are present in the compounded and the uncompounded atom in just the same way.)

(38) All this is alien to Aristotle. For him, a compound (mixtum) of simple substances is through and through homogeneous, not only in the sense that physical division never

---

[32] See *De Gen. et Corr.*, I.10, II.6–8; H.H. Joachim, 'Aristotle's Conception of Chemical Combination', *Journal of Philology* XXIX, 1904, pp. 72 ff.; the same author, *Aristotle on Coming-to-be and Passing-away*, pp. 175–89, 230–46.

reaches a part that does not have the same observable properties as the larger mass, but also in the following sense: the
mixtum cannot from any point of view be regarded as structured, or as consisting of structured units (like molecules)
that are systems of "interlocking" component structures.
This conception of a compound may be due in part to the
difficulty of seeing how a structure of interlocking components could differ from a mechanically assembled aggregate: in the absence of some account of the special nature of
a chemical bond,[33] the original distinction between synthesis and mixis would be threatened. But the path towards
any theory of compound masses as structured is for Aristotle
even more fundamentally blocked by his own view of the
simple elements as essentially characterized by locomotion
each in a given cosmic direction. On these terms it would be
absurd to treat a compound as consisting of elemental particles that actually instantiate in full the same essential
natures as uncompounded particles of the same elements, or
in other words the same natures as they themselves would
have instantiated prior to entering the compound. Such a
situation would imply a compound that was either so unstable as hardly to exist at all for any length of time, or else
was held together by a continuing miracle. We might conclude that Aristotle's doctrine of the elements simply cuts
him off from the concept of a compound altogether, and in
our sense of 'compound' we should be right. Yet he does distinguish between mixis and synthesis, and what is more,
holds that mixis produces those stuffs that are the immediate matter of the organic parts of organisms: flesh, bone,
etc. These are homoeomerous compounds of all four elements in varying proportions. But how can he even coherently
conceive of such stuffs? Only by dispensing with the assumption that the elements that make up a compound *are actually
present in* the compound once formed. The compound is

---

[33] Cf. Joachim, *Aristotle on Coming-to-be, etc.*, p. 183: 'The reader will observe
that μίξις, as Aristotle conceives it, demands a more thorough union of the
constituents than that assigned to the constituents of a chemical compound by
modern chemical theory. In so far at least as modern chemistry regards a compound
as a mere arrangement or shuffle of the atoms of the combining constituents,
Aristotle would accuse it of confusing μίξις with σύνθεσις.'

actual only when its components (the elements) are not fully actual. But this is not to say that they in no sense are, or that they are destroyed out of all possibility of existence when they form the compound, for when the latter exists actually, they are present potentially, in that the compound can be transformed back into the separate elements.[34]

(39) Only in this way does Aristotle achieve a concept of 'chemical compound' that is not logically at odds with his ascription of essentially locomotory natures to the elements when free. The solution is not without its difficulties, however. To mention only one, it is implausible to hold that a compound wholly lacks the locomotory characteristics of all its elements. Flesh and bone have weight, i.e. tend towards the centre, like earth their major component. And how is this to be explained except on the supposition that earth is not totally absent, i.e. not merely potentially present in the sense in which 'being potentially F' is compatible with the total absence of the corresponding actuality? A good craftsman builds taking maximum account of the continuingly actual forces of the primitive components,[35] and the stability of the finished product depends as much upon their presence as upon the balance which if left to themselves they could never have achieved. How can something like this not be the case with natural complex structures such as organisms and organs? But if this is so, standard senses of the formula 'potentially but not actually present' cannot do justice to the fact that the independent natures of the four elements are not totally 'suspended' in flesh, bone, etc., but are permitted limited expression, the bounds of which are set by requirements of organic· functioning.[36] Thus the earth-composed roots of the plant tend sufficiently downwards to

[34] Cf. Joachim, locc. citt., Cherniss, *Aristotle's Criticism of Presocratic Philosophy*, pp. 140–3; L. Robin, *Aristote*, pp. 138–9; S. Sambursky, *The Physical World of the Greeks*, p. 144; E. McMullin, 'Four Senses of Potency', *The Concept of Matter in Greek and Mediaeval Philosophy*, ed. McMullin, pp. 305–8, 315–17; E.J. Dijksterhuis, *The Mechanisation of the World Picture*, pp. 23–4 and 200 ff.

[35] E.g. of the house-wall in II.9, 200a1 ff., quoted para. (23).

[36] Cf. Joachim, *Aristotle on Coming-to-be*, etc., pp. 180–1 and McMullin, p. 306. For the later history of the problem see Dijksterhuis, pp. 200 ff.

give it necessary stability, but not so as to part company with the other organs, thereby ceasing to be roots.[37]

(40) But we need not reach a decision on how precisely to conceptualize the status of earth in this example in order to see that for Aristotle there can be no question of explaining the structure and behaviour of organisms and organs by reference to the properties of their simple components. The reductionist programme presupposes that a knowledge of the independent natures of the components (i.e. of laws concerning them which have been established independently of the organic context) would, given known boundary conditions, make it theoretically possible to predict organic structure and behaviour. But we now find that the elements in the organic context either totally lay aside their original natures or modify them so as to fall in with the needs of the whole. On the first alternative they are not actually present at all in the organism, so that it would be absurd to attempt explaining it and its behaviour, which are actual, by reference to the non-actual properties of the non-actual. On the second alternative, while the elements may in a sense be *there*, the ways in which they manifest their presence are deducible only from a prior knowledge of the organism and its requirement, not vice versa as the reductionist would have it. The whole, moreover, is inexplicable not only in terms of its simple ultimate components, the four elements (this answers the second (elemental) materialist position, *v.s.* para. (10)), but in terms too of its immediate materials, the homogeneous compounds (which answers the first position). For these, being (as they must be) absolutely free of configuration at any level of physical analysis, could never alone explain organic *structure* and the functioning that depends on and maintains structure. Such is the basis of Aristotle's position in *Physics* II.8, and insofar as the materialists share his

---

[37] Many writers find irresistible the metaphor of the organic form 'compelling', 'constraining', 'bending', 'harnessing', the behaviour of the materials. This wrongly suggests that the latter are present in the full actuality of their independent natures so as to need repressing. If a metaphor is needed, 'voluntary self-subordination' better describes the normal case. Or: the well-functioning organism is to its matter as the σώφρων to his passions, as opposed to the ἐγκρατής.

view of the elemental locomotions, they too are bound by its consequences.[38]

(41) So in a modern discussion of mechanism *versus* teleology there is no point of entry for Aristotle. This debate gets off the ground by means of considerations such as these:

The physical sciences are concerned with a hierarchy of structure and patterns resulting from very different processes: the fusion of the fundamental particles within the nucleus of the atom; the association of various numbers of electrons with atomic nuclei of different net charge to produce over 100 different elements; the combination of these elements to produce millions of different chemical compounds; the interaction of elements, compounds and energy in various forms to make the large scale features and phenomena of the natural world, mountains and seas, stars and planets, storm and earthquake. Living organisms continue to persist in the world by imbibing less organised material from outside (in respiration and feeding) and when they cease to exist their organization breaks down into chemical compounds such as salts, carbon dioxide, ammonia and water which are structurally not different from those obtained by mining, combustion, or the synthetic processes of chemical industry. It seems therefore legitimate, and a reasonable *prima facie* assumption on which to base further study, to regard living organisms as matter organised in a special manner, and not as matter invested with a special property 'life' beyond the scope of the physical sciences. (A.R. Peacocke, in 'The Molecular Organization of Life', in *Biology and Personality*, ed. I. Ramsey, p. 17.)

[38] I have not discussed Aristotle's explanation of elemental combinations in terms of the four contrary powers and their combinations in the simple substances and compounds of these. This topic raises fundamental problems, not least that of the conceptual relationship between the theory that defines fire etc. as Hot-Dry etc., and that which defines them by reference to natural places. Has Aristotle his own version of the wave/particle problem? See F. Solmsen, *Aristotle's System of the Physical World*, pp. 363-4. But I do not see that a full discussion would affect the present argument. The theory of contrary powers is supposed to explain (*a*) the mutual transformation of the simple bodies, (*b*) their transformation into mixta with different properties from the components'. But it does not allow us to say that e.g. Fire (= Hot-Dry) is actually present in a mixtum. For Hot and Dry are supposed to have merged with their opposites contributed by other elemental components, so as to form a new intensive property. The λόγος of a given type of mixtum refers to the proportions of the elements that went into it, but (unlike a modern chemical formula) not to any actual resultant *structure* in which, say, two discriminable units of fire are bonded with three of earth, one of water, etc. Thus the introduction of the contrary powers leaves us as far as ever from being able to explain the structural properties of an organic whole by reference to its constituents.

So many things are 'matter organised in a special manner', so why should not the same be true of living things?[39] This is where the controversy starts between the modern mechanist and the 'emergence' theorist, or between reductionists and organicists. But from an Aristotelian point of view the fundamental problem occurs a long way back: How can inanimate matter be *organized* at all? Living things, from this point of view, are no more surprising than inorganic compounds: in a way less so, for whereas the character and behaviour of the former *can* be explained teleologically, those of the latter cannot, nor by reference to the behaviour of any actual constituents either.

(42) I have argued that within the framework of his theory of the simple bodies, Aristotle's refutation of contemporary materialism in *Physics* II.8, 198b10–199a8, can be seen to be cogent. It follows (within this framework) (*a*) that there is a sound basis for applying teleology to at least some natural phenomena, and (*b*) that organic creatures can properly be regarded as ontologically fundamental substances in their own right, rather than arrangements of other, physically more primitive, substances. They are, in other words, *per se* unities. This conclusion does not make it illegitimate to say that they are also combinations of components. In the first place, they have organic parts, both the structured organs and the various homoeomerous stuffs such as flesh that the organs are made of. But these are not self-sufficient substances having each its own inner principle of change which it exhibits in actual change whenever not physically prevented. That would imply that even (if not especially) when separated from the organic context the objects in question would change naturally so as to express autonomous natures. But in fact organs and flesh etc. are never found except in the organic context, and if separated they begin at once to decay. Thus although the organic whole is in a sense a combination of them, it is not a *per accidens* combination of

[39] Cf. also H. Hein, 'Molecular Biology *vs.* Organicism', *Synthese* XX, 1969, p. 242: 'The molecular biologists claim . . . that the dynamic, system building character of organisms can be accounted for in terms of a basic architectonic tendency inherent in the fundamental particles of matter itself.'

independent *substances*. Secondly, the organic whole does in a sense consist of the simple bodies, and these are indeed autonomously natured substances (at least in the *Physics* they are so treated). But they, unlike the flesh and organs, are not actually present in the organism, i.e. not as the autonomous beings that they actually are when actual. Hence the organism, which *is* actual, cannot be viewed as a *per accidens* combination of them either. The *per se* unity of the whole is not diminished by its being composed of different things, for the actually present components are not substances, while the substantial components are not as such actually present.

(43) Despite the close relation between conclusions (*a*) and (*b*) above, they are distinct. This is clear once we realize that so far as (*b*) is concerned, it makes no difference to Aristotle's argument whether his reductionist opponents view the simple bodies as necessitated to behave as they do, or as *meaning* to. They may or may not have thoroughly disengaged these two concepts from one another: the English word 'will' itself bears witness to a proto-concept in which the ideas of purpose and of predictability as such had not yet parted company. It is possible that 'by necessity' and 'for an end' express opposing concepts only when the latter is applied to creatures that act for more than one end, or that do not always achieve the same end in the same way. Thus even if someone says that earth falls in order to be at the centre, perhaps he need not deny that it must fall, since for earth there is no other end and no other way of getting there.[40] Suppose, then, that the materialist notion of the necessary movements of the elements was not wholly untinged with teleology (in which respect it may have resembled Aristotle's own). In that case there would be no need for Aristotle to prove that some phenomena are teleological, since this (by the supposition) has never been clearly denied by either party to the controversy. Aristotle would therefore be wasting his time in arguing in II.8 for a teleological account of organic structure and behaviour if his only purpose in so arguing were

---

[40] The conceptual question is whether we can speak of an 'end' even where nothing resembling choice is possible.

to show that teleology has application to nature. But his purpose, I suggest, is also to refute those who in II.1 were described as holding the simple bodies to be 'the whole of substance, and everything else to be affections and states and arrangements of these'. This position is compatible with a theory of goal-directed simple bodies. It might also be compatible with a theory of organisms as goal-directed.[41] But it is not compatible with viewing organisms as genuine unitary substances in their own right. From this point of view, the importance of Aristotle's argument in II.8 does not lie in the bare conclusion that organic phenomena are teleological, but in the proof that they *cannot be explained as combinations of simple substances*. The proof is the same whether we think of the latter as having wills of their own, or as necessitated in some more clinical mechanist sense. Either way, coincidence would for Aristotle be the only cause of combination; and either way, combination would mean one of two alternatives: totally unstable synthesis or totally unstructured mixis.

(44) A number of writers have stressed the empirical basis of Aristotle's philosophy of organic substance. I refer in particular to a strong statement by A. Gotthelf,[42] who has shown clearly how Aristotle's teleology of organisms depends on a theory of the irreducibility of their behaviour to that of inanimate components.

Philosophers of science today are in increasing agreement that the question of reduction is an empirical one; they insist that one cannot legislate the precise form of the laws in which our understanding of nature is expressed. Aristotle's attitude is similar: he does not attempt to legislate a priori the particular form which a successful account of the natures and potentials of living organisms must take. His arguments for his teleological doctrine make this clear. What he insists is that the facts as we have observed them, and the identification of the natures and potentials of things that these observations have led us to, entail

[41] One can conceive of a teleological reductionism that would account for the behaviour of an organism by reference to a "composite end", i.e. the set of ends individually pertaining to each element. Cf. egoist theories of society.

[42] Op. cit., pp. 253–4. With this passage compare F.S.C. Northrop, *Science and First Principles*, p. 18. See also A.P.D. Mourelatos, 'Aristotle's "Powers" and Modern Empiricism', esp. p. 97.

the irreducibility thesis which is at the core of the concept of final causality asserted to obtain in nature. Though the simplicity and the non-mathematical character of Aristotle's chemistry (and physics) eliminates for him any real possibility of a successful reduction to element potentials [i.e. to the natures of the simple substances] of the complexities of the organic world, this makes his thesis no less empirical — for his view of the inanimate world is equally subject to revision. There is nothing in the fundamentals of Aristotle's philosophy, and nothing in his philosophical or scientific method, that would prohibit the adoption of a reducibility thesis, should the scientific evidence be judged to warrant it.

The long tradition of bitter attacks on Aristotle as arch-enemy of the true spirit of science may still have life enough in some quarters to merit sharp reaction. But Mr. Gotthelf's defence of the 'empiric Aristotle' (an image whose increasing vogue parallels that of 'Aristotle the philosopher of ordinary language') is exaggerated.[43] It is true that observation supports the theory of elemental locomotions, as well as the distinction between aggregates and homogenenous compounds. But observation could not teach Aristotle that the latter must be absolutely homogeneous, any more than it could dictate that the elements themselves must be simple. (This is a deduction from the teleological consideration that a substance whose nature it is to move straight up or down does not need to be anything more complicated than a homogeneous mass.) In general, observation may have seemed to confirm, but it could not enforce,[44] the conception of a world of substances whose natures are expressed each in some *single pattern of behaviour* to which external objects are relevant only negatively as possible hindrances. This view, developed as it is by Aristotle, leaves no *conceptual* room for a view of basic physical units whose character is shown in and through all their specific combinations. Thus chemistry and biochemistry as we understand them have no beginnings of a purchase. One of the recurrent motifs in Aristotle is conceptual pluralism.[45] We have in logic the mutually irreducible

[43] I agree however with the bulk of Gotthelf's article and have found in it encouraging confirmation of a number of points made here.

[44] Cf. J.D. Logan, 'The Aristotelian concept of ΦΥΣΙΣ', *Philosophical Review* VI, 1899, pp. 18 ff., esp. pp. 32-3; 'The Aristotelian Teleology', ibid., pp. 386 ff., esp. pp. 392 ff.

[45] Cf. G.E.L. Owen, 'The Platonism of Aristotle', *Proceedings of the British Academy* L, 1965, pp. 125 ff., esp. pp. 140 ff.

categories, in metaphysics the four types of cause, in logic of science the autonomy of subject-matters. His philosophy of nature adds a striking example to the list: there is no single sub-class of laws from which all other laws and generalizations could theoretically be deduced. The four elements are all-pervasive, but their natures cannot account for those of living structures, and in each type of case the explanatory gap is filled by a different form or telos, of which there are as many as there are species of organism. To exchange this view for a reductionist alternative, Aristotle would have had radically to alter 'the fundamentals of his philosophy'.

III

The Analysis of Change

PART I

(1) Having examined the concept of nature as a principle of change, we turn now to change itself.

Since nature is a principle of process (κινήσεως) and change (μεταβολῆς), and nature is the subject of our inquiry, we must consider what process is. For if we do not know this, then we cannot know what nature is either. And having defined process, we must try to deal in the same way with the concepts next in order. Process is held to belong to the class of continuous things, and the infinite makes its appearance first and foremost in the continuous. For this reason, when people define the continuous they often bring in the concept of the infinite, saying that the continuous is what is divisible to infinity. Moreover, it is held that there cannot be process without place and void and time. Thus it is clear that for these reasons, and because these are common and universal to all [sc. physical] things, we must take each of them up for discussion, since enquiries into specific topics cannot precede enquiry into common concepts. So first of all, as we said, we must examine process. (III.1, 200b12–25)

(2) From the methodological pronouncement in the last sentence but one, we might suppose Aristotle here to be undertaking the most general and comprehensive inquiry into change. Yet the very wording of the preamble just quoted might also cause us to doubt this. In the first line he uses 'μεταβολή', his most general word for 'change'. But he uses it as interchangeable with 'κίνησις' and similarly a few lines below (200b32–3, 201a2, 8–9). In *Physics* V.1 Aristotle distinguishes the two terms, restricting 'κίνησις' to non-substantial change. This somewhat technical distinction we should not expect him to be observing here at the outset, nor does he. Here in III.1 we find him using 'κίνησις' to cover changes ruled out by the meaning stipulated in V.1.[1] Even so,

---

[1] 201a8–15; cf. 2, 202a9–12.

it is surprising that in advance of any discussion he should treat the terms as interchangeable, since in their ordinary senses too they are not equivalent. Briefly, '$\mu\epsilon\tau\alpha\beta o\lambda\dot{\eta}$' means change from one state of affairs to another (cf. V.1 224b35-225a2), while '$\kappa\dot{\iota}\nu\eta\sigma\iota\varsigma$' implies or even means 'process'; and to describe an event as a change from one state to another is not necessarily to describe it as a process. So is Aristotle here using '$\kappa\dot{\iota}\nu\eta\sigma\iota\varsigma$' to mean the same as '$\mu\epsilon\tau\alpha\beta o\lambda\dot{\eta}$', the wider term, or is it the other way round? And what are we to make of the fact that despite the apparent equation of the two, he shows in the subsequent discussion an overwhelming preference for '$\kappa\dot{\iota}\nu\eta\sigma\iota\varsigma$'?[2]

(3) Aristotle's use of '$\mu\epsilon\tau\alpha\beta o\lambda\dot{\eta}$' expresses his determination to let nothing that could be called change from one state to another fall outside the net of the definition he is about to propose; whereas '$\kappa\dot{\iota}\nu\eta\sigma\iota\varsigma$', creeping in from the first and soon taking over, is symptomatic of a restriction controlling his entire approach to the concept of change. A few lines on from the passage quoted above, and just before Aristotle proposes his famous definition of $\mu\epsilon\tau\alpha\beta o\lambda\dot{\eta}/\kappa\dot{\iota}\nu\eta\sigma\iota\varsigma$, he tells us insistently that changes are to be exhaustively classified in terms of the categories: the categories and the categories alone determine all the respects in which change is possible (200b32-201a9). What better evidence of Aristotle's aim that his definition should be fully comprehensive? But there are more ways than one of dividing the class of changes: there can be division, for instance, in terms of *cause* as well as in terms of *respect*. Some changes are from the natures of substances, some from conscious purpose, some from neither: and just as a proper concern for comprehensiveness leads him to take account of each categorially determinate type of change, so it should deter him from concentrating exclusively on changes caused in one of several possible ways. But this, as I shall argue in this chapter, is precisely what does not happen in *Physics* III. Here Aristotle has come to consider change in general because of his interest in *nature*, since change is that of which nature is the inner principle. But

[2] On Aristotle's varying uses of '$\mu\epsilon\tau\alpha\beta o\lambda\dot{\eta}$' and '$\kappa\dot{\iota}\nu\eta\sigma\iota\varsigma$' see Ross, *Aristotle's Physics*, pp. 7-8, 45-7.

considered as *changes*, the changes which spring from natures instantiate a concept whose other instances have other sorts of cause. Thus we should expect an adequate analysis of this concept to abstract at some stage from the differences entailed by the differences in sorts of cause, and to display a conceptual nucleus common to change as such. But in fact it turns out that in Book III Aristotle treats *natural* change as the type and model of change as such. As a result, his account there suits only natural changes and changes formally analogous to these, namely ones that stem from purpose. Yet in his pluralistic universe the paths of different individuals meet and cross, and there is no single all-embracing Nature or Purpose guiding these encounters and shaping their results. That new situations should arise in this incidental way is not only possible but inevitable in the common framework of space and time. The III.1 definition makes no provision for such changes. It is not merely that the *definiens* fails to cover them. Aristotle's preoccupation with nature and purpose appears even in his choice of *definiendum*. For, as I shall now argue, it is this conceptual bias that dictates his unquestioned assumption that the task of defining change as such is one and the same with that of defining *process*.

(4) The difference in meaning between '$\mu\epsilon\tau\alpha\beta o\lambda\acute{\eta}$' and '$\kappa\acute{\iota}\nu\eta\sigma\iota\varsigma$' with which I am here concerned rests on a difference between ways of individuating changes. Change necessarily involves the emergence of a new state of affairs B, to the exclusion of some prior state A. (Thus to indicate that there is a *change*, we should describe A and B by means of incompatible predicates, either contraries or contradictories, as Aristotle says in *Physics* V.1.) Now (*a*) we can regard the actual emergence of B as *the change*. From this point of view, there is no change to B either before or after the moment when B emerges. Thus before the emergence, there was no event describable as a 'change to B'. No doubt there were conditions C causally related to the emergence of B, but these were not the change to B itself, nor any part of that change. Again, someone with knowledge of the causal relationship would have been justified in saying, when C was present, that a change to B would occur, but if the change

itself is being identified with the actual emergence, he would
not have been justified in saying that the change was occurring.
Nor would it be correct to say that the change was occurring
at the moment of the emergence itself, since 'was occurring'
implies that what occurred took a length of time, whereas
the emergence itself happens in a moment. Thus according
to this way of regarding change there is no use for the continuous tenses. On the other hand, (*b*), we frequently take
'*the* change to B' as including the conditions that causally
led up to the emergence of B. Far from being all of the
change, the emergence itself is the culmination of a prior
state of affairs which as a whole is regarded as the change to
B. Thus in this sense the change to B is, or was, going on
before the emergence of B. I shall call these two concepts of
change the E(emergence)-concept and the L(leading to)-
concept. Now in ordinary Greek usage the difference between
'μεταβολή' and 'κίνησις' is this: the former simply means
change from one state of things to another, and leaves it undetermined whether this is to be viewed E- or L-wise; whereas
'κίνησις' means change in the L-sense.

(5) It is to be remarked that this initial explanation of
'κίνησις' (which in this chapter I usually translate as 'process')
leaves a number of issues open. I shall mention two of particular relevance (as will appear) to Aristotle's account.
Firstly, the process leading up to the emergence may or may
not be usefully described as continuous in the *mathematical*
sense. It is correct to speak of it as going on for a time, but
so far nothing forces us to decide whether this entails that it
(or the time) is infinitely divisible. This is not to say either
that we hereby sanction analysing it as a succession of
mathematically discrete units. The point is that we are not
yet committed to applying the dichotomy 'Either (mathematically) continuous or discrete'. Secondly, in speaking of
the process which leads up to the emergence of property P
in object Y, we may but need not focus only on those conditions of which Y itself is the subject. If another object, X,
is in a condition which if continued is sure to result in P in
Y, then X can be said to be in course of bringing about that
result. Nor would it be improper to describe X as 'in course

of changing (transitive) Y'. But this entails that Y can be described as 'in course of being changed (by X)', and hence as 'in course of changing (intransitive)'. Here 'change' is used in the L-sense, and it is predicable of Y in virtue of a condition in an external subject X even at a time when no flurry of activity is discernible in Y itself.

(6) It is true that Aristotle generally seems to regard a κίνησις or L-type change as an identifiable process occurring in the same individual that will eventually be subject of the emergence or E-type change. But as we shall see, it is to his advantage if the III.1 definition of κίνησις can be interpreted in the wider way just indicated. For instance, one apparent inconsistency immediately disappears. On the one hand, the very meaning of 'κίνησις' implies a process taking time. On the other hand, Aristotle occasionally speaks of κινήσις from one state A to a contrary B as happening all at once, apparently meaning by this that the subject spends no time in passage between them.[3] On the assumption that Y can be said to be in course of changing only on account of an activity of change in Y itself, Aristotle has contradicted himself. For while Y is still in state A, the *a quo* of the change, no change-activity in Y itself has yet begun, and once Y is in B, the *ad quem*, Y's change-activity must be over; so that if its being in B followed without interval on its being in A, there was no change in Y that took any time at all. Thus it seems that what happens to Y might be correctly described as a change (μεταβολή), for it *is* an emergence (of B, or being in B), but not as a κίνησις. But there is no contradiction if we allow that Y can be said to be changing even during a period when its state is uninterruptedly A, provided that some other object X is meanwhile engaged in a process that will result in the emergence in Y of B. From this point of view, Y is already changing even while in the *a quo* condition; thus its process of change takes time even though none of that time elapses *between* Y's being in A and in B.

(7) Many phenomena can equally be described as changes in

[3] E.g. *Physics* VIII.3, 253b21–30; I.3, 186a15–16; *De Sensu* 6, 447a1–3. *V.i.* paras (35) and (65)–(69).

the E-sense and the L-sense. We may think of the change as
the emergence of a new state, to which the preceding condition is conceptually external though causally related, or
we may include the latter in what we call 'the change', considering this as a process. Which way we individuate seems
often to depend on the epistemic context. If we perceive the
emergence of B but do not know what led up to this causally, then we think of the immediately preceding conditions
as 'whatever caused B' and regard them as that in which the
coming about of B, or the changing to B, consisted, or as
the leading-up to B; for no other specification is available.
Again, if the causal conditions are known but uninteresting
by comparison with the emergence of B itself, they may not
attract the attention implied by a conceptually self-sufficient
specification, even when such is possible; we shall therefore
tend to think of them, again, simply as 'what leads up to B'.
Thus we describe actions leading to an intended result (even
when these can be separately described) as the process of
'bringing about that result'. However, there are some changes
in which the event immediately leading up to the result *cannot* be described in conceptually independent terms. These
are changes of spatial position. Take the case in which the
new property B to emerge in Y is the property of being at
place P_n. What immediately led up to the emergence of B
was Y's going (or being taken) to P_n. And there seems to be
no alternative description of this leading-up event which both
(*a*) allows us to say that the event so described was the immediate cause of B's emergence, and (*b*) is conceptually independent of 'B'. If we describe it as 'going to P_n' it is not
conceptually independent. If we describe it as 'going to
P_{n-1}', where 'P_{n-1}' designates some place not far short of P_n,
the description cannot be regarded as the immediate cause of
B's emergence, since more is needed for this than that Y
should go only to P_{n-1}. And although going to P_n can take
many different forms (walking, swimming, being thrown to
P_n, etc.) there does not seem to be anything in which going
there *consists*, the description of which would not entail
'going to P_n'. For instance, the process of coming to the boil
consists in (is the same concrete event as) being in contact
with the fire (under given conditions, for a given time etc.).

But 'sitting on the fire' does not *entail* 'coming to the boil', and for this reason, what is described as a process of coming to the boil can also be described as an emergence (of boiling) caused by sitting on the fire. But with 'arriving at a place', there appears to be nothing that corresponds to 'sitting on the fire'.

(8) Since change of place can be described only in L-terms, or as a process, it is not surprising that so many discussions of process (including much of Aristotle's) should revolve round this paradigm case. But this fact cannot justify Aristotle's assumption that the concept of change in general will be adequately dealt with by means of a definition of *process*. That assumption would be legitimate only on one of two further assumptions: either (*a*) all changes are changes of spatial position, and must in the end be described as such, and therefore as processes; or (*b*) even those changes which can be described as caused emergences are nonetheless best or most properly described as processes. Now Aristotle of all people is in no position to assume (*a*). It is true that for a number of reasons he regards locomotion as the primary type of change (see *Physics* VIII.7, 260a26 ff.), but not because all change is reducible to locomotion. That theory could be held only by a philosopher who takes all large-scale phenomena to consist in the spatial configurations and displacements of microscopic constituents. But we have seen how Aristotle's theory of nature as form rules out any such reduction. Therefore, if his approach to the concept of change has a rational basis at all, it must lie in (*b*) above. But why should he assume (*b*)? This is easily explained on the hypothesis for which I am arguing, i.e. that his entire conception of change in Book III is governed by the logic of *natural* change.

(9) Let me begin to support this claim by recalling the distinction expounded in Chapter I (paras (18)–(19)) between appropriate and inappropriate descriptions of the same fact. There we saw Aristotle employing this distinction to solve the paradox of becoming. We saw too that the solution could not satisfy unless it was assumed that the choice of one type of description as appropriate was not arbitrary, but rested in

the end on an absolute metaphysical difference between substance and accident, or between substance-constitutive characteristics and accidental ones (*v.s.* Ch. I, para. (27)). I shall now argue that the concept of a natural substance developed in Chapters I and II cannot be sustained except on the assumptions (i) that natural change is more properly described as L-change, or as process; and (ii) that this type of description is superior precisely because it best reflects the structure that must objectively belong to any change that can reasonably be regarded as manifesting the nature of a substance. In other words, the concept of natural change entails that some phenomena necessarily and of their own nature have the character of leading up to others, while others equally necessarily have the character of being led up to, while not themselves leading further. The idea is of course familiar to us from Aristotle's teleology, but is even more pervasive. For it is not certain that Aristotle saw all natural change as teleological. It is not clear, for instance, how the simple bodies, fire etc., could be said to move as they naturally do for the sake of their own good. When he calls these movements 'necessary' (in the sense in which this contradicts 'for the sake of an end') he may only be conceding a point for the sake of argument (*v.s.* Ch. II, para. (33)); but then again he may not. But what *is* certain is that even these cases involve a relation of phenomena whose status is objectively intermediate to phenomena in which the former objectively culminate and which are not themselves steps to some ulterior culmination. This is the basic structure of natural change as such, whether or not it always makes sense to describe the culminating state as a good.

(10) Except for the simple bodies, natural substances display many different kinds of change.[4] The more highly organized the substance the wider the variety of changes. If the events are treated as emergences of perceptibly new states (which often will follow one another in quick succession), it becomes impossible to identify any single type of such change as natural to the substance, since none has higher claim to

[4] Cf. *Physics* VIII. 4, 255a10–11.

this status than another. If on the other hand they are *all* to count as natural, there will be no empirical basis for assuming a *single* substantial nature manifesting itself through change. A substance is unitary and as such is expressed through unitary change. Thus if the complex behaviour of organisms is viewed simply as series of distinctly specifiable, emergences, it is nonsense to attribute these changes to *the* nature of a substance, and nonsense therefore to regard their subject as an Aristotelian substance at all. But if as a matter of fact the various changes of a particular natural object can instead be described so as to bring out in all or most of them a common structure or pattern, then the situation is saved for Aristotle's basic concept. And in fact such description is possible. The simple bodies do each behave in a way that can be perceived to be uniform and the same each time. Organisms display a bewildering variety of emergences which are neither bewildering nor so various once they are seen as having in common what (as a matter of fact) they do have in common: a tendency to contribute to the life and on-going of individual and species. Thus the primary and most proper description of these perceptibly quite different emergences must be as 'stages in a process towards' some condition T, where 'T' denotes the mature or healthy state of the organism, or some more narrowly specified condition implying health or maturity. Unifying descriptions of this latter type have a different epistemological status from the descriptions of the simple bodies as 'falling', 'moving up', etc., which can be applied on the sole basis of immediate perception. In the organic case, application of a unifying description requires experience of trains of apparently quite different events drawn from many different instances. Thus as a rule natural κίνησις is not straightforwardly *perceived*. Not only are we generally unable, merely by immediate perception, to know whether a change is or is not externally determined: nor are we able to identify *what* the κίνησις is (what life-supporting condition of what organism it is a process towards). But we can of course perceive the "matter" of the process, i.e. the particular emergence in which it happens at a given stage to consist.

(11) In Chapter I it was necessary to take an oversimplified view of the part played by external conditions in natural change. There it was said that these must be such as to permit the change, but without determining its character. But the distinction between "matter" of the change (the perceived emergence) and "form" (corresponding to the overall process-description) allows for a less schematic and more realistic view of the way in which external conditions contribute to the change. For although they do not determine the form of change but only make possible changes of that form, they can now be regarded as helping to determine its "matter" at any given stage, and this without prejudice to the self-sufficiency of the form. For it is because of the external conditions that maturing, reproducing, getting healthy, etc. consists on one occasion in a change of temperature, on another in a change of position, on another in a different change of position, etc.

(12) By contrast, the natural behaviour of the simple bodies, earth, fire, etc., is itself simple and consists always in the same upward or downward movement. From this point of view it is easy, in their case, to describe the behaviour in a way that brings out its substance-expressive unity. But at the same time the simple bodies present a difficulty which does not arise for any other kind of natural substance. Natural change expresses the specificity of substance, not only its unity, or not only some *un*specific unity (*v.s.* Ch. I, para. (40)). The difference, then, between the uniform movements of fire and earth must be as absolute as the difference between fire and earth as substances. For if they are not different substances, what explains the fact that unimpeded they move always in different directions? Either fire should (sometimes anyway) behave like earth or vice versa, or both should exhibit some common free behaviour in fact exhibited by neither. Or can we say that although they are different substances, the difference is not exhibited in their unimpeded locomotions, so that we need not believe in an absolute difference between upward and downward movement in order to maintain that fire is one type of substance, earth another? But if not in these locomotions, in what changes are

these different substantial natures expressed? What other obvious ones are there? And even if there are others, what of the methodologically disastrous precedent set by dismissing certain frequent and universally recognized changes as 'accidental', and looking for something more recondite to fill the role of substance-expressive behaviour? The doctrine that only one kind of behaviour is natural to a given type of substance effectively ties Aristotle down to identifying the natural change with whatever behaviour is most familiar and typical in the eyes of common sense. For once he leaves the beaten track, he requires a principle for selecting the one and only natural change from all the other strange and uncharted manifestations that may or may not be significant; a task which none of his established principles can begin to help him perform.

(13) It was inevitable then that Aristotle should regard the difference between upward and downward motion as absolute. The difference cannot lie in the shape of the motions, since in both cases this is the same: rectilinear as far as possible. It must then lie in what each is directed *towards*. They differ because each homes in on something different in kind. Could the homing points be determined by physical substances, different in each case? But why should these substances *be* where this theory demands that they should, one kind high up to receive fire, the other below to constitute a terminal for earth? If the substances simply happen to be where they are, we might as well have said at the outset that fire and earth merely happen to move in their usual directions, so that their directions are not intrinsic to their natures. It is for this reason that Empedocles' principle of 'like to like' does not account for the natural motions. For granted that experience supports the view that e.g. fire moves upwards to where more fiery matter already is, nothing in this fact shows it not to be arbitrary that the latter is where it is. Why does it not lie to the north, for instance, so that the motion of the smaller homing masses would be sideways; or itself change position, so that the smaller masses go first one way then another to rejoin it? Since in fact these go always in the same direction, and it is absurd to suppose that

they merely always happen to, then even if their motion is governed by the principle 'like to like', it follows that the larger mass does not merely happen to be always where it is. So there must be something about where it is that determines its being *there*. This something cannot, by this very argument, be a physical object or landmark: it must, then, be the very character of the region itself considered simply as a part of space, independently of whatever physical object it holds. But how can different parts of physical space differ intrinsically from one another? This makes sense only on the assumption that the space of the world is shaped. Probably the simplest hypothesis is the one which Aristotle accepts, namely that it is spherical. We have now the absolute difference for which we have been looking. For the centre of a sphere differs from its periphery regardless of the observer's point of view: what is right from one standpoint is left from another, but what is the centre of S from one standpoint cannot from any other be peripheral to the same sphere S.

(14) Thus it is that Aristotle reinterprets 'upwards' and 'downwards' as 'towards the periphery' and 'towards the centre'; a reinterpretation necessitated by his theory of substantial nature as expressed through change. But before returning to the main discussion, I must try to remove a false impression. The argument just presented seems to attribute to Aristotle the view that physical space and its parts have a reality prior to and independent of particular extended objects: i.e. that there is *something*, which is the geometrical centre of the physical universe, and *something* else, its geometrical periphery.[5] But Aristotle was of course as far from holding any such theory as he was from holding that the characteristic directions of the simple bodies could just as well have been different or variable. To account for these directions by reference to the absolute geometrical difference between the "elements" of a sphere (centre and periphery) may be a useful corrective to the idea that there is no intrinsic difference between up and down. But if this

---

[5] This picture seems to be implied by statements to the effect that Aristotle sees different regions of space as exercising 'attraction' on different kinds of body. See e.g. A.E. Taylor, *A Commentary on Plato's Timaeus*, p. 665.

commits us to hypostasizing the geometrical sphere, we have
moved right away from Aristotle. But there is a way out of
the difficulty if we consider the variety of meaning that
Aristotle himself attaches to the word 'because'. Fire does
not happen to move in the direction that we call 'up'. It
moves thus *because* that direction is intrinsically different
from any other, so making manifest the intrinsic difference
of fire from the other elements. But the 'because' clause
need not refer to an already constituted fact concerning a
periphery regarded as some kind of distinct reality. It can
mean, and I suggest does mean, that fire moves upwards
because *by so doing* it will form the physical periphery or
spherical outer shell of the (sublunary) world. It is in the
nature of fire to encircle the other three elements. It is in
the nature of air and water to range themselves in concentric
shells encircled by fire and encircling earth as the centre; and
it is in the nature of earth to be encircled by the rest. Thus
earth tends towards the centre of the universe for no other
reason than that it is the tendency of earth to *make* the
centre of the universe by assuming the central position relative to the other elements. This has the interesting consequence that the natures of each of the four are not conceptually self-sufficient (and in this it may be that they differ
radically from more complex substances). For the place to
which earth tends would not *be* the centre unless the other
three elements were themselves tending to take up positions
encircling earth in their successive layers; and so it is for each
element in relation to its three peers.

(15) The natural movements of the simple bodies illustrate
with particular clarity the special connection with *terminus*
which for Aristotle gives the fundamental structure of all
sublunary process or change. The terminus is intrinsic to
change: for without the terminus there would be no direction,
and direction is not an extrinsic determination added to some
per se directionless change. Change without direction is sheer
abstraction, like being as such. In III.1 Aristotle puts this in
terms of the categories.

There is no process independently of definite respects of change. For
in every case what changes changes either in respect of substance, or

quantity, or quality, or place. Our doctrine is that there is no common factor running through all these that is neither substance nor quantity nor quality nor in one of the other categories. So there is neither process (κίνησις) nor change (μεταβολή) in any respect apart from those mentioned, for there *is* nothing apart from what has been mentioned. (200b33–201a3)

And the point is made even more strongly in *Physics* V.4, where he insists not only on definite categories of change, but within each category on definite genera and infimae species. These are given by the genera and species of that terminal state which it is the essence of the change to be towards. This conception entails that a given change could not have continued past its terminus, since from then on "it" (the change) would have had no identity.[6] It follows too that a distinction is possible between 'complete' and 'incomplete' that would be meaningless in connection with static conditions, such as being green or being a house. For a process of change can come to an end either because the terminus is reached, or because it is interrupted part-way. In the latter case it is incomplete by contrast with the completion that would have been achieved had it been allowed to continue for the necessary time. But if a house is demolished or a brown wall painted white, the wall's previous whiteness, the bricks' and planks' previous arrangement, were for as long as they lasted as complete as they would ever have been however much longer they had been permitted to last. And so these static conditions are not self-terminating, since to be so would presuppose being incomplete (because further completable) for as long as they "went on".

(16) It is this self-terminating[7] character of change that makes it so puzzling to comprehend. Change must be real since it is the manifestation of the primary realities, substances. The difference between the occurrence .and non-occurrence of a given change must be as genuine as the

---

[6] So when a change ceases in a given subject, this is not because "it" has been "passed on" to objects in the environment. Cf. D.M. Balme, 'Greek Science and Mechanism I', esp. pp. 137–8. The point is all the more startling in that Aristotle believes that the simple bodies accelerate as they near their natural regions, so that on arrival the up-to-then on-going impulse vanishes when at its maximum.

[7] Cf. Ch. I, para. (13), and L.A. Kosman, 'Aristotle's Definition of Motion', *Phronesis* XIV, 1969, pp. 40 ff., esp. pp. 57–8.

difference between the existence and non-existence of some substance. Yet how can a real thing or a real condition be of a nature to head for its own finish? Static conditions, we have seen, are terminated only by external interference. Organic substances exist for their own continued existence, and since this is not possible indefinitely they make up for it by the power of producing individuals as like as possible to themselves.[8] Nor is this self-propagatory tendency uniquely the property of substances. Qualities too such as heat generate new versions of themselves in patients available to receive them.[9] But a change of a given type does not of its nature generate another similar change in the same subject, nor yet in another subject. Once the terminus has been reached the first time, what need to reach it all over again by another such change; and how can it help one individual substance to produce in another changes similar to its own? It is true of course that one individual by changing in certain ways will generate another of its kind, which in turn will behave in the same way. But this is not change generating change; rather, substance *by* changing generates substance: change, then, is directed not to its own continuance or the continuance of its like, but to the continuance of *substance*.[10]

(17) The paradox is that whilst change must be real on account of its necessary connection with substance, it is this same connection, spelt out so as to reveal the unity and specificity of substantial nature, that ties change down to an inbuilt terminus, and hence to the dubious status of a being vowed to its own non-being. On this matter Aristotle's position stands in curiously exact contrast to one strand in the Platonic view of change. In the *Republic* and *Timaeus* change and becoming are refused any place of their own in the domain of true being and substance. Yet there is a sense in which Plato's becoming, relegated to a limbo peculiar to itself, is just such an ontological constant as Aristotle's cannot be. Becoming, on Plato's Heracliteanized view, is never superseded except by further becoming. In its own

[8] See e.g. *De Anima* II.4, 415a25 ff.; *De Gen An.* II.1, 731b31–732a1.

[9] Cf. *Physics* VIII.5, 257b9–10; *Metaph.* Z 9, 1034a21 ff.

[10] Cf. *De Part. An.* I.1, 640a18–19.

way it is as unperishing as the Forms. Here, however, I am speaking of becoming in general, and it might be said that even for Plato its particular instances are necessarily transient. But the *Timaeus* account can be read in terms of a *single* unbroken and intrinsically undifferentiated process which successively takes on different patterns. There is but one source of becoming, the 'receptacle', whose natureless nature is a metaphysical factor in all empirical objects. Since these objects are only quasi-existent, it is no paradox if their particular changes are ontologically so tenuous as to arise and then vanish without self-transmission. In any case, these passing changes are simply diversifications of the one primary Becoming, and *this* never gives out. Here we are not many steps away from the line of thought which culminated in the principle of conservation of energy. Plato himself would have started down this line if besides postulating for his elements geometrical structures to enable their orderly transformations, he had also assigned rules by which the all-pervasive Becoming converts itself from one to another form of empirical energy or motion. But for Aristotle this path is closed. If particular natural objects are substances, and if substance is the ultimate source of change, there is no Becoming more fundamental than the gamut of particular natural processes. Hence if for whatever reason these seem to defy metaphysical analysis, the issue must be directly faced; there can be no escape by pointing to some deeper level of process for which the problem does not arise.

(18) It is time to turn in detail to Aristotle's definition of κίνησις.[11] He introduces it as follows:

We distinguish between what is only actual, and what is potential and actual. This may be substance, quantity, quality, or in one of the other categories of being. Under the category of 'relative to something' fall excess and defect, agent and patient, and in general mover and mobile. For the mover is mover of the mobile, and the mobile is able to be moved by the mover. There is no κίνησις independently of definite respects. For in every case what changes (τὸ μεταβάλλον) changes either in respect of substance, or quantity, or quality, or place. Our doctrine is that there is no common factor running through all these

[11] For a close study see L.A. Kosman, op. cit.

that is neither quantity nor quality nor in one of the other categories. So there is neither κίνησις nor μεταβολή in any respect besides these, since there *is* nothing besides these. Each of these applies in two ways to a subject, in all cases: for instance, as regards substance, there is the shape of it and the privation; for quality there is [e.g.] white and black, with quantity, the complete and the incomplete. Similarly in loco-motion too there is up and down, or the light and the heavy. Thus there are as many kinds of κίνησις and μεταβολή as there are of being (III.1, 200b26–201a9)

(The last statement will be modified later by the arguments in V.1–2, where Aristotle shows that the only categories in respect of which there can be change are the four he explicitly mentions here.)

(19) This passage leads up to the definition at 201a9–15. There Aristotle will state that change is a certain type of *actuality*. Uncompromisingly, this means that change is real, as real as anything else actual is real. But the point must be carefully prepared since it contradicts so much of the philo-sophical tradition. And this means too that the definition it-self will fail unless it manages to give due weight to just those considerations (however vaguely in the past expressed) that led so many of Aristotle's predecessors to deny the reality of change. In part their problem lay in not seeing how the concept of change could involve 'not-being' without thereby consigning itself to its own non-being and absurdity. Already in Book I.7–8 Aristotle has shown one way out, in terms of substance and accident and the subject that remains. But, as he said at the time (I.8, 191b27–9), the concept of potentiality also carries a remedy, and this is what he invokes here. Something comes to be what previously it was not. But to say simply that X was not-P is misleading. This bare state-ment contrasts X with things (including itself later) which *are* P in a way that takes no account of another and equally essential contrast, namely between X's being not-P and the not-P-ness of things that never can be P. Even when X lacks the actuality, it has the potential; and this is something. Change then must be conceptually located in the domain of things that are sometimes actually and sometimes poten-tially P, and this is Aristotle's point in the first sentence of the last quotation. But what sort of 'something' is a potentiality?

If it is anything definite then surely it is a way of being, not of not-being; but unless it retains something in common with not-being (so that 'potentially P' carries some of the same message as 'not-P') it will be of no use to explain change. Is potentiality then simply indefinite, a kind of being without being anything in particular? Aristotle has already made clear his repudiation of any such concept, when in I.4 he argued against Anaxagoras' Infinite.[12] But the positive answer lies of course in the categories. What is actual is actually P, where 'P' is a predicate in one or another category; and the potential is potentially just what it would be if actual. Thus potentiality in any given case is as definitely specifiable as actuality, being specifiable in exactly the same terms. There can be no indescribable potentiality for the reason that all actualities are specifiable by categorially pigeon-holed predicates. An indescribable potential would be one for which there was no corresponding actuality; which is impossible, since the potential is, precisely, potentially nothing but the actual.

(20) This is the obvious point of the passage just quoted: that change is from potential to actual in some definite respect. But the emphasis here on 'actual'/'potential' has also, I think, a different bearing, and one that would explain the apparently inconsequential third and fourth sentences.[13] The passage would read more smoothly if these were omitted, but (so far as I know) there is no independent evidence of interpolation. And in their absence Aristotle could not so easily pass as he immediately does in the next section to a definition of change itself as a sort of *actuality*. To show that change is respectable and real it is not enough to explain it as the *passage to* a real property, an actuality, from a no less definite potentiality. For any ground thus gained would immediately be at risk if a critic were to insist that this does not yet warrant the claim that *change itself* is something

---

[12] See especially 187b7 ff.; also *Metaph.* A 8, 989b6 ff.
[13] Cf. Ross ad loc., p. 535; 'The connexion of this section with what precedes is not very close'. The plausibility of my interpretation depends on taking seriously 201a2–3, 'μηθενός γε ὄντος παρὰ τὰ εἰρημένα'. I do not deny that in general Aristotle presents change as falling under no category; which is proper, since the categories are of *being*, hence cover the termini of becoming but not becoming as such. But his special problem here is to show that *becoming* in some sense *is*.

actual. The main drift of the passage as a whole is to tie 'actual' to the categories (thereby anchoring 'potential') in such a way that nothing not in some category can be said to be actually anything. So he ought to show that change is not only *in respect of* categorial properties, but also *itself* finds a niche in some recognized category or other. Now Aristotle is bound, I think, to choose for change a category *in respect of which* there is no change. If a change-condition were classed as (e.g.) a quality (a category with a fairly mixed bag of members), then since change is possible in respect of qualities, there could be change in respect of changes. But Aristotle cannot admit 'change of change' to be a coherent concept, notably because he holds that if something is said to change to changing in a given way, it must also be said to change to the change to this change, and so on (cf. V.2, 225b33 ff.). Now the category of *Relation* is one in respect of which it makes no sense to speak of change, for all so-called relational changes are already taken care of by changes in other categories. If X dyes his hair darker than Y's, no extra relational change is needed to account for the fact that Y's has "become" lighter than X's. So the category of Relation (which like that of Quality already includes a lot of different kinds of properties) is chosen to house change. But this will not do unless change *is* relational! Now when agent acts upon patient, this is a kind of relation. Also it involves change, since the agent causes some new condition in the patient. Logic alone, it is true, cannot take us from this to the conclusion that *every* change is by agent upon patient and therefore necessarily relational. But Aristotle need not believe this inference valid in order to embrace the conclusion. If I am right, the pressure on him is metaphysical. Even natural change, where the object changes of itself, must, he now implies, somehow involve an agent and a patient: in fact natural change above all, since this is the primary type without which there could be no other. *How* agency and patiency find a foothold in natural change is a problem which, as we shall see, Aristotle is very far from being able to brush aside. Yet it seems that he has no choice but to take it on, since the only alternatives would be to deny that change is strictly real or else to admit realities not covered by any category.

(21) He continues:

Given the distinction (which applies in each category) between that which is actually (ἐντελεχείᾳ) [sc. so and so] and that which is potentially (δυνάμει) [sc. so and so], κίνησις is the actuality (ἐντελέχεια) of that which is potentially [so and so], insofar as it is potentially [so and so]. Thus the actuality of the alterable insofar as it is alterable is alteration; of what can grow and contrariwise shrink (there is no common word for both) it is growing and shrinking: of what can come into being and pass away it is coming into being and passing away; of what is spatially mobile it is locomotion. That this is what κίνησις is may be shown as follows: when materials that can be built up into a house possess actuality insofar as they are as we have just specified [sc. capable of being built into a house], then they are being built up, and this is the process of building. It is the same too with learning, healing, rolling, jumping, maturing, ageing. (III.1, 201 a9–19)

Here Aristotle gives his formal definition of κίνησις. He first puts it in general terms, then in terms of specific types of processes, and then appends examples. The definition is obscure in both its formulations, and the examples do nothing to make it clearer.

(22) The main difficulty concerns the meanings of 'potentially [so and so]' and 'alterable', etc. However, let us begin with the 'actuality' ('ἐντελέχεια') that κίνησις is here stated to be. Some[14] render this as 'actualization' and 'realization': misleading terms, in that they can mean the *process* of becoming or making real or actual. Aristotle cannot be read as defining process by 'actualization' in any such sense, since that would be blatantly circular.[15] Circularity apart, to offer such a definition would be to give up the fight to show that process and change are themselves real and actual. For if one says only that a change tends towards some eventually actual end-state, one is left with no basis for maintaining that the tending itself is real while it continues and of an ontological status commensurate with that of the actuality brought about. But process must itself be an actuality even though it is the making or becoming actual of some state not a process;

---

[14] E.g. E. Zeller (or his translators), *Aristotle and the Earlier Peripatetics*, vol. I, p. 381, note 1; P. Wicksteed and F.M. Cornford, *Aristotle, The Physics* (Loeb ed.) vol. I, p. 195; Ross, *Aristotle's Physics*, pp. 45, 359 ff.

[15] Cf. Kosman, p. 41.

thus Aristotle aptly calls it an 'ἐντελέχεια', a word which says that becoming, *when* it takes place, does so not because it itself is becoming, but because it successfully manages to *be*.[16] However, those who translate 'ἐντελέχεια' here as 'actualization', when 'actuality' would be more appropriate, may be impelled by the sense that process and change are *activities*, as opposed to the apparently static and inert actual conditions in which processes start and terminate. That is, 'actualization' and 'realization' capture the dynamism of change, whereas 'actuality' leaves this out. And here one might wonder whether this too does not show Aristotle's definition to be circular from the start. Seeing that the most obviously active activities are changes and processes, one might conclude that 'activity' and 'change' mean the same. In that case one will not be impressed at being told that change is an activity. But that this is a mistaken reaction is clear when we consider that being active may take the form of preserving some state of affairs rather than changing it, so that the man who keeps his head is no less actively exercising a potentiality than 'all about him', who exercise their potentialities for panic and hysteria. A physical object which, on the Newtonian view, continues indefinitely to move with constant speed and direction thereby evinces what is just as truly described as '*behaviour*' as its change of velocity in reaction to external force; yet the former by comparison with the latter is a mode of staying the *same*. I have not here drawn upon Aristotle's own favourite examples of activities that are not changes, such as exercising a skill (as opposed to learning it), and perceiving and thinking,[17] since their non-kinetic status may require to be justified by

---

[16] "Ἐντελέχεια' is preferable to the equivalent 'ἐνέργεια' (used of process at III.2, 201b32-202a2) because, Aristotle tells us, 'ἐνέργεια' in its original and most usual sense means the actual occurrence of *process* (see *Metaph.* Θ 1, 1046a1-2; 3, 1047 a30-3). C-H. Chen, in 'The Relation between the terms ἐνέργεια and ἐντελέχεια in the Philosophy of Aristotle', *Classical Quarterly* N.S. VIII, 1958, takes *Physics* III.1, 201a11 as evidence that 'ἐντελέχια' has a secondary 'kinetic' meaning. However, he supports this from no other contexts, and the present one proves, if anything, the opposite of Chen's contention, for if the word did have a kinetic meaning this would *ipso facto* render it unsuitable to stand on the right-hand side of a *definition* of 'process'.

[17] Cf. *Metaph.* Θ 6, 1048b23-4; *De Anima* II.5, 417b8-9. *V.i.* Ch. IV, paras (27) ff.

argument, in which case they would be poor illustrations. But it is enough that there are *some* illustrations for us to grant that in calling change and process 'activities' or 'active exercises of potentiality', Aristotle is not simply allotting them to a class of which it is analytically true that all its members are changes.

(23) But a more likely prey for the circularity-spotters[18] is provided by that part of the definition where Aristotle speaks in general and then in more specific terms of the *potentiality* of which process is said to be the actual exercise. Here the issue cannot be settled by examples, only by analysis of the concepts involved. Consider in particular the more specific formulations. Alteration, he says, is the actuality of the alterable insofar as it is alterable; growth/shrinkage is the actuality of what can grow and shrink insofar as it can do so, etc. But 'alterable', it is pointed out, means 'capable of, or having the potentiality of, altering'. So Aristotle is defining each type of process as the actuality or actual exercise of the subject's potential for: that type of process.[19] Now in a way this is indeed exactly what he is doing, because the potentiality of which change is defined as being the actual exercise is indeed the potentiality for that change itself. But that potentiality can also be spelt out in terms that make no reference to *change*, and for this reason the definition is not circular. The part of the *definiens* in which the *definiendum* reappears can be further analysed so that the latter no longer occurs in it explicitly or implicitly. To see this, consider what has to be true of a given subject (taken in abstraction from external conditions) if it is to be properly described as having the potentiality for a certain change. If the change is a process towards being in some new condition C, then the subject must (i) lack that condition but (ii) be suitable 'for being in

---

[18] E.g. P. Duhem, who makes the charge without particularizing, *Le Système du Monde*, vol. I, p. 160.

[19] This is Ross's interpretation, p. 536 (although Ross vacillates; see Kosman, pp. 43–6). Ross is followed by J.L. Ackrill, 'Aristotle's Distinction between *ENERGEIA* and *KINESIS*', *New Essays on Plato and Aristotle*, ed. Bambrough, pp. 121 ff., esp. 138–40. For criticism based on what I take to be the correct interpretation, see especially T. Penner, 'Verbs and the Identity of Actions', *Ryle*, edd. Wood and Pitcher, pp. 393 ff., esp. 427–31; also Kosman, pp. 44–5.

it. Thus a healthy man lacks the potential for convalescing
since in his case (i) is not fulfilled; and water cannot be made
into a pair of gloves through non-fulfilment of (ii). But these
conditions (i) and (ii) of the subject not only constitute the
latter's potentiality to *change to* the state in question: they
are also what is meant by saying that it has the potential
to *be* in that state.[20]

(24) The point will be clearer if we consider the passage immediately following the one just quoted, where Aristotle
speaks of the actuality and potentiality of states brought
about through change, states such as being hot and cold.
He says:

> . . . in some cases the same things are both potentially and actually [so
> and so], but not at the same time, or not in the same respect: for
> instance, what is hot is potentially cold. (201 a19–21)

These words show that this is one of the many contexts in
which 'actually F' and 'potentially F' are being used as
mutually exclusive, or in which 'potentially F' means '*only*
potentially F', i.e. 'suitable to be F, but not actually F'.[21]
In this sense, the potentiality to be in condition C is identical
with the potentiality to come to be in C. Thus in saying that
alteration is the actuality of what is alterable insofar as it is
alterable, Aristotle is saying that alteration is the actuality of
a subject truly described as having the potential *to be* in
whatever final condition the alteration in question is an alteration *to*. And although this condition will come about through
alteration, its nature can be specified without reference to
alteration or the way it came about, i.e. as *white*, *hot*, etc.
And in the more general formula or definition ('Process is the
actuality of what is potentially so and so insofar as it is
potentially so and so') we may, if we like, fill in 'so and so'

---

[20] That the potentiality is (primarily) the potentiality to *be in the end-state*
is the interpretation of Themistius; see esp. Schenkl, p. 70, 33–71, 5. It is also
presupposed by Simplicius' remarks at Diels p. 414, 1–6. Recently Kosman,
pp. 44–5, and Penner, pp. 429–31, have come to the same conclusion. This interpretation is supported by *Physics* VIII.5, 257b6–10, which makes sense only
if 'τὸ δὲ δυνάμει' in 6–7 means 'that which has the potentiality to *be* (so and
so)'; *v.i.* Ch. V, para. (38), n. 27.

[21] Cf. Bonitz, *Index Aristotelicus*, s.v. 'δύναμις' (2), p. 207b33 ff.

with a phrase like 'undergoing process' and thus obtain a circular definition; but this does not matter, since 'potentially undergoing process' is then cashable in terms which make no reference to process, i.e. as: 'suitable to be in some new (non-processive) condition C but not actually in C'.

(25) The power of Aristotle's definition begins to emerge only when we consider the following problem: How are formal distinctions to be drawn between the three actualities involved in change, namely the actual change, the actual subject and the actual result or product of change? An adequate definition of the first of these should supply an analytic contrast between it and each of the others. On the difference of change from *subject* Aristotle writes:

. . . κίνησις is the actuality of that which is potentially so and so: an actuality which occurs when something actual is active (ἐνεργῇ) with an activity that belongs to it not insofar as it is what it is, but insofar as it has the potentiality for κίνησις'. (201a27-9)

Here he makes two points. First, the subject of change is not a mere shadowy locus of potentiality: it is also in itself something actual and describable as such, e.g. as a piece of bronze. Secondly, he implies a contrast between the actuality or activity of change and a different activity, that which belongs to the subject insofar as it is what it is. For instance, if it is a piece of bronze, then its activity as this is simply: being actually bronze. This is a tautology, but useful because it enables him to delimit the activity of change, which belongs to S not *qua* bronze but *qua* potentially changing in a given respect (i.e. *qua* potentially *being* in some new condition). Aristotle continues:

By 'insofar as' I mean this: the bronze is potentially a statue, but the actuality of the bronze insofar as it is bronze is not κίνησις. (201a29-31)

Here he is saying that although that which is bronze is identical with that which has the potentiality, the activities corresponding to these aspects of the one subject are different. For the activity of being bronze is not the activity of changing in any respect. But this difference between the activities depends on a difference between the aspects manifested in each, and this cannot be taken for granted. At any rate he now makes moves to show that the aspect of being bronze is different (i.e. different in formula) from that of being potentially a statue. First he simply repeats (31-4) what in effect he has stated: that otherwise, to say that the bronze is actually changing would be to say neither more nor less than that it is actually bronze. He does not pause to point out that on these terms the Eleatics and the extreme Heracliteans are neither of them in the wrong, but goes on to argue (201a34-b3) that if being bronze were the same as being potentially a statue, we should be equally obliged to say that being bronze is the same as being potentially anything that the bronze can be, a dish, a helmet, a heap of coins, etc. But in that case the potentialities would be the same as each other, which entails a corresponding identity for the actual κινήσεις whose bases they provide. Yet in fact the processes are not only different but incompatible, being in mutually exclusive directions. To merge their differences would be in effect to deny that there is any such thing as a single, determinate change. Hence the reality of change, its existence in distinct specifiable forms, turns out to rest on the same ground as the difference of actual change from actual changing subject.

(26) To display the difference between the actuality in which change consists, and the actuality that comes about through change, it is enough to attend to the sense of 'potentially F' already explained. The changing that turns bricks into a house holds of the bricks insofar as they are not a house but suitable to be so formed. The actuality of the house-form itself also holds of the bricks at a later stage, but not insofar as they are potentially a house. Or, if we wish to say that they are, a different sense of potentially' must be called in, referring only to the bricks' suitability and the positive characteristics, hardness, weather-resistance, etc., that render them suitable. For the bricks built up are not now potentially a house in the sense in which this implies that they are not actually so formed. Thus the change-actuality differs from the product-actuality in that the former holds of its subject in virtue of an irreducibly negative condition. This phrase 'in virtue of' cannot be understood in standard logical terms.

Aristotle's definition of change does not state the obvious falsehood that the subject's not being F is a *sufficient* condition for its becoming F (cf. III.2, 29-30). That would imply no difference between the actuality and the mere potentiality of change. But it says more than that becoming F is that for which not being F is *necessary*. It is not the case that every actuality that obtains only if the subject is in some negative condition is a change towards the corresponding positive one. The actuality of statue-form belongs to the bronze only if e.g. helmet-form is lacking; yet the actuality of being formed as a statue is not that of becoming a helmet. If it were, by the same argument being a statue would be the same as becoming a set of coins, a set of nails, etc., and all the things that the bronze logically cannot be if it is a statue. The relation between the negative condition of the subject of change, and the actuality of change itself, is stronger than necessary but weaker than sufficient. The change is the active expression of the negative condition and is grounded in it. Changing to F is what something does on account of being not-F, and the change is the manifestation of the absence of F. But when 'being a statue' holds good of the bronze, this is not on account of the bronze's not being something else, nor does being a statue express this negative fact. Being at Athens entails, but does not express not being at Sparta, whereas going to Sparta both entails the latter and expresses it.

(27) In general we may say that the following holds of actualities that are not processes: just as we give no information about what or where or what-like a thing is by stating what, where, etc., it is not, so we give none about the *basis or ground* of its being as it is by saying what it is not. But with process-actualities the opposite is the case. We give the ground and basis of what actually *is* true of the subject (namely, that it is changing) by saying what it is not. We can deepen the contrast by noting that the terminal condition whose absence is the ground of the change is such that its presence will necessarily exclude the change itself. Being a statue is incompatible with becoming just such a statue. Hence becoming a statue is an actuality grounded not only in its

subject's potentiality to be a statue (which it is not), but in its potentiality to be in a state in which the former actuality no longer exists. In short, change is the active expression of a subject's potential to be no longer changing. Whereas it would be absurd to say of a non-process actuality A that it expressed its subject's potential to be, eventually, without A. In this way, Aristotle's definition of change and process succeeds (a) in avoiding circularity, (b) in defining change as something real and actual, and (c) in preserving a fundamental type-distinction between process and non-process. This last requirement is as essential as the others, if only because the definition must give some explanation of the problematicity of change. If becoming were simply a subclass of being, differing from other sub-classes no more radically than they from one another, how could anyone have been so misled as to think that becoming made best sense when dispatched, by one argument or another, to the realm of non-being? We have now seen how the definition meets requirement (c) by exhibiting the subject of change as essentially (*qua* subject of change) in a state of privation.

(28) Aristotle sums this up by typifying process and change as '*incomplete* actuality'. He does not mean that they are not fully real but that what they really are is incomplete. This, he says, is 'because the subject of whose potentiality [κίνησις] is the actual exercise is incomplete' (III.1 201b31–3). We might object that the subject's negative condition does not necessarily render it *incomplete*. For 'incomplete' here can hardly be understood except evaluatively, but positive properties acquired through change may not enhance or fulfil the subject: sometimes they are neutral, sometimes damaging. Thus this latest formula can only be guaranteed to cover *natural* and *purposed* changes to states valuable or proper or life-enhancing for the subject. Aristotle could have avoided this objection by simply stating the special structure of process-actuality in terms of the subject's negative condition without committing himself to an evaluation of the corresponding positive. But there is little point in amending him on this, for (as we shall continue to see) his entire analysis is moulded so as to fit not change as such but natural and purposed change.

(29) But before this charge is spelt out in full, some account should be taken of the relationship between Aristotle's formal definition of process in *Physics* III and the positions variously reached by his predecessors; and also of its connection with his own main conclusions in Books I and II. So far as the earlier philosophers are concerned, he is anxious to show that the very feature of his own account that guarantees an ultimate distinction between process-actualities and others also explains the bafflement which drove his forebears sometimes to deny change altogether and sometimes to define it in strange terms conveying not much more than their inability to grasp its nature. His own words make the point.

A proof of the adequacy of this account may be found in what others say about process, as well as in the fact that it is not easy to define it in any other way. For the only heading under which process and change find a place is the one suggested here. This is clear if we consider how some thinkers[22] define it: as otherness, and inequality, and not-being. Process is not a necessary property of things describable in any of these terms, i.e. as other or unequal or not-being. Nor is change to or from these properties rather than to and from their opposites. But the reason why they locate process among these is that it does seem to be something indefinite, and the principles in the second column are indefinite on account of being privative.[23] For none of them is a this or a such or in any of the other categories. The reason why process is regarded as indefinite is that it cannot be straightforwardly allotted to the domain of potentialities, nor to that of actuality. For something that is potentially of a certain quantity is not necessarily in process, nor is something that is actually of that quantity. Process emerges as a kind of actuality but incomplete. This is because the subject of whose potentiality it is the actual exercise is incomplete. And because of this it is difficult to seize what it is. For it has to be either privation or potentiality or actuality in the strict sense; but it cannot be included among any of these. So our approach is the only remaining one, which is to say that it is a sort of actuality, but an actuality such as we have explained: difficult to grasp but capable of being. (III.2, 201b16–202a2)

It was the privative aspect of κίνησις that the earlier thinkers were groping towards when they tried to identify it with one or another member of the class of 'indefinites'; but it was Aristotle's achievement to pin this down in a way that

---

[22] See Ross, *Aristotle's Physics*, pp. 538–9, for probable identities.
[23] Cf. *Metaph.* A 5, 986a22 ff., on 'the second column'.

does justice to the negativity without undermining the claim of κίνησις to rank amongst things indisputably 'capable of being'.

(30) Turning now to the relation between the account of change in III.1-2 and the doctrines of the earlier books, I shall take space here to touch on only one large issue. This concerns the coherence of the concept of *subject of change* which emerges in III with the earlier schema in which change was related to the idea of substantial nature. Much has already been said about the way in which Aristotle's concept of substance as unitary and specific determines his notion of change, and of natural change in particular. But examination of III.1-2 enables us to detect an equally close dependence in the reverse direction, this time of the idea of substance itself upon the account of change formulated in III. This connection comes to light if we raise the question whether there is not a contradiction between the Book II doctrine of change as expressing substantial nature, and the Book III doctrine of change or process as the activity of the subject insofar as it lacks the property gained as a result of the change. For if natural change expresses substantial nature, which if knowable at all is susceptible of positive specification and definition, how can it also express some negative property possessed by the subject for as long as the latter is changing but no longer? The two positions are easy to reconcile in fact, but the basis of reconciliation deserves attention. Aristotle means that whereas it belongs to the positive substantial nature to dictate the kind of end-state to be reached through change, it is the present lack of this state that accounts for the change's actual occurrence. The nature determines *what* change will be *if* any will be, but the privation determines *that* it will be, circumstances permitting. The difference between the roles of nature and privation is clear if we recall that nature is a principle equally of change *and stasis*. Which alternative is realized on a given occasion depends then not upon the nature, but upon the presence or absence of the natural end-state which the natural stasis is *at* and the natural change *towards*.

(31) But the main point of interest to emerge from this answer is this: were it not for the assumption that the change terminates, Aristotle would find it difficult if not impossible to disentangle the positive and essential substantial nature expressed through change from the accidental negative condition which, by the account of III.1-2, is also thereby expressed. Given a terminus or intrinsically determined stasis, there is a "moment" of change in which the negative condition can no longer be actively exercised, for the simple reason that the stasis has superseded it with its own positive, so that it is no longer there to *be* expressed. This being so, we can conceptually sift out the substantial nature from the negative property by insisting that the former is still expressed even when the latter cannot be, i.e. through the terminal condition. And we can add that unless the same substantial nature is supposed operative then as during the change, there is no basis for regarding the now changing, now static, subject as one and the same individual. But now let us consider the conceptual impact of denying an inbuilt termination to change. Suppose for instance that the direction of change were dictated by an ideal end or goal which the subject by nature is unqualified to be able to reach. Plato's concept of imitation might be construed in this way, the particulars being regarded as embodied aspirations rather than inert copies. In that case, the subject would necessarily always be subject of change and as such never free from the privation. Thus it is not surprising that the Platonists should have committed what Aristotle evidently takes to be a serious mistake in equating the Great and Small (which in their system he sees as filling the role of matter or subject of change in his) with not-being, i.e. with the privation opposed to the form towards which becoming tends. He takes them to task for thus reducing the number of principles involved in change from the Aristotelian triad (subject–form–privation) to an inadequate *pair* in which subject and privation coincide (*Physics* I.9, 192 a3-25). In this Aristotle makes no allowance for the fact that within the Platonic framework the reduction was reasonable not to say inevitable, if only because there is never a time when the extensions of the subject-concept and the privation-concept could ever fail to coincide.

Aristotle on the other hand assumes that the subject of change, e.g. a man, will emerge on the other side of the change as no longer changing, i.e. as a now cultured man. Thus he can dissolve the paradox of becoming by insisting that although the troublesome 'What is not comes to be' is not false, it fails to reveal the true structure of change by describing the subject by a term true of it only *per accidens*, the appropriate description being the positive 'man'. For the best proof that 'not cultured' holds only *per accidens* is that it, unlike 'man', is *superseded* in the change. In this way the individual that was subject of change emerges as *per se* positively describable; its essence then can be given by saying what it is, not what it is not.

(32) Here we have the basis for the doctrine of the categories, whereby negative properties are negations of positives in some category or other. There would be no categories other than Substance unless there were the category of Substance: this then *must* comprise positive terms (substance-constitutive characteristics), since otherwise the whole doctrine collapses. This means that the concept of substance as kingpin of the categorial division of Being is reconcilable with the concept of substance as subject of change only on one assumption: that change (depending as it necessarily does on its subject's privation) *cannot continue indefinitely towards an unattainable end*. Change must be structured so as finally to release its subject de-negativized, thus showing that the negative property was never intrinsic to the latter. Change and process then must be as the definition of III.1 prescribes: an actuality incomplete in itself and hence *self-terminating*. These considerations give special significance to the fact that the Greek term for 'potential' is also the term for 'possible'. Verbally, it is no doubt tautologous to say that what is potentially so is possibly or not impossibly so.[24] But a substantial point emerges when we consider that within the context of Aristotle's definition of process, 'potentially F' has the function of stating the *direction* of change. In other words, 'potentially F' harbours one purely intentional element, which it might be more apt to call 'gerundive',

[24] Cf. *Physics* VI.10, 241 b3-11.

stating what *is to be* and would be *if* the change were to reach completion. But that the subject *can* attain to the state of being F (which gives the gerundive its specific content), is a synthetic proposition. An indication of direction does not in itself entail the possibility of arrival. But this synthetic union of the two aspects of 'potential' is in no sense contingent for Aristotle. On the contrary, it is an assumption necessary *a priori*, for the reason already explained: namely, that the categorial doctrine of substance rests on the conception of change or process as actually terminable. In the *Physics*, as for instance in the *Ethics*, Aristotle usually treats his doctrine of categories as a starting-point already settled prior to the task of conceptualizing the specific subject-matter in hand. That of course is why he can then use it as a tool. But the issue just raised shows that in one case at least, the dependence runs the other way too. Aristotle's definition of change, a physical concept, sustains his theory of the categories.

(33) We must now return to the definition itself and its consequences. So far I have attended only to the formal statement in III.1, 201a9 ff. But there are two ways of interpreting this. On the one hand, it can be understood as analysing the common meaning of process-words. These form a fairly obvious class in Greek, as in English, the verbal nouns being usually of the '–σις' ending. On this interpretation, 'κίνησις' on the left-hand side of the definition may be regarded as a variable ranging over the class of "entities" individually named by specific process-nouns. Taken in this sense the definition presupposes that language already marks off the class of actualities falling under it. The job then of the definition is to tell us what these linguistically specified actualities have that is common and distinctive. On the other hand, the definition can also be taken as laying down the conditions under which we are entitled to regard an actuality as a process whether or not the standard linguistic expression for that actuality is a typical process-word. On this interpretation, if it is actually true of a man that he is standing still, but this actuality holds only insofar as something else is not yet actually true of him, as for instance when he stands

on the door-step waiting to be let in, so that his being there is the expression of his not yet being where he is going — then under these conditions, the definition tells us, the standing is a process, and the standing man may be regarded as 'ἐν κυνήσει'. And indeed the ordinary speaker might describe him as 'on his way inside'. Similarly if an animal lies in wait for its prey; in lying in wait, it is 'on the road' to some end, and the lying in wait is grounded in its not having got there, since this is the means.

(34) It is hard to think of examples illustrating this last point in which the behaviour is not purposive or does not lend itself to description in purpose-like terms. However, the fact that Aristotle's definition of process can be interpreted so as to fit even a narrow class of examples such as the above shows that in one area at least, the difference between process-actuality and non-process-actuality does not depend upon any immediately perceivable on-goingness or moment to moment emergence of new properties. Thus although in III.1, 200b16–20, Aristotle names 'the infinite' as one of the concepts to be examined in his philosophy of nature, on the ground that process is continuous, and infinity rears its head in connection with continuity, his actual analysis of process does not compel him to treat it as mathematically continuous or infinitely divisible. This is an advantage, for had he restricted 'process' to situations which it makes sense to describe in terms of mathematical continuity, he would have consigned to conceptual limbo a vast range of occurrences that we should naturally class as processes and becomings; including many examples of his own. How could we begin to apply the model of the continuous series to getting healthy, or to house-building? It is not clear how any type of change apart from locomotion (and increase and decrease so far as they imply locomotion of an object's boundaries) could be handled in this way. And for Aristotle, not only is change in general not scientifically reducible to locomotion (v.s. para. (8)), but even if it were, conceptual reduction would still be out of the question. A given change is of the kind that it is on account of the type of end-state in which it terminates. Unless the latter not only empirically depends

on but essentially consists in some spatial arrangement, macro- or microscopic, the change itself cannot be characterized as locomotion. Being healthy may as a matter of fact consist in a certain disposition of "primary" qualities, but to call this 'health' is simply to evoke a *per accidens* identity. This is not *what* the convalescent is regaining insofar as he is so described. One might as well say that health is the same thing as coolness, on the ground that getting better in his case involves a fall in temperature.

(35) In (5) above we noted that an apparently static object Y may coherently be said to be in process, or in course of changing, on account of some condition in another object X which leads to the emergence of a new property in Y. (Thus someone is already 'getting his hair cut' when the barber is only fetching the scissors.) In this way it is possible to preserve the ordinary implication of 'process' as *taking time* while applying the term to changes where one state of the subject immediately succeeds another. But does the III.1 definition formally sanction this? The answer is surely Yes. Suppose a time in which only X is perceptibly busy; if the stir is because the as yet quiescent Y is (merely) potentially F, then X's behaviour is an actual exercise of *Y*'s potentiality as such. But then Y, by the definition, is the *subject* of an actually occurring process of change, even though that process may be said at this stage to *consist of* the doings of X. Hence by the definition Y may be said to be 'ἐν κινήσει'; for the actual condition leading up to F-ness, though housed in X, *is grounded on privation in Y*. This point is of importance for Aristotle's system, since it is only by some such analysis that he would be entitled to class as 'processes' one vital group of changes, those switches of quality-pairs that constitute the mutual transformations of the simple bodies. These must be instantaneous in the subject; for Aristotle does not hold that between every pair of qualities terminating a change there is another quality "through" which the subject must "pass", thereby taking time to get from one terminus to the other.[25] And there is an extra reason why elemental

---

[25] *V.i.* para. (46). On the finite number of sensible qualities in a given range, see *De Sensu* 6, 445b20–446a20.

transformation involves no temporal separation of the termini. The termini here are quality-pairs constituting the physically simple substances, and apart from such terminal pairs there is no further substance for the subject to *be*. This means that if for any time "it" were "between" termini, there would exist something without nature, form, or character.

(36) Thus far, then, the III.1 definition can be shown to be usefully flexible: but is it a definition of change in general, or even, in general, of led-up-to change (*v.s.* para. (4))? By now, I suppose, the answer is fairly obvious. Where it makes sense to say that the change's occurrence is grounded in the subject's lack of a given property which it is capable of possessing, there the definition applies: otherwise not. Hence, natural and intelligently purposed changes immediately fall under it, for if something's nature or purpose is to be P, being not-P grounds and explains the actuality of P-wards change. Moreover, certain changes neither natural to the subject nor purposed can also be brought within the fold: these are ones that stem from the nature of some external agent. Thus if bees bring pollen to the hive, the pollen's displacement is unnatural to itself but nonetheless grounded on its not being already on the spot; what destines it for this new location is the nature of the *bees*. But what about changes dictated by no nature or purpose external or internal to the subject? Say a stone (S) happens to be kicked sideways by a walker, and rolls until it gets stuck. The motion is not natural to it, nor does it contribute to the inadvertent agent's purpose or to some phase of his natural development. Can we say that the displacement of S from P_1 to P_2 is an actuality belonging to it *qua* potentially at P_2, i.e. which was grounded on its not being actually there? This would imply that the movement would cease of itself at P_2, the grounds being no longer present. But this case is not like that, since S could have been displaced in the same way from P_1, yet not stopped at P_2. The identical kick would have sent it somewhere else but for the position of the obstacle. The passage is informed by no single gerundive from the start. Indeed the only reason for saying that the motion was 'to' P_2 is that this is where it ceased in fact; but this event is extrinsic to the beginning

of motion, and therefore the reference to P_2 in no way specifies *what* it was that unfolded from P_1. By contrast, a directed
process has its end dictated from the first, whether actually
reached or not. To Aristotle the notion of intrinsic direction
is of logical, not merely teleological, significance; or we might
say rather that the teleology is grounded on the logic. For, as
he conceives it, the specific and definite character of a process is given by *both* its termini, and nothing exists or takes
place that is not of a definite nature. Hence *before* the process
is over (at which point it no longer exists), and indeed from
the outset, it must already "have", in some sense, an *ad quem*
regardless of the outcome. For whatever the outcome, there
must already be something determinate whose fate this is:
if a describable event is said to reach completion, it is also
true that that same bearer of that same description might
have failed to reach it.

(37) Hence accidental events such as the displacement of the
stone in our example are conceptual anomalies: they are not
static conditions — something new comes about — but nor
are they κινήσεις in accordance with the definition. The
latter, in effect, excludes all events not explicable under the
headings of nature and purpose. Since these headings cannot
be applied in the abstract, one would need in practice to have
evidence of a particular substance or purpose at work before
being in a position to classify an event as a 'process'. And
even if one could know in a general way that an inner principle of change and stasis (i.e. of self-terminating change) was
the cause, the event's kinetic status would still be indeter-
minate unless one could identify that principle. A pile of
stones on the ground is in a condition of natural stasis if we
have regard to the earthy substance of stone; but if a builder
has dumped them there as the position most convenient from
which to hoist them to an arch under construction, then
from his point of view they are there only on account of not
yet being somewhere else, and are therefore 'in process'.
Again, kinetic status varies with the description: if we focus
on 'being on the ground', and regarding 'being just here at
the foot of the wall' as incidental, then we treat the stones
as a case of earthy substance whose condition is static: for

it is the nature of earthy masses to lie low, but not in one particular place rather than another; whereas if 'being just here' is not incidental (because central from the external agent's point of view), then under this description we are dealing with a κίνησις. But without causal knowledge of the agents or substances concerned we cannot divide essential from incidental descriptions; hence 'κίνησις' in the sense of III.1 is predicable only from within a framework of such knowledge. We have already seen how the concept can be correctly applied even when nothing is visibly 'going on' (*v.s.* para. (5)); and it is now clear that this is not because in those cases the alteration is too minute to be observed, but because a κίνησις is not, as such, a datum even for the sharpest senses, any more than the causality of a cause or the substancehood of a substance.

(38) If Aristotle had intended this result he would surely have signalized it by some attempt to conciliate ordinary users of process-terms, who do not regard themselves as unable to apply the words correctly unless they are causally in the know. For them Aristotle might have marked off a secondary sense (although first in the order of knowledge), the one used simply to *report* what is *observed* to happen when a stone (for whatever reason) rolls. That he makes no such distinction to save the linguistic phenomena is clear evidence that he was unaware of having produced an analysis which on its own gives rise to the dilemma: either rolling is not a κίνησις (it is one of his own examples at 201a18-19) or we cannot know whether S is rolling or not until we know the cause . . . cause of *what*? His definition leaves us without a word. But although this is embarrassing it is also in a way appropriate, since if we consider even the phenomenon of rolling we seem to encounter something defying description, although for reasons which have nothing to do with ignorance of the cause. Motion as such is something of a mystery, whether the case be directed or accidental; and it is this, I think, that Aristotle has partly in view when framing the III.1 formula. The rolling object is not nowhere, but nor is it at any moment somewhere either, in the full-blooded sense in which it was and will be somewhere before and

after the passage. This is one of the paradoxes to which Aristotle alludes at the beginning, where he says that continuity and infinite divisibility are topics for study in connection with process (III.1, 200b16-20). Soon we shall follow him some way through the very precise discussions in which in *Physics* VI and VIII he formulates, criticizes, and reformulates the doctrine that motion is infinitely divisible. But even if only vaguely stated (as above), the paradox seems a perfect subject on which to exercise the dichotomy 'actual'/'potential'. Rolling is an actuality whereby the subject is not actually anywhere, nor yet nowhere, but (surely) potentially somewhere. But potentially *where*? There are many positions (perhaps we have to say infinitely many) which the continuously moving object neither was nor was not at: should we not then say that it was potentially at each? But the problem is not that of producing an infinitely long list, for a single formula covers all the positions: 'all those between A and B'. It is that the different positions cannot be occupied simultaneously: there is therefore no single actuality consisting in being at P_m and at P_n and at P_o, etc. But potentiality is for the possibly actual; hence there is no such thing as *the* potentiality to be in P_m and P_n, etc. Should we then speak of the potentiality to be in them successively, or rather (as continuity demands) in a different one at each moment? But the actuality that would correspond to this is the actuality of motion itself, since this simply *is* being in a different position at each moment; and the original problem survives, because this 'momentary being at' was just what seemed insufficiently real to be classed as 'really being somewhere'. Should we say then that the motion is an exercise of many potentialities, as many as there are positions? If so we lose the right to call it *the* exercise and *the* motion. In short, the logic of 'actual'/'potential' demands a *single* filling for 'is potentially at —'; and since potentiality is for things in the future, not the past,[26] the reference will inevitably be to the latest position, or that where the motion ends.

(39) Thus we arrive at a formula verbally identical with the

[26] Cf. *Rhet.* III.17, 1418a3-5; *Eth. Nic.* VI.2, 1139b7-9; *De Caelo* I.12, 283b13; *De. Int.* 9.

one in which reference to the terminal condition specifies the inner direction of the process. But the meanings are very different, and the second is actually incoherent. It mimics the first by referring to a single last state, but the reason for this is simply that 'potentially —' demands a single, or at any rate a self-consistent, filling; not that the last state has any real priority over the intermediate stages with respect to the structure of the process. For where this is not intrinsically directed, or not considered as such, the last state can only be identified (and the process therefore fully specified) *ex post facto*. But this means that the process literally has no fully determinate description while taking place. But then it cannot count as an *actuality* while occurring — and if not then, when? Nor can it count as an incomplete actuality, for an incomplete actuality is one whose essential description requires a gerundive reference to a specific terminus *ad quem*. By contrast, a true account of the non-directed process *as* it is unfold*ing* ought to supply a description complete (or not incomplete) without any such reference, since in itself the process is not towards anything in particular. Such a description, if it is possible, should display the 'neither anywhere nor nowhere' aspect in coherent fashion; but this poise between being and non-being is not the same as the incomplete (or privation-based) actuality which Aristotle's formula in III.1 successfully defines to the satisfaction of certain special metaphysical requirements concerning natural substance. What he, strangely, fails to see is that this success is limited to only a sub-class of events that would ordinarily be regarded as 'processes'. That failure may be due to confusion engendered by the verbal coincidence just explained.

PART II

(40) Enough has been said about the limitation of the Book III definition for it to be no surprise that Aristotle elsewhere mounts another attack on the problem of change. I refer to *Physics* VI, where he approaches the question from a standpoint very different from the one coherently represented in

III. In VI the metaphysical concepts of substance and nature, act and potency, have sunk out of sight for the time being, and the analysis depends instead on the notions of space, time, and the magnitude of the changing object, and above all on the infinite divisibility of these. As he says at III.1, 200b22-3, these are common and universal properties: in particular they are shared by accidental changes. Here, then, we may hope to find an improvement on the account of change as 'incomplete actuality'. However, there is no reason to think that Aristotle himself at any stage saw this as deficient. Book VI shows only that at some point (whether earlier or later[27]) he believed that change could be profitably discussed in a different way. The conception of III is the one to which in the end he returns (if he ever left it), in VIII.[28] Moreover, in VI he never departs from the fundamental assumption of III, that change is properly to be described as *process*: not as emergence, but emergence-led-up-to, where the leading-up is itself the change, or rather the chang*ing*. The assumption was necessitated by the metaphysic of nature, but is present even where this is least in evidence. He also, in VI, represents process as demanding analysis under two aspects, each of which found a place in the III.1 account: a process is (*a*) of a fundamentally different structure from a non-processive actuality, but (*b*) in common with the latter it has (in any given case) a unity and identity of its own. The rest of this chapter centres on the question whether in VI Aristotle succeeds in developing a non-metaphysical concept of process that does justice to both these aspects. It will turn out that he fails, as he himself came to realize: the reason being that in VI he analyses the first aspect in terms which makes nonsense of the second.

(41) Assuming that change is to be regarded as essentially a chang*ing*, the problem as always is how to characterize this. On such a view it necessarily takes time; so how is it distinguishable from non-process conditions which also last for a time? In III.1, drawing on the concept of 'nature', Aristotle

---

[27] Ancient tradition assigns Books III and VI to different works, but their chronological order is uncertain. See Ross, *Aristotle's Physics*, pp. 1-8.

[28] Cf. 251a8-10; 257b6-9. On internal evidence VIII postdates both III. 1-3 and VI.

was able to define process in a way not entailing its mathematical continuity. However, if process is now to be marked off from non-process in metaphysically neutral terms, what is left but to attempt a distinction by means of *temporal* structure? On reaching the discussion of Zeno's paradoxes in Book VI, the reader of the *Physics* may find it surprising that Aristotle, with his sensitivity to differences of conceptual level and his constant insistence that each subject-matter be treated in terms proper to itself, should have so enthusiastically accepted Zeno's initial assumption that the concept of the mathematical continuum applies to physical space, time, and motion. We should expect Aristotle to query this,[29] even granted that his main concern in VI is to meet the paradoxes on their own terms. But his attitude becomes intelligible once we see that the concept of the temporal continuum seems to be exactly what he needs to make out afresh the distinction of process from non-process. A process necessarily lasts for some time, as do non-processive conditions, but the difference between them is now held to lie in the *temporal variegation* of the former. What distinguishes process is its many stages, at each of which something different is true of the subject. The non-processive is now, by contrast, identified with the static, i.e. with a condition such that for as long as it lasts what is true of the subject is always the same. And since the difference between process and non-process is assumed to be absolute (it is still the difference between being and becoming), an adequate account must ensure the irreducibility of process to a series of static conditions.

(42) The concept of time as infinitely divisible seems the ideal instrument for this purpose. For suppose, rather, that time is composed of indivisible units. These must have duration, for otherwise together they could not compose duration.

---

[29] Cf. G. Vlastos, 'Zeno's Race Course', *Studies in Presocratic Philosophy*, edd. Allan and Furley, vol. II, p. 218, n. 25 (the article first appeared in *Journal of the History of Philosophy* IV, 1966): 'To humour Zeno's claim that the sequence of Z-runs is infinite we must allow that any point reached after traversing a finite number of Z-intervals would be physically distinguishable from the terminal point, G, as also from infinitely many intermediate points.' Aristotle is not in the habit of humouring his adversaries; that he does so here requires some explanation.

Hence every stage in a process would necessarily endure for at least one unit's length, during which there could be no change, because no room for a 'before and after'. In that case the large-scale process would be a series of non-changes. But if instead time is infinitely divisible, no amount is too small to house change or to exhibit different stages of a process. The way is now open for a concept of process involving as many stages as there are divisions of the time. According to this, within any period of an object's change there is no sub-period in which it is not changing, and therefore no sub-period not terminated by a moment at which it is true that *there has already been change*. It follows too that within the period of change, for every moment at which this is true, there was a prior moment at which the same was true. This is the position which Aristotle has reached half-way through the sixth chapter of VI.

(43) He now draws the conclusion crucial for his entire account of change and process in that book. It depends on a certain interpretation of the perfect tense in 'there has already been change'. The position just stated could be taken to amount to this: 'Within the period of change from A to B, there is no moment when it is not true that the object has already been engaged in changing from A to B'. However, Aristotle, helped no doubt by the special nuance of the Greek perfect tense, uncovers a further meaning: ' . . . there is no moment when it is not true that the object has already *completed* ("perfected") a change'. Now, obviously a change completed *within* this period of change from A to B is not a change to B but to something in some sense (for we are not dealing only with locomotion) "nearer" to A than B is. So it has a terminus other than B, and is therefore a different change from the one terminating in B. This follows from Aristotle's never questioned assumption that *the* way to specify a change or process is by reference to its termini, and especially the *ad quem*. In this we can perhaps again detect the influence of teleological meta-physics even here in one of the least metaphysical sections of the *Physics*. At any rate, that assumption is what inspires his conclusion:

In half the time it will have performed another change (ἄλλο ἔσται μεταβεβληκός') [i.e. other than that performed in the whole], and in half that another, and so on *ad infinitum*. (6, 237a26-8; cf. also 15-17)

Thus a process is said not only to take place during an infinitely divisible period t_0-t_1, but to incorporate within its duration an infinity of distinct lesser processes, one for each sub-period t_0-$t_{n < 1}$. We can now draw a general distinction between process and the static, using some supposedly neutral word like 'condition' to cover both. A specific condition C is a *process* if its temporal structure is such that: for every period t_0-t_n throughout which X has been in C there is a period t_0-$t_{m < n}$ throughout which X has been in a specific condition C', where C' is (*a*) of the same type as C, and (*b*) distinct from C. Thus if throughout some period X has been engaged in the specific locomotion described as 'from A to B', then throughout the first half it has been in locomotion from A to an intermediate point I, this being a condition of the same type (locomotion) as the first, but specifically different. By contrast, a specific condition C is *static* if its temporal structure is such that for every period t_0-t_n throughout which X has been in C there is no period t_0-$t_{m < n}$ during which X has been in a condition of the same type but specifically different. For if something was, say, of a particular shade of green throughout a period, then it was not any other colour during any part of this time.

(44) This concept of process could hardly be more different from the limited one successfully presented in III.1. The focus has shifted from the subject's incompleteness with respect to a future state to its series of changes already at any stage accomplished and past. It is the infinity of this series that now guarantees the *sui generis* status of process, rather than a special connection with potentiality as such and privation. Regarding the question of the unity of a given process, the situation is much the same. In III the unity was derived from the singleness of the end-state specifying inherent direction, and since the direction was dictated from the start, the object may be said to have been in process to (= in the direction specified by) T even if T was not reached

in fact. But in VI, 'to T' has no other ground than the actual issue of the process at or in T, and its unity prior to the moment of issue can be made out only by reference to the mathematical ordering of process-stages. These are correlated one-one with temporal instants, which are simply points of division in the time considered as a continuous magnitude. Just as the instants are specified in quantitative terms (the limit of half the time, of a quarter, etc.), so the stages are corresponding divisions in the process, which has now itself come to be treated as a sort of magnitude. Thus every stage can be given a designation which is unique but also conceptually homogeneous with the designation of every other, since each can be picked out by a different value of some one variable such as 'degree of remoteness from the starting point'. Their amenability to this kind of ordering is all that is relevant to their claim to be considered stages of the one process. In III, by contrast, infinite divisibility by mathematically ordered stages is an entirely optional feature of process as there defined: it is not a sufficient condition (since accidental "processes" can have it, and these do not fall under the definition; nor is it necessary. A process, as presented in III, may involve a countable succession of non-instantaneous stages or phases whose descriptions are quite heterogeneous. Going to the house consists in opening the gate, walking up the path, ringing the bell, etc., and these are related by no algorithm but as concrete events whose community in the one process derives from their all (in the particular situation) being grounded in the current absence of one and the same terminal condition; while their continuity consists simply in the fact that this end is approached without interpolation of phases belonging to some differently directed change. It should also be observed that 'process' has different contraries on the views of VI and III. We have already analysed the *static*, which is the contrary in VI. On this conception it is evidently impossible that an object in some condition that is contrary to process should as such have different descriptions true of it from moment to moment. But the contrary of process in III is: actuality *not* grounded on privation. And under this heading come not only so-called static conditions, but also non-self-terminating activities like the pursuit of an investigation for its own sake or dancing for enjoyment, whose continuing for any length of time necessarily entails that different things are true of the subject from one moment to the next.[30]

(45) Finally, the two accounts differ not only with regard to the temporal structure of process and its opposite, but also over the demands made (or not made) concerning their relative positions in time. Book III permits the time of the process itself to coincide with (or anyway overlap) the time of the *a quo* condition, (*v.s.* paras (6) and (35)). By VI this is logically impossible. Stages of process are now identified by their distance from one or other terminus; hence the subject cannot be at a stage and at a terminus simultaneously, even if it is 'at' the former only in the sense of passing through. Not only terminus and terminus, but terminus and stage, are logical contraries. But the object is not in process unless already at a stage (has completed a lesser process). So: since being at the *a quo* condition excludes being at any stage, it excludes being in process. Hence the process begins only as the *a quo* condition ends, and occupies a temporal interval between the termini. There is no such requirement according to III, since there there need not be logical contrariety between the terminus *a quo* and the process. A dish of water is put in the freezer: after a time its surface is frozen. Aristotle regards the transformation from liquid to solid as instantaneous (his physics excludes the sort of corpuscular theory that could represent it as gradual).[31] Is he then bound to deny a time-taking process? No, because by III the process can be said to consist in the water's simply standing there, provided that this was explicable by the future solid state, as for instance if someone had put it there with this intention. Hence in this case the becoming frozen is an actuality coincident with the liquid state. Being liquid does not

---

[30] These are the ἐνέργειαι contrasted with κινήσεις in *Metaph.* Θ 6. For a discussion of this text see below, Ch. IV, paras (28) ff. Aristotle's examples ad. loc. have often been disputed; it is now clear why this is inevitable. Just as nothing is a κίνησις (as defined in III) (or phase of one) *per se* and in the abstract, but only when circumstances are such that absence of the end-state prompts *this* particular move or stance, so it is with ἐνέργειαι, *mutatis mutandis*.

[31] Cf. *Physics* VIII.3, 253b25-6.

logically exclude standing in a certain place; why then should it exclude becoming frozen, when there can be circumstances in which this process simply consists in the standing?[32]

(46) We have now to consider the merits of the analysis in VI. Its best illustration is, of course, locomotion. But Aristotle intends it to cover change of whatever kind. Infinite temporal variegation is, in his present view, the distinguishing mark of change as such (see VI.6, 237a34 ff.). If so, all types of change must be mathematically continuous. But there is a difficulty which he himself notes: not all properties in respect of which there is change belong to continuous ranges. Qualities, he says, are 'indivisible' (VI.5, 236b1-6), by which he means that it is not the case that between any pair of a kind there is necessarily another. In this Aristotle is surely right, for on what grounds could it be credibly maintained that there must be always an intermediate? A perceptible change of quality may involve a *perceptible* gradation between termini, but perception cannot discern a shade between every pair of perceptibly distinguishable shades. Nor have we, as with spatial position and magnitude, a mathematical method of designating an intermediate for every pair in terms of fractions of some size or distance. And in any case, even if between any two qualities a third could theoretically be found, in what sense are the intermediates actually *passed through* in a particular qualitative change? The nature of space dictates (or so we assume) that all positions on a line must be traversed by an object moving from one end to the other. But even if between (say) any two musical tones there *is* an intermediate, in the sense that a note might be produced lower than one and higher than the other, it would be ludicrous to insist that every actual passage from F to A must 'go through' all these, as if a player could only ever move from note to note *glissando*.[33]

(47) Yet in VI Aristotle maintains that even in qualitative

---

[32] Standing, but not becoming frozen, may continue once the ice has appeared. The standing "survives" as "matter" of the process no longer "informed" by an unattained end.

[33] Cf. *Physics* V.3, 226b29-30.

change what changes has already performed another change, and in this another, etc. His argument is that although the *respect* of change is indivisible, the time is not (VI.5, 236b2-8; 6, 237 a35-b3). This is a bid to save the continuity model by reading into the transition itself stages entirely borrowed from the divisions of the time.[34] Thus (granting for the moment that time does elapse) we are meant to say that in half the time X has completed a change to half-way being red and so on. But apart from reducing qualities in the Aristotelian sense to primary qualities in the Lockean, there is no independent method for identifying infinitely many degrees of qualitative change. It is meaningless to say that at t_n X was one thousandth more red than at t_m and millionths more for every thousandth part of the interval. In any case why should we suppose in the first place that qualitative change requires time? Aristotle has no choice in the matter as long as he takes change to be essentially graduated *ad infinitum*.[35] But although qualitative change is often 'continuous' in the sense of smooth and unbroken, so that to describe it as a series of discrete states gives entirely the wrong impression, this does not entail mathematical continuity. If we do not observe a succession of A and then B this need not be because there intervened a time-taking transition, which presumably we could have watched advancing. On the contrary: a change from, say, pain to relief or from loud to soft is typically noticed as having happened, not as happen*ing*. But

---

[34] He also hopes to solve this by insisting on the spatial divisibility of the object changing (VI.4, 234b10 ff.; cf. 6, 237b10 ff.). He here prefers to forget not only that water freezes in an instant but that at that instant *some* water must *all* be frozen (if any is at all). For a different view see I.3, 186a13-16 and VIII.3, 253b19-30.

[35] Aristotle's attempt to apply this analysis to all types of change, including qualitative, runs into a further difficulty consequent on his account of time in *Physics IV*. There (11, 219 a10 ff.) he plainly argues that the divisibility of the time of a κίνησις derives from the divisibility of the κίνησις itself, which in turn is seen as having μέγεθος on account of its traversing a divisible spatial interval; cf. G.E.L. Owen, 'Aristotle on Time', *Motion and Time, Space and Matter*, edd. Machamer and Turnbull, pp. 3 ff.; esp. pp. 19 ff. But in VI.6 Aristotle's general thesis requires him to revise the conceptual order in the case of qualitative change, making the latter's divisibility depend on that of the time. For further discussion of Aristotle's treatment of change over non-continuous ranges, see R. Sorabji, 'The Instant of Change', in *Articles on Aristotle*, vol. III, edd. Barnes, Schofield and Sorabji, especially pp. 168-70.

it is not only the detail of ordinary experience that conflicts with Aristotle's universal contention, for there are also philosophers who will seize on this experience to reinforce an opposed universal view. Given Aristotle's own premises (*a*) that every change is necessarily divisible into changes, and (*b*) that quality is an 'indivisible' respect of change, a physical atomist now has the perfect opportunity for concluding that apparent change of quality is really change in some divisible respect, hence is nothing but the locomotion of particles.

(48) The onus is therefore on Aristotle to *argue* that all change without exception takes time between its termini (so that the change is divisible because the time is). And he does argue.

Not only is it the case that what is changing (τὸ μετάβαλλον) has changed, but it is also the case that what has changed was changing before. For whatever has changed [i.e. completed a change] from something to something has changed in a period of time. To see this, suppose that it has completed the change from A to B in an instant. Then it has not completed the change in the same instant in which it was at A, since in that case it would be in A and B at the same time. This is supported by our earlier conclusion that what has changed, when it has changed, is not in the terminus *a quo*. But if it has completed the change in a different instant from that in which it was in A, then there is a period of time between, since instants are not together. So since it has changed in a period of time, and all time is divisible, in half the time it will have performed another change, and by the same reasoning in half of that another, and so on *ad infinitum*. Thus what has changed was previously changing.' (VI.6, 237a17-28)

The earlier conclusion referred to was reached in 5, 235b6 ff., where he showed that whatever changes 'leaves' ('ἀπολείπει') the terminus *a quo*. There and in the course of the argument just quoted Aristotle uses spatial terminology to talk about change in general. More specifically, in speaking of the object as being at or in (ἐν) the termini A and B, he invites us to imagine these as places, therefore as spatially distant, so that the passage from one to the other would inevitably take time. But since his purpose now is to *prove* that this is a feature of change in general, I shall take it that in reaching this conclusion he intends the spatial terms to be understood as metaphors only. Accordingly, in the present passage 'being at (or 'in') A etc.' is to be read as equivalent to 'having the properties A etc.', where 'A' etc. designate qualities as well as attributes of spatial position; and the earlier phrase 'X has left A' means simply that X has A no longer.

(49) The argument just quoted from VI.6 rests on the Law of Non-Contradiction. It is because 'A' entails the contradictory of its contrary 'B' that the subject of change from one to the other cannot be in both at once, and so must have 'left' A by the time it has 'arrived at' B. Therefore, Aristotle argues, there must be an interval of transition between the two states. For if they were immediately consecutive the first instant of B would be identical with an instant (the last) of A. This is because instants cannot be contiguous; if I_1 is other than I_2 they must be separate in time. But the first instant of B and the last of A cannot be identical, since if so the subject would have A and B simultaneously. Hence there is no *instant* of transition,[36] but in all cases a measurable time taken, and it is only the between-ness of this that saves the concept of change from the incoherence of entailing that the subject is in contradictory states at the same time. However, the argument proves too much. On the same principles an interval can be demonstrated between a state and its contradictory. But no interval is possible between not-Q and Q, at any rate not for Aristotle, who holds by the Law of Excluded Middle (cf. VI.5, 235b15–16). Suppose, however, that we ignore this law, and allow the object to be neither Q nor not-Q in becoming one from the other: the reasoning in 6 would make change impossible even on these terms. If there has to be a period of transition between contradictories because instantaneous change would entail the object's having both at once, then there must also be such a period between each contradictory and N (where 'N' = 'neither not-Q nor Q), since 'N' and 'not-Q', and 'N' and 'Q' are no less mutually exclusive than 'Q' and 'not-Q'. So there must also be a period of neither not-Q nor N between

---

[36] On Aristotle's handling of this concept see G.E.L. Owen, 'τιθέναι τὰ φαινόμενα', op. cit.

not-Q and N, and so on, proliferating to infinity the consecutive periods required for any single change.

(50) Aristotle himself considers a similar difficulty in the preceding chapter, i.e. VI.5. His problem there is the transition from rest to process. An instantaneous transition seems to entail a moment when the object is both at rest and in process. But this time Aristotle cannot step out of it by postulating a non-instantaneous transition. This would produce the infinite regress: a $process_2$ from rest to $process_1$, and $process_3$ from rest to $process_2$, etc. His answer consists in the assertion of instantaneous transition from rest to process together with the denial that this implies a moment when the object has both the properties characterizing the periods on either side. The object, he says, must not be described as in process of changing *at* the instant in question. It is changing *as from* this instant, and at every subsequent instant (up to the latter end of the change) it is true of it that it has already been changing. And however early a subsequent instant we select, there was always an earlier one likewise subsequent; thus he is able to phrase his conclusion: 'There is no moment which is the first at which the thing has changed'. (VI.5, 236 a25-7; cf. 3, 234 a34-b5).

(51) Here, then, Aristotle breaks the paradox by prohibiting the inference from 'Instant I limits the period during which X is in process' to 'I is a moment when X is in process'. In this way he ensures that rest and process are not separated by an interval, while avoiding commitment to a moment when they coincide. But he fails to see that the same treatment can be meted out against his own argument in VI.6 refuting instantaneous change between contrary static conditions. It is true that the logical situation is different in the latter, since a time-taking transition is not in all such cases absurd *a priori*; but nor is it absurd in some cases (e.g. the qualitative) to suppose the change-over to occupy no time at all. Aristotle's argument in 6 to the contrary can be defused by treating the moment when e.g. loud replaced soft as a limit in the sense explained, i.e. in the sense in which 'being a limit of the period of loudness' does not entail 'being a moment *when*

or *at* which loudness was present'. However, perhaps he has good reason not to attend to the possibility of this move. If he were to concede that ordinary contraries (i.e. not process and rest, but the termini of process) may be divided only by a limiting instant, he would then face the question of what to say *does* obtain at that instant. There seems no clear reason to assign to it one of the contraries and not the other, in which case we have the contradiction which he actually exploits. But if neither is assigned, nothing is true of the object at that instant. Yet how is this possible, given that it exists throughout? There is only one way of sidestepping absurdity. This is to draw a categorial distinction between instants and periods to the effect that only the latter can meaningfully be treated as times *when* a predicate *is* true of its subject. In that case the role of the instant of transition is simply to be a limit marking the end of one period and the beginning of another, and not to be any kind of property-location for which could be posed the dilemma: either the subject is *then* in contrary states, or it is *then* in none.

(52) At one point Aristotle approaches this position, when at VI.3, 234a31–b9, he says that for a state of rest to obtain, i.e. a condition of statically being so and so, measurable time is required no less than for a process. However, if he were to go the whole way and declare that *being* P, no less than *becoming* P, takes a length of time, it would be good-bye for ever to the analysis of change as an infinite nested set of distinct lesser changes. The universal application of this would cease to be a problem because there would now be no coherent concept at all. Since the object is supposed in any one change to have completed others, it must have reached and *been* at the terminus of each; but since the other changes are infinite within any finite period, there can have been no lingering when they were complete. But this not lingering at T must (if the account is coherent) allow nonetheless for the object's having *been at* T. For otherwise T is not a change-defining terminus. That is to say, if '*being* at T' fails to make sense, then so does '*coming to be* at T', and there is no such thing as a *T*-wards change, but at most a change *through* T

somewhither else.[37] In short, the account of change in *Physics* VI latently depends on the concept of instantaneous being at a terminus.

(53) I say 'latently' because *Physics* VI is remarkable for the degree to which it combines intense precision of reasoning with a pervasive ambivalence concerning the fundamental concepts involved. The position is incurably incoherent, as Aristotle himself came to see in Book VIII, where a particular problem of cosmology forced him to reconsider the entire project of defining process in terms of its infinite divisibility. I shall turn to this presently, but not without first observing that trouble in any case would now be inevitable, even if the view of VI were sound in itself. We have already seen how radically this differs from the definition of III, and how the extensions of the two conceptions fail to coincide. But so far it might perhaps have been hoped on Aristotle's behalf that the difference does not amount to incompatibility, and that certain paradigmatic cases of process can usefully be handled in both ways. The locomotion of an intentionally driven billiard-ball surely illustrates both accounts. And so it does, but it is now clear that adopting the one entails dropping the other, even for those concrete instances where the extensions intersect. If, as VI implies, a terminus can (and in infinitely many cases must) be possessed or dwelt in only instantaneously, then *stasis* in some terminal condition bears at most a logically contingent relation to the process thus terminated. On this view, the contrast between process and stasis turns out to be superficial, plausible only on the level of unexamined sense-experience. For analysis now shows that in VI the real contrast (and also the real connection) is between process and *terminus*, and if *stasis* is to fit into this scheme at all, it can only be as a kind of optional (in some cases) extension of the terminal condition. However, in view of the conceptual difficulty of representing that which takes time as any sort of prolongation of that which is instantaneous, there would seem to be no

[37] See e.g. VI.10, 241 a26–b12 for an exposition of the point that process is only to an attainable terminus. See above paras (31)–(32) for the metaphysical background.

point in even considering this, were it not for what is at stake: namely, Aristotle's continuing entitlement to the notion of natural substance as a principle of self-terminating activity in the sense defined in III.1. For in this connection the terminus *ad quem* can scarcely be regarded as a point of possibly momentary dwelling. If the non-negatively-based actuality were to last for no time, it is difficult to see how its prior absence could ground the actuality of process towards it. Privation functions as a motive only to the extent that the positive terminal state, if reached, would remove it. But if the privation is a type of condition that exists for a finite time if at all, *instantaneous* possession of the terminus could not meet the lack. If, on the other hand, privation too were instantaneous, and were a motive, then (since there is no interval between privation and possession, and instants not separated by an interval are the same) it follows that privation, possession, and process would coincide in a single instant: for the process cannot extend beyond the privation.

(54) So internal evidence amply confirms the ancient reports that III and VI belong to different works:[38] even to the point of implying that neither view could have developed except in isolation from the other. The inevitable tension begins to surface only in VIII. Yet perhaps there is no such thing as complete isolation, and one may even wonder whether Aristotle would have been able to push the mathematicized scheme of VI to such confident lengths were he not *also* the metaphysician of III. The point of this remark will be clearer once we have stated the fundamental error of VI. What Aristotle fails to see there is this. If X in passing from A to B through the intermediate point I completes a change terminating at I, then there is no single change occurring throughout the time of passage from A to B. For if one change (distinguished by reference to one pair of termini) is over at I, then at I *another* begins, even if X does not halt. It gets from A to B by a succession of changes A–I and I–B. Yet the account was intended to display each and every *single* change as "containing" infinite others. Aristotle wanted to say not only that at each moment of the change from A to B the

[38] *V.s.* n. 27.

object has already been in process of change *from A to B*, but also that at each moment it has already completed a lesser change than the change to B. In effect, every intermediate point is a terminus *ad quem*. But the *ad quem* of one change must be the *a quo* of another, unless the object now stays for ever. And even if it stays at I for no time at all, I cannot function as a terminus one way and not the other. Hence B, strictly speaking, is reached by a change not from A but from I. But here one can never speak strictly enough, since by the same argument the change to B is not really from I, but from another terminal point I' between I and B. Thus infinite divisibility ensures that although in the end the object will *be* at B, it will not have arrived there by any single identifiable change; nor by a succession of these, since no change is single. One might ask why it should matter, seeing that the infinite proliferation does not entail that the object will never be at B. But it does entail that B is not reached by *change*. For only the specific is real, and there is no specific change or set of specific changes in which the passage consists. This amounts to a proof that the very concept of 'change' is incoherent: for change is nothing if not that by which something passes from one condition to another.

(55) As Aristotle later saw it (in VIII.8), this infinite fracturing of change by instantaneous intermediate termini is the real nerve of Zeno's first argument[39] for the impossibility of motion. What on further reflection he took to be at issue is not the possibility of traversing infinitely many points in a finite time, but that of retaining any meaning at all for 'traverse' if intermediate points are regarded as termini. But, as the text of VIII shows, Aristotle had to struggle for this insight, since it depends on dissociating 'terminus' from 'stasis', concepts which even now he can hardly bring himself to separate. Not only the naive imagery of ordinary language but his own previous physics and metaphysics work against the discrimination. We need only recall the coupling of 'change' with 'stasis' in the Book II account of 'nature'. But

---

[39] 'Nothing is in motion, because what travels must reach the halfway mark before it reaches the end.' VI.9, 239b11-13; cf. 2, 233a21 ff.

if he only just grasps the distinction in VIII it could not have been clearly to the fore for him when he wrote VI, the gist of whose central position reappears (as target) in VIII. Hence despite the fact that objectively that position presupposes the highly abstract concept of 'instantaneous terminus', it would not be surprising if alongside this we were to find in VI traces of the familiar notion of terminus as *resting*-place. Indeed it would be surprising if not. At any rate, it is the presence of this, I suspect, that sustains Aristotle's temporary illusion that the Book VI theory of process is coherent. For how was it that he failed to see that if the intermediate point I is a terminus *to* which X passes in passing from A to B, then there not a single (although internally variegated) change from A to B, but (leaving infinite divisibility aside) two, one that ends and one that begins at I? I think it was because he judged the unity of a change by one standard and its distinctness by another. The longer transition A–B, and the shorter one A–I, are seen as distinct changes because the termini *ad quos* are different. At the same time A–B is seen as a single unpunctuated progression because the object is not at rest for any length of the time taken to get from A to B. So A–I and I–B appear as phases of one unbroken process. The assumption is that a new process would be preceded by rest. However, this surely entails that A–I is not after all a distinct complete change unless there is rest at I. To presume the contrary, as Aristotle does in VI, is to treat I as an *ad quem* that somehow manages not to function also as an *a quo*. Thus the change to B seems to be unbroken from A in that it has no starting point but A, yet is at the same time distinct from the change to I because its end-point differs. But if I is the *ad quem* of one change, how can it not be the potential *a quo* for another, and if, as in the example, change beyond I actually occurs, how can this not then have actually started from I? Aristotle's placidity in the face of what, on analysis, turns out to be a paradox threatening the entire conception of 'terminus', whether this be interpreted statically or instantaneously, is easily explained on the hypothesis that he is using both interpretations at once: the static in connection with the 'outside' change A–B, and the other in connection with those which it allegedly "contains".

(56) Nor is this the only ambiguity in the Book VI account, for two senses of 'continuous change' are in play here, and to distinguish them Aristotle would need to have been as clear at this stage about the notion of 'terminus' as he only later started to become in VIII. To say (i) that throughout a certain period X is continuously engaged in change in a given respect, say place, is not to say (ii) that throughout the period it is engaged in the same continuous change of place. The first amounts to the claim that X is not at rest during any portion of the time, i.e. that it is always engaged in some locomotion or other; while the second means that throughout there is some single locomotion (between a single pair of termini). The inference from (i) to (ii) is formally invalid, but the invalidity is unlikely to show up as long as 'terminus' tends to be interpreted as 'stopping-place'. On that interpretation, (i) cannot be true and (ii) false, for (i) now implies that no change terminates within the period, and from this follows (ii), that there is a single change.

(57) I turn now to VIII itself, where a new and special interest brings Aristotle again to the question of the divisibility of change. His main problem in the relevant section is to identify a kind of process capable of continuing for ever. His concern now is not primarily with change and process as such, but with the requirements of rational cosmology. Foremost among these is that there be always change in the universe, and this, he holds, is possible only if there is at least one body engaged in some single unbroken process. Hence the need to decide what sort of process this could be. Despite the fact that this question is reached and answered in the course of a long and massive argument, it cannot but seem an afterthought in relation to his first principles of physics. Having defined nature in II as an inner source of change *and stasis*, and change in III as (in effect) the sort of thing of which nature is the source, he is ill-equipped, it would seem, to deal at all with the topic of *unending* process otherwise than by simply forgetting about those definitions.[40] But far from this, he reverts in VIII to both (3, 253b7-9; 1, 251a8-10; 5, 257b8-9), and especially tries to capitalize on the

[40] Cf. below Ch. V paras (43) ff.

second. But whatever the difficulty of adapting these themes of II and III to his new concern, their presence should lead us to expect a general reaction away from the Book VI account of process in which they have no consistent part to play.

(58) The reaction takes definite form in the final section of Aristotle's demonstration that the everlasting process is circular locomotion (7, 261a27 ff. and 8 *passim*). What interests us here is not so much the proof that it is locomotion, but the proof that it is circular. In reaching this conclusion Aristotle is forced to take the idea of *unbrokenness* more seriously than ever before, and this has repercussions for his understanding of change and process in general. There is no denying the infinite divisibility, in some sense, of all locomotion, even of that which continues for ever. But this is not at all the place to treat the internal variegation of process as its feature of greatest significance. That is relevant, perhaps, in a context where a contrast is to be drawn between process and rest. But now the conceptual opposition of rest and process is overlaid by their resemblance. There has to be eternal *motion* to account for the *life* of the universe, but, that being said, the motion must be exhibited as so solidly self-identical through time as to be almost indiscernible from a state of eternal rest. For the particular endless process which Aristotle's cosmology primarily demonstrates belongs, of course, to the heaven or outermost sphere of the world. This motion physically sustains and metaphysically epitomizes the unity through time of the entire universe, representing in spatial terms the absolute simplicity of the unextended Prime Mover. The important contrast now is not between motion and rest, but between the absolutely continuous and the successive.

(59) In order to chart the conceptual revision effected in VIII we need not follow Aristotle step for step towards his conclusion that the endless locomotion is circular. He proceeds by the method of exhaustion: either it is rectilinear in one direction or in opposite directions successively, or it is circular; and the rectilinear alternatives are eliminated. The

first of these is easily dismissed on the familiar ground that (in Aristotle's world) there are no infinite distances to provide the condition for endless rectilinear motion in one direction. But the second alternative[41] requires, in his view, an elaborate argument to refute it. What makes the refutation more complicated and obscure than it might otherwise have been is the difficulty he finds even here in prising apart the concepts of 'terminus' and 'resting-place'.[42] In general he still tends to conflate these when thinking of sublunary finite changes such as those involved in organic development. But in the context of the everlasting process he is bound to distinguish them, since in this case there can be no rest and yet there must be a terminus. This follows from Aristotle's never questioned assumption that the specific nature of a process is given by its terminus *ad quem*. (The eternal process that cosmology requires is in no sense an abstraction, but as real, and hence specific, as terrestrial changes.) In this case, moreover, the terminus cannot be regarded as in any sense a break-point; not only is it not a physical stopping-place, but it cannot even be considered to function as the purely *geometrical* starting-position of a new process. This is because the process which proceeds *from* it cannot be distinct from that which proceeds *to* it, since in that case we should have a succession of processes as opposed to one that is absolutely unitary and continuous.

(60) But even if a terminus need not be a resting-place, how can it not be in some sense a break-point? For whereas logically a given process can end without being succeeded by rest, it cannot end except at a terminal point of discontinuity with whatever comes next. And if all the same one tried saying that in general the terminal point need not be considered a point of discontinuity, one could not then prove the conclusion which Aristotle must certainly have set his heart on in advance, viz. that the unbroken eternal motion

---

[41] This stands for the entire class of non-circular returning motions.

[42] See 7, 261a36–b26; 8, 262a12–b8; 264a22–32. Note especially 261b1–2 and 264a22–8, where he argues that if X has not always been engaged in one particular process it must previously have been at rest. This is the fallacy which, I have suggested, made the VI.6 view seem plausible (*v.s.* paras (55)–(56)).

must be circular. For ceaseless rectilinear to-ing and fro-ing between opposite places would also fill the bill if motion specified as from A to B is not necessarily discontinuous with motion specified as from B to A. But this must be excluded. We are dealing now with substances, not mathematical abstractions, and it is metaphysically absurd that any substance, let alone the eternal one in question here, should act out its unitary nature through motion in different and opposite directions.

(61) Hence under some logical conditions the terminus by reference to which the direction or pattern of change is specified functions also as a break-point between distinct changes, or between change and rest; and under other conditions it does not. The problem now is to determine the conditions. We can say that a specifying terminus O is not a break-point if and only if:

(*a*) some process or other goes on from after as well as up to O; and

(*b*) what goes on after and what goes on up to O can properly be described as phases of one and the same process.

So the question is: When can P_1 and P_2, falling on either side of O, be considered consecutive phases of a single process? The criterion is ready to hand: it is based on a proposition which Aristotle originally formulated in *Physics* V.4, 227 b20-9 (cf. 228b1-3), and which he now repeats at VIII.8, 261b36-262a2:

We have already defined [*sc.* numerically] single and continuous process as a process of a single subject in a single time [i.e. not on different occasions] and of a unitary form.[43]

Now the form is given by the termini, so a single process has a single pair of termini. Therefore P_1 and P_2 are earlier and later phases of a single process if and only if in both phases

---

[43] Cf. V.4, 228b7-10, where he says that if there are different successive forms of process, then *even without a temporal interval between them* they do not constitute a continuous whole. In VIII.9, 267a21-b15, he strengthens the continuity–condition so that it entails a single *agent* for P_1 and P_2.

the same object is in process between the same set of termini. That is: if and only if at every moment of P_1 it is true to say that X is moving towards the *ad quem* towards which it is moving in P_2, and at every moment of P_2 it is true to say that it is moving from the *a quo* from which it is moving in P_1.[44]

(62) Now if O, which divides P_1 from P_2, is a specifying terminus for these phases, it is the *ad quem* of P_1 and the *a quo* of P_2. Hence if the phases are phases of a single process, O is also the *ad quem* approached in P_2 and the *a quo* receded from in P_1. Hence P_1 and P_2 are each to and from the same point, O. But a process from and to the same point is circular; hence the phases are consecutive revolutions returning to the same point. The same argument may be repeated for any number of consecutive phases. Thus it is proved that only iterated circular motion is endless, since it is the only case in which the specifying terminus is preceded and succeeded by phases of numerically the same motion. This is all that Aristotle needs for his immediate purpose in VIII. But he also draws a corollary concerning unitary noncircular process, namely that a point intermediate between two termini is not itself a terminus *a quo* or *ad quem* of the phases which it divides. The logic is as follows: suppose a single process A–B, where A is different from B, and with an intermediate point I. Since the phases A–I (P_1) and I–B (P_2) belong (*ex hypothesi*) to the same process, the termini receded from and approached are the same in both. Hence, since A is the *a quo* of P_1 and B the *ad quem* of P_2, the *a quo* of P_2 (= that of P_1) is different from the *ad quem* of P_1 (= that of P_2), since A is different from B. Hence if the intermediate point I is the terminus *ad quem* of P_1, and the *a quo* of P_2, I is non-identical with itself, given the supposition of a single process between different termini. Thus since I is one point and self-identical, the supposition entails that I is not a terminus specifying changes to and from itself.

(63) In this way, an analysis inspired by the metaphysical

---

[44] The point is explicitly made for the *ad quem* at VIII.8, 264a9–13.

need to conceptualize in its absolute unity the eternal ultimate process of the universe led Aristotle to recognize the
incoherence of VI.6 as an account of any process whatever,
no matter how transient or trivial. But what of infinite
divisibility now? The most that can be said is that in any
single continuous process, e.g. locomotion, the total distance covered contains potentially the halves, quarters, etc.
of that distance. That is to say, we can (mentally or physically) divide it. But it does not therefore actually contain
or consist of halves, etc. (VIII.8, 263 a11-263 b9). Nor does
it if it *is* divided, for then there is no "it", not one distance
but two, or however many. And what is true of the distance
is true also of the change. An actual change that took time
could have been stopped or deflected (physically "divided")
half-way. But it does not follow that if not "divided", the
whole actually has that half-change distinctly present in it.
And as with space, if the division were to take place, so that
the lesser change was actual, it would not be an actual half
of a larger change, because the larger one would not have
happened. If the parts are actual, the whole is not (in which
case they are not properly called parts), and vice versa.

(64) With regard to space, Aristotle draws the conclusion:

One who moves continuously has traversed infinite stages *per accidens*,
but has not traversed them strictly speaking. For it is *per accidens*
that the infinitely many halves [halves of halves, etc.] are in the line,
whereas its essence and being are different. (VIII.8, 263 b6-9)

A line along which something travels is not definable as
halves, quarters, etc., any more than an animal is definable
by reference to the substantial natures of the simple bodies
'in' it only in the sense that they emerge on decomposition.[45]
Similarly with respect to change: *what* a given change is, is
not any or any set of the lesser changes that might have
occurred through interference. It is absurd to define a specific
actuality in terms of the remnants that would have been left
had it been destroyed or prevented from fully being. Thus

---

[45] Cf. Simplicius, ed. Diels p. 1293, 3-5: 'κ᾽ἂν ὁριξόμεθα . . . τὸ συνεχὲς τὸ
δυνάμενον ἐπ᾽ἄπειρον διαιρεῖσθαι, τὸ ἐνεργείᾳ ὄν κατὰ τὸ ἐν αὐτῷ δυνάμει
ὁριξόμεθα, ὡς εἴ τις τὸν ταῦρον ὁρίζοιτο τὸν δυνάμενον μέλισσαν γένεσθαι.'

mathematical analysis into its temporal fractions could not give the essence of a change, even if it were a necessary truth that such analysis is always possible. However, once it is clearly seen that division does not give the essence, there is no longer the pressure felt in VI to insist on divisi*bility* into stages as a universal property of process. In any case the general difference between change and non-change must be made out anew; or rather, by recourse again to the contrast of complete and incomplete actuality (cf. VIII. 5, 257b6-9). For in VI the difference was grounded on the *actual* temporal variegation of process as opposed to rest (v.s. (41) ff.), and this characterization has turned out incoherent.

(65) Aristotle's recognition of this in VIII leads to a further shift from the position of VI, although the revision in this case is implied rather than stated. It was a theorem of VI that a process from contrary to contrary occupies a temporal interval between the termini. This was argued for in VI.6 on the ground that otherwise (i.e. if contrary succeeded contrary immediately) there would be a moment when the object was, absurdly, in both states. This argument was weak, as we saw (*v.s.* para. (51)), since the absurdity could also be avoided by treating the moment of transition as a limit of (rather than an element in) one or both the periods occupied by the contrary conditions. But at the time Aristotle was dominated by the mathematical model of process as proceeding through an infinite series of stages. He had really no room for the idea of process without such a series, since on this hung the essence of process as contrasted with non-process. Since the stages were conceived in mathematical terms alone, they could only be represented as "distances" from one and the other terminus. It followed that at no stage of its process could the object have been still in the terminus *a quo*. From this point of view, then, to suggest that being at the *ad quem* should immediately succeed being at the *a quo* would be as much as to deny that any *process* of change occurs at all. There would simply be the emergence of the second condition, but not an emergence led up to by process; a conception which is thoroughly alien to Aristotle, although not, perhaps, to a British empiricist.

In Book VIII, however, once Aristotle has seen that the mathematical schema must, on pain of absurdity, fail to convey the essence of process as this actually occurs, it is only to be expected that the idea that process must be temporally intermediate should also lose its hold.

(66) Thus at VIII.3, 253b14 ff., we find him arguing against those who hold that all things are always in motion, on the ground (amongst others) that in some changes, e.g. of quality, contrary succeeds contrary all at once (at which point the change is *over*). In asserting 'all at once' here he seems mainly to mean that in some cases (as e.g. freezing) the object is taken over by the new condition as a spatial whole, not point by point. But the denial of qualitative gradation seems also to be implied. However, we need not lean heavily on this passage, for there is a later one in which it is clearly assumed that change from contrary to contrary need not be gradual between the termini. This occurs at 8, 263b9 ff., a passage which follows without break the discussion of distance and motion as only potentially containing lesser distances and changes. At first sight it may seem that 263b9 ff. will not shed new light on processes from contraries to contraries, since the question raised here concerns transition between contradictories. We shall see, however, that the way in which Aristotle deals with this implies that he has abandoned the Book VI view of process between contraries. The problem is familiar: when X becomes white from not-white or not-white from white (these are his own examples), what are we to say of it at the moment of transition? Aristotle continues to regard it as absurd to say that at that instant X is in both states, but in avoiding this he does not follow his own lead in VI, where he argued (*v.s.* para. (50)) that at the instant of transition from rest to process or vice versa X is in neither condition. Instead he now lays it down that although the instant dividing white from not-white belongs to each period as a limit, it belongs only to the later 'as far as the fact is concerned' (263b12–15). That is: the factual content of the instant is that of the later period only. But why does Aristotle take this way out?

(67) The alternatives of saying that at the instant neither property obtains, or that the earlier does but not the later, are closed to him because he describes what happens as X's *becoming* not-white (*ceasing* to be white) or *becoming* white (11-12; 21 ff.; 264 a2, 5, and 6). There is a process of becoming. And becoming, logically, is over just at the moment when X has become whatever it was becoming. But it cannot *have* become so and so at *t* unless at *t* it *is* so and so.[46] Thus if *t* were only a limit of the later condition and not also a moment when it obtains, the becoming would never have completed itself, neither at *t* nor (by construction) at any earlier moment. But in that case the later condition would be present, as from *t*, but without ever having *come to be*: in short, it would be a sheer emergence not led up to by any process of becoming. The case is different when X is described as passing from rest to process or vice versa. X cannot at the instant of such a transition be in the subsequent state, whichever this may be. For 'rest' has no application where 'process' has none, and at that instant 'process' can have none. This can be deduced, as in VI.5, 236a7 ff., Aristotle did deduce it, from the premiss that time is infinitely divisible together with the assumption that 'changes' entails 'has changed'. But the same conclusion follows also from the notion itself of process (in the sense of 'becoming'), by reasoning that makes no reference to infinite divisibility. Logically there cannot be a process to process in this sense, or a becoming of becoming (cf. *Physics* V.2). This follows from the definition in III.1, whereby process is the actual exercise of the privation of some state S whose own actuality (when it has come about) is not itself the exercise of a privation (*v.s.* paras. (26)-(27)). This is only another way of saying that becoming is coming to *be*; but for Aristotle this is far more than a verbal point. For suppose that becoming becomes, i.e. that in some subject X there becomes$_1$ a 'state' of becoming$_2$. Then the second becoming is the defining terminus *ad quem* of the first. But in that case the first is a

---

[46] Aristotle by no means rejects all the findings of VI. The point just made has already been argued for at VI.5, 235b6-30. Then (235b 31 ff.) it is proved that the moment of having become must be indivisible: a conclusion reaffirmed at VIII.8, 264a1-6.

process without any genuine direction of its own, hence not a genuine process at all. For if we ask what is the direction of becoming$_1$ we can only be told that it is directed towards being directed towards some terminus not its own. For that is what becoming$_2$ is: it is a being-directed-towards some terminus which cannot be the same as that of becoming$_1$. This is because the latter's terminus, by the supposition, just is: becoming$_2$; hence if the two becomings had the same terminus, becoming$_2$ would be, *per absurdum*, directed towards itself. Or should we say that 'being directed towards itself' means only that it is an actuality not directed to anything else? In that case becoming$_2$ is not a becoming but a state of being. Thus the moment of transition to process cannot be the moment of having become of that process; hence in such a transition we necessarily lack the reason which holds in other cases for making the transitional instant a locus of the later condition.

(68) Aristotle's insistence in VIII.8 on this solution[47] to the problem of transition between contradictories shows that when he speaks here of 'becoming' he is using the term with its full logical weight, not merely as shorthand for e.g. 'X was first white, then not-white'. It was: but through having *become* not white. Yet since the termini are contradictories the transition is necessarily instantaneous. But the transition is not itself the process of becoming, for the transition is when becoming is over. It can only therefore have not been over when X was still white. Perhaps the process consists in some external agent's preparations to paint X green (cf. paras. (5) f. and (35)). At any rate it cannot consist in a graduated passage through shades between white and some final colour. For the object cannot be white and an intermediate colour at the same time, whereas it *is* white and in process at the same time. As soon as it comes to be some shade S, however "close", that we are willing to regard as distinct from white, then at that moment we are bound to say that the process to not-white is over. The same goes, as it happens, for the process from white to S, a contrary of white. So this

[47] Which Ross at 263b9–26 (*Aristotle's Physics*, p. 714) remarks strangely is as 'difficult' as the view that X at transition has both contradictories.

process too, to the contrary S, coincided in time with X's being in the *a quo* condition. Thus in this case process from contrary to contrary is 'between' its termini only in a logical sense: a sense which (*contra* VI) need not go hand in hand with *temporal* intermediacy.

(69) In conclusion, then, we must reject the statement of O. Hamelin:[48]

Ce qu'il y a de plus essentiel dans le changement aux yeux d'Aristote, ce ne sont pas les deux contraires que lui servent de limites, c'est l'intervalle de progrès qui s'étend entre ces deux limites, et cet intervalle est, selon lui, contenu.

Hamelin writes as if Aristotle's first and last word on the essence of change had been said in *Physics* VI. But according to the position set out in III, which emerges again in VIII, those features which Hamelin claims to be most essential are no more than incidental. They are not inherent in process or change as such, but are due, presumably, to the special nature of locomotion, which in VI is taken as the paradigm of change. However, III makes the same mistake of assimilating all cases to one type of case, for the paradigm there was change dictated by nature as inner principle. In his study of change Aristotle has mined from two quite different veins, each as narrow as it is rich.

[48] *Le Système d'Aristote*, p. 308.

IV

Agent and Patient

(1) We turn now to the most puzzling part of Aristotle's theory of change, the topic of agent and patient. It is difficult to determine his position on this matter, and difficult to see its philosophical sense. Yet these problems have a special claim on the attention of anyone concerned with his notion of change, because for Aristotle, 'agent-patient' more than any other concept is bound up with his account of change itself. The connection is so close that his analysis of change can hardly escape the reach of any charges of confusion and obscurity that might be levelled against his views on agency and patiency. No one would dispute the relevance of these to change, any more than that of space, time, infinity, and the problems of the vacuum (cf. III. 1, 200 b15-25). But Aristotle does not deal with agency and patiency as he does with these, devoting to each a methodical discussion whose beginning and end are clearly marked. This procedure means that the original definition of change in III.1 enjoys a certain measure of immunity from difficulties arising independently in connection with these separate studies. But his remarks concerning agent and patient in III.1-3 are so embedded in the discussion of change itself that it is hard to resist the impression that for him the two notions stand and fall together.

(2) We have seen, for instance, how he refers to agent and patient, changer and changed, even at the very moment of introducing the definition of κίνησις (200 b25-32; v.s. Ch. III, para. (20)). And he has no sooner proposed the definition than he turns briefly to the question 'Is the agent of change necessarily also a patient?' The definition is then discussed in detail and compared with accounts of change in earlier thinkers. This leads, with no indication of a diversion, to a more expansive treatment of the question just mentioned, which in turn leads to an argument designed to show that

'the κίνησις is in the patient (not in the agent)' (III.3, 202 a13–b22). Immediately after this Aristotle gives formal notice that the section on the definition of change is at an end, winding up with the following words:

It has been stated that κίνησις is, both in general and as regards its particular species. For it is clear how each of its kinds will be defined. Alteration is the actuality of the alterable insofar as it is alterable. But it is more perspicuous (γνωριμώτερον) to say that κίνησις is the actuality of the potential agent and patient (τοῦ δυνάμει ποιητικοῦ καὶ παθητικοῦ) insofar as they are potentially so, whether we say this *simpliciter* or in application to particular types of case such as building or healing. (202 b23–8)

So Aristotle concludes the account of κίνησις with what amounts to a *reformulation of the original definition in terms of agent and patient*. The potentiality so central to the definition is now explained as the potentiality of agency and patiency. But if change by definition involves a potential agent and patient, then the actuality of change must be the actuality of agency and patiency (since it is only in actual change, caused or suffered, that something is an actual agent or patient). In effect, then, these concluding lines declare that change is by definition the actuality of agency and patiency, these actualities being grounded on their own corresponding potentialities.

(3) What moves him to this reformulation, and how can it be supposed even to make sense as applied to change in general, and in particular to the primary type of change, viz. natural change? These questions will engage us in this and the next chapter. But it should be said at the outset that the text of the *Physics* offers hints rather than answers. In particular Aristotle never explains how it is that the very definition of change as such is supposed to involve the agent–patient relationship. In the discussion of Book III the transition is made as if justification were unnecessary. This situation is not remedied by an argument in VIII.4 purporting to show that everything that changes is changed by something; for, as we shall see, Aristotle can only achieve this conclusion by departing radically from the meaning he has assigned to 'agent' and 'changer' in III. In *De Generatione et Corruptione*

he devotes several chapters (I.6-10) to just such an independent discussion of agency and patiency as we might have expected him to instigate in the *Physics* along with similar discussions of space, time, infinity, etc. But it is noteworthy that in *De Generatione et Corruptione* he never tries to delineate an essential relationship between agent–patient and change as such. He is there concerned only to state what agency involves when it occurs, not to show that it occurs of necessity whenever change does (although no doubt this is taken for granted). These defects of exposition would hardly matter if in the *Physics* the agent–patient concept figured only as an unimportant offshoot from the account of change. But nothing could be further from the truth, since it is this concept that has to bear the weight of the massive argument in VIII for a supreme immaterial unmoved mover.

(4) We shall consider that argument in the next chapter. Meanwhile we must examine the general position from which Aristotle is able finally to reach his conclusion in VIII. But a word first about terminology. I am translating Aristotle's pairs '$\pi οιοῦν$'/'$\pi άσχον$' (and cognates), and '$κινοῦν$'/'$κινούμενον$' (and cognates) by 'agent'/'patient' (etc.), and 'changer'/ 'changed' (etc.) respectively. In the present discussion the pairs will be used interchangeably, in accordance with Aristotle's own usage in III.1-3. As a rule, he tends to reserve '$\pi άσχειν$' etc. for changes in respect of quality.[1] However, when in III.3, 202 b26-7, he casts the definition of $κίνησις$ in terms of '$\pi οιεῖν$' and '$\pi άσχειν$', he is obviously using the latter word to cover all the categories of change covered by '$κίνησις$' itself. Now his general position concerning agency and patiency may be summed up in the following propositions:

(i) Everything that changes (intransitive) is changed by a changer.

(ii) A changer is a source of change distinct in some way

---

[1] Bonitz s.v. '$\pi άθος$', 3 (556 b44-557 a4). For Aristotle's own discussion of wider and narrower senses of '$\pi οιεῖν$' see *De Gen. et Corr.* I.6, 323 a15 ff.

from that which is changed. (For this, see especially *Physics* VIII.4–5.)

(iii) To act as a changer is not to change (intransitive).

I shall begin by considering (i) and (ii).

(5) Although in III.1 Aristotle speaks as if '*κίνησις*' and '*μετα-βολή*' were synonymous, he conducts his analysis almost entirely in terms of '*κίνησις*'. Hence it may have seemed a necessary truth that every change that takes place, takes place in a subject that is chang*ed*. For the verb '*κίνεῖν*' can express a meaning equivalent to the intransitive 'X changes' only when used in the passive voice. (It is otherwise with '*μεταβάλλειν*', which may be used intransitively in the active, and is often so used by Aristotle, as e.g. in Book VI *passim*.) However, his reformulation of the definition of *κίνησις* in III.3 entails that for every change there is not only a chang*ed*, but a chang*er*. It might seem that this too follows from the linguistic rule for '*κινεῖν*'. For if change is predicated of the subject of change by means of a verb in the passive, does not the grammatical relation between active and passive ensure that there is a logically equivalent sentence with the same verb used transitively in the active, and the subject of the previous sentence functioning now as grammatical object? This however is not so obviously true. Grammar alone dictates that where the verb of change is '*κινεῖν*', the subject of change must be described as a 'chang*ed*' ('*κινούμενον*'). But it is not obvious that *grammar* alone forces us to accept the corresponding active-voiced sentence, and so to acknowledge a chang*er*. Linguistic rules oblige us to suppose an object chang*ed* for every chang*er*, but not the reverse. For where 'changes' is transitive, 'X changes —' is grammatically incomplete, as much so as e.g. 'X is with —'. The same is true of 'X is changed by —'. But in using the passive, there is no need to append the preposition that asks to be completed by an agent-term. We can simply say: 'X is (being) changed (*κινεῖται*)'. This is a grammatically complete sentence, fulfilling the basic requirement of 'saying something about something'.[2] It

---

[2] Cf. *De Int.* 5, 17a20–1.

may indeed *be* a necessary truth that for every changed there is a changer, but if so, the necessity is not grammatical: it is more like that of the sentence: 'For every changed, there are possible conditions whose presence would have prevented it from being changed'. The rules of *language* do not demand that a well-formed sentence make reference to the conditions whose presence would have hindered; nor do they demand reference to an agent, even when the verb is grammatically in the passive.[3]

(6) '*κινεῖσθαι*' then is passive as to its grammatical form, but not necessarily passive as to its meaning, and I have just argued that the grammatical form does not grammatically require the construction of an equivalent sentence with the verb in the active and an agent-term as subject. But it may be that conceptual if not grammatical considerations justify the inference from 'change' to 'changer'. Every change, after all, is dependent on something, and every change takes place in a subject. Is it legitimate to equate *subject* with *changed*, and *that on which change depends* with *changer*? The second of these questions is the difficult one. For it seems clear that the subject of change is the chang*ed*, i.e. the patient – on one proviso. The proviso is that there *be* an agent or chang*er*. For if there is no agent, then although there may be change and a subject of change, the subject is not a *patient*, or a chang*ed*, in any but the weak grammatical sense displayed in the linguistic behaviour of the Greek verb '*κινεῖν*'. But it is safe to say that *if* there is an agent, then it is the subject of change that is the patient. So the question is whether there is in every case an agent, and, more specifically, whether the fact that every change is causally dependent proves that every change has an agent.

(7) Aristotle is given to speaking of *the* agent or *the* changer of a given change. Thus he does not see any and every condition

---

[3] Cf. J. Lyons, *Introduction to Theoretical Linguistics*, p. 378: 'If there is any function that is common to the passive in all the languages that are customarily said to have a passive voice (and in certain languages this seems to be its sole function: e.g. in Turkish), this is that it makes possible the construction of "agentless" sentences: e.g. *Bill was killed*.'

on which a change depends as its agent. There are many such conditions, so none as such is *the* condition. '*The* agent' makes sense only if used of some factor uniquely related to the change. Given Aristotle's scheme of concepts, the uniquely related factor ought to be identified with that which determines the form or pattern of change. For there are many conditions without which the change could not occur, but what determines the type of change is a single individual embodying a single principle, whether substantial nature or purpose. This conclusion is borne out by Aristotle's words at III.2, 202 a9–12:

> The changer will in each case introduce a form, whether of substance or of quality or of quantity, which form will be the principle and cause of the change whenever the changer operates. For instance, an actual man makes what is potentially a man into a man.

Now this remark is intended to apply to all changes as such, or (given the inbuilt restrictiveness of the defintion in III.1) at least to all dictated by nature or purpose. But natural change, which is presupposed by all other kinds, typically involves only one individual substance. The man begotten by man in Aristotle's example must also grow. In this case the same individual substance is the subject of growth and also its source, being not merely the locus of change but *such as to* change in that way. Does this mean that the substance is agent (and therefore also patient) of its change? An affirmative answer would seem to entail abandoning the second of the three principles set out in paragraph (4) above, viz. that there must be some distinction between agent and patient. Where source and subject are the same individual, as in natural change, there appears to be no room for the agent–patient relationship as defined by those three principles. This problem is especially disconcerting in the context in which it occurs: namely, Aristotle's reformulation (as he takes it to be) of the III.1 definition in terms of agency and patiency. In the last chapter we saw (paras (36) ff.) how the original formula in fact fits only natural changes and their purposive analogues. Now it seems that the new (agent-patient) formulation fits this primary kind of natural change not at all.

(8) But to avoid this latest difficulty perhaps we should identify the agent in natural change with the nature itself or principle embodied in the changing substance. In arguing against the Eleatics in I.2, Aristotle remarks that a principle cannot be identical with that of which it is the principle (185 a3–5). Since nature is a principle of change, we can infer that a thing's nature is other than any of its changes. Can we also infer, though, that the nature is other than the subject of those changes? And if in some sense this is true, is it a sense of 'other than' that would license saying that the nature is the *agent*? Our earlier discussion revealed no grounds for saying that the nature is a special kind of *thing* 'inside' a particular substance. Indeed, if *'thing'* is interpreted precisely to mean 'particular substance', Aristotle's concept of nature decisively forbids any such view. If a nature were itself a particular substance, it would not be, as he says in II.1, 192 b34, 'in a subject'; hence the subject of change of which a nature is supposed to be a nature would not have the nature 'in' it. The subject of change, then, would either be identical with the nature (which in that case cannot stand to the subject as agent to patient) or not; and if not, the subject, it seems, would be without a nature, hence without substantial character, hence no substance. A nature, then, is not a distinct thing from the individual natured. No doubt we can say that it is an aspect of it, distinguishable in thought from other aspects. But is this distinction strong enough to justify regarding the nature as an agent? In cases of externally determined change, Aristotle identifies the agent or changer with the concrete individual substance that is sufficient cause, the begetting parent, the house-builder, etc. It would therefore be risky to suppose that where the change is *not* externally determined he assigns the agent-role to a nature, which in itself is only an abstraction. How could the nature stand to the subject in a relation sufficiently similar to that which holds between concrete external agent and subject for it not to be sheer confusion to speak of 'agent and patient' in both cases?[4]

---

[4] Cf. Mansion, pp. 226 and 233, for a strong statement of the view that (on Aristotelian principles), the efficient cause of change is not, strictly speaking, the principle (nature or art) but the concrete substance that embodies it.

(9) We shall recur to these questions in the course of the next chapter (paras (7)–(9) and (34)–(36) in particular). We are not obliged to pursue them at present in order to interpret Aristotle's general theory of agency–patiency. For, as we shall see, he does not indulge in any general identification of natures with the agents of natural change. Hence the problems of this identification are for the moment a side-issue. What concerns us now is whether he can make good the principle that for every change there is a changer, or, rather, whether he can make it good without giving up some other principle or assumption. For instance, if changer and changed need not be distinct, natural change would present no problem; the same concrete individual would function as both. Or if the changer need not be the *determinant* of change, but only a *sine qua non*, natural change could be put down to an external concrete agent (or set of agents). In the end it is this last assumption, that the agent determines the form of change, which Aristotle drops so as to save principles (i) and (ii). This takes place in *Physics* VIII.4.

(10) The context there is an argument designed to demonstrate that whatever changes is changed by something. (It is assumed that what something is changed *by* is its chang*er*.) The reasoning has an ambiguous flavour; it betrays an *a priori* resolve to save at all costs the conclusion to be proved, while at the same time proceeding as if this conclusion were no longer self-evident or true by virtue of the very definition of '$κίνησις$'. The argument parades as empirical; it is an induction from cases, but with a foregone conclusion. The types of change are divided into enforced and natural, and natural change is subdivided into organic and inorganic. Aristotle then argues that in each division change is change *by* something. Enforced change presents no problem; obviously it is by something, an external physical substance. Nor does Aristotle find any difficulty in supposing agents for the natural changes of living things. These are changed 'by themselves', and although the meaning of this is not fully explained, he takes it as intuitively certain that a living thing (and especially an animal) contains an agent of its natural changes which differs from the subject of change in a way which may, as he says, be difficult to

analyse, but which clearly permits us to regard the subject as a genuine 'chang*ed*'.

The proposition that whatever changes (κινεῖται) is changed by something is most obviously true in the case of things changed against their nature, since it is apparent that they are changed by something else. The next most obvious cases after these are things that change by their nature but are changed by themselves, such as animals. For what is difficult to make out is not *that* they are changed by something, but in what way the changer in them is to be distinguished from the changed. (VIII.4, 254 b24-30)

The whole question of 'self-change' in *Physics* VIII will be a major topic of the next chapter, but meanwhile let us see how Aristotle deals here with the remaining class of cases, the natural changes of the simple inanimate bodies. These present the worst problem ('μάλιστα δ'ἀπορεῖται', 254 b33) for anyone who maintains that whatever changes is changed by something. For here there is no external determinant, yet Aristotle refuses to class the simple bodies along with substances changed 'by themselves'. Self-changers, he says, are alive, they naturally change in diverse ways, they are physically complex (255 a5-18). This is enough to show that the mere fact that a substance has a *nature* is not for him a sufficient ground for holding that it has "within" itself an agent. For the simple bodies no less than organic creatures have natures giving rise to change. If every nature as such were an agent of natural change, all natural change would be self-change in substances of every type.

(11) So what are the changers responsible for natural changes of simple bodies? Aristotle can solve the problem only by a conceptual shift: i.e. by breaking with the original meaning of 'changer' laid down in III.2. The natural changes of the simple bodies are not, he argues, totally independent of everything else: in the first place, a mass of earth or fire owes its natural motion to the agent that generated it and made it be what it is, fire or earth; and secondly, the realization of the motion depends on the absence of external interference, so that whatever removes an obstruction is also responsible for the change. In these changes then, he concludes, the subject is chang*ed*, not by itself, but by something, whether

the generator or the remover of hindrances (255 b13-256 a2). But neither of these "changers" can possibly be said currently to determine the motion while it is happening. The generator (according to his theory of elemental transformation) no longer exists,[5] and the remover of hindrances not only does not determine the form of the change, but might rather be said to gain its character *as* remover of hindrance from the very change of which it is supposed to be the agent. For what constitutes a hindrance, and what (therefore) the removal of one, depends on the direction of the tendency pre-existing in the simple body.

(12) It is perhaps no accident that during this argument Aristotle speaks only of *that by (ὑπό) which* the simple body is changed and not of its chang*er* (κινοῦν). For the latter expression unavoidably suggests a currently acting cause, whereas the former permits the interpretation that the change itself (the natural motion) is an intransitive event resulting from the earlier action of an agent. On this interpretation, the body is only a patient with respect to the earlier action, say of releasing: this it "suffers", but not the intransitive *change* that thereby becomes open to it. However, Aristotle decisively blocks this interpretation when he writes in 255 b29-31:

> It is clear that none of these [the simple bodies] changes (transitive) itself. But each has a principle of change, not of (transitively) changing something (τοῦ κινεῖν), nor of making something come about (τοῦ ποιεῖν), but of suffering (τοῦ πάσχειν).

Since the principle investing the simple body is primarily a principle of *change* (not a principle for being released by some external agent), Aristotle must mean that the change itself is a "suffering". But he cannot logically mean to assert this merely on the ground that the change owes its being to the prior action of an external agent. For by that criterion many things would count as "sufferings" which for him are conceptually *opposed* to "suffering". For instance, where the

---

[5] As Simplicius puts it (*Comm. in Phys. ad* 255 b31-256 a3, ed. Diels, p. 1220, 9-11): 'εἰ τὸ γεννῆσαν καὶ ποιῆσαν πῦρ πέπαυται ἐνίοτε καὶ οὔτε πάρεστιν οὔτε ἐφάπτεται τοῦ κινουμένου, πῶς ὑπ'ἐκείνου λέγεται κινεῖσθαι τὸ πῦρ;'

activity of an *agent* results from the agent's release from constraint, this would be a "suffering". (Even the activity of the
changer within the self-changer might turn out to be one, at
this rate.) In 4, 255 b1-11 and 20-3, Aristotle carefully compares the natural motions of the simple bodies when released
with the knower's exercise of knowledge, which is supposed
to occur whenever nothing prevents it. Yet the exercise of
knowledge is an ἐνέργεια in the special sense in which Aristotle contrasts this term with 'κίνησις' (*v.i.* paras (28) ff.). It
is like thinking, seeing, and being happy, all of which occur
'unless prevented' (given the appropriate state of the subject);
but these are the very last conditions that Aristotle would
connect with 'suffering'. Not only is this term's suggestion of
subjection to the undesirable wholly inappropriate in their
case, but so is its broader and more neutral meaning of 'condition that does not come from the subject itself'. For these
activities are the highest expressions of the natures of beings
capable of them. It is clear then that Aristotle's only reason
for classing the principle within a simple body as a principle
of "*suffering*" is that it is a principle of *change*; the reason is
not that it owes its manifestation to a releaser. In other
words, he is simply identifying change as such with patiency
for no apparent reason other than that change is change. For
seeing and the exercise of knowledge are not patiencies
because, as we shall see, they are not changes (κινήσεις) but
ἐνέργειαι. (The difference between these categories turns on
the difference between the complete and the incomplete. An
ἐνέργεια is essentially complete as long as it lasts, a κίνησις
essentially incomplete.)

(13) We shall presently investigate this last-mentioned distinction in some detail; meanwhile let us summarize the
position to have emerged so far. (*a*) Aristotle's doctrine of
nature makes it impossible for him to hold that every change
has a changer in the sense of a *concrete* agent (other than the
subject) that determines the shape of the change. (*b*) It
remains to be seen whether in some cases the nature of a
substance might not fulfil the role of changer. However (*c*) it
is clear that in some cases (the natural changes of the simple
bodies) the nature is *not* seen by Aristotle as an inner agent.

(*d*) Since in these cases there is no external concrete substance shaping the change either, Aristotle can only preserve the principle that for every change there is a distinct agent by diluting the concept of agent so that it no longer implies 'currently acting determinant'. Thus (*e*) even the generator and the releaser are now seen as agents, and the change is considered to be a "suffering" in relation to them. On the other hand (*f*), it is not because of what these so-called agents do (i.e generate and release) that the subject is said to "suffer", but because of what happens as a result, viz. a *change*. In effect, Aristotle cannot or will not recognize such a thing as *intransitive* change that is neither an acting upon nor a being acted upon.[6] His assumption appears to be that since the nature manifested in e.g. the typical movement of fire is obviously not a principle for acting upon other things (save *per accidens*), it must be a principle for *being* acted upon. He admits no third possibility. But it cannot simply be the event's dependence on the action of prior agents that justifies equating it with suffering. For states of natural rest (the fire's at last being where it belongs) are likewise dependent, as are various non-kinetic activities. Perhaps it is the *incompleteness* of change that provokes this classification of it as essentially passive. But Aristotle does not bring into the open the conceptual connection between passivity and incompleteness, and it remains thoroughly mysterious.[7]

(14) So far then we have failed to uncover any sound basis for Aristotle's assumption that change is essentially dependent on an agent. However, there is one aspect of the original definition of κίνησις in III.1 which we have not yet considered at all and which might serve to bridge the gap between this and the agent/patient version at the end of III.3. The original

---

[6] Hence his notorious problem at VIII.10, 266 b27 ff. in accounting for the motion of missiles. The special difficulty here is that since the motion is counternatural, there must be not merely an external agent in the extended sense, but a currently acting external determinant.

[7] Simplicius tries to explain as follows (ibid. lines 21 ff.): 'θαυμαστῶς ηὗρεν καὶ ἐν τοῖς κατὰ φύσιν κινουμένοις τὸ ὑπό τινος κινεῖσθαι τὸ κινούμενον, ἐπειδὴ τὸ κινεῖσθαι πάσχειν τί ἐστι, τὸ δὲ πάσχειν δεῖται τοῦ ποιοῦντος. ἡ μὲν γὰρ τελεία ἐνέργεια ἐκ τῆς τελείας οὐσίας προϊοῦσα οὐ δεῖται τινος ἄλλης τῆς παραγούσης αἰτίας, ἡ δὲ κίνησις ἀτελὴς οὖσα ἐνέργεια καὶ πάθος μᾶλλον καὶ πολλῷ τῷ δυνάμει συγκεκραμένη δεῖται τοῦ ποιοῦντος αὐτήν.'

version has a defect, noted with unease by the ancient commentators,[8] which it might seem can only be remedied by
reference to the concept of agency. If κίνησις is defined simply
in terms of the subject's potentiality to be in a state that it is
not actually in, then it follows that the concept of κίνησις is
co-extensive with that of potentiality: to every potential condition there corresponds a possible change defined as the
actuality that holds of the subject insofar as it is potentially
in that condition. But there would appear to be at least one
class of potentialities to which there do not correspond
changes or κινήσεις. These are comprised under the category
of Relatives. There seems to be no good reason for refusing to
extend the 'actually/potentially' distinction to this category.
Thus it ought to make sense to speak of X as potentially
smaller than Y, etc. Suppose now that it comes to be true of
X that X is actually smaller than Y. According to the definition, this transition from the mere potentiality to the actuality ought to count as a change on the same logical level as
that of bricks becoming a house or a boy growing to full
height. But intuitively we reject the idea that 'coming to be
smaller than Y' describes a *change* in X. For, as we say, it
could be true of X even though *X* has not changed, but only
Y. Aristotle endorses this common-sense reaction later on, by
excluding Relation from the list of categories in respect of
which κίνησις is possible (V.2, 225 b11-13).[9] Yet this is not
justified by his own original definition of κίνησις. The conceptual elements of that definition, viz. potentiality and
actuality, occur in all the categories including that of Relatives.
So if Aristotle's manipulation of these elements can succeed
in producing a formula that covers, say, qualitative change,
how can it fail to cover, at the same time, "changes" under all
the categories?

(15) Our unwillingness to count the acquisition and loss of

---

[8] *Ad Phys.*, 202 a3–7; Themistius, ed. Schenkl, p. 75, 3 ff.; Philoponus, ed.
Vitelli, p. 367, 8 ff.; Simplicius, ed. Diels, p. 436, 26 ff.

[9] It is clear that here Aristotle excludes the acquisition of new relational
properties from the class of μεταβολαί as well as from the class of κινήσεις (which
in this context are regarded as a sub-class of μεταβολαί). He also argues in *Cat.* 5,
4 a10 ff., that change of truth-value is not real change. See S. Waterlow, *Passage
and Possibility, A Study of Aristotle's Modal Concepts*, Ch. VI.

relational properties as "real" changes may have no single simple reason.[10] But perhaps the most obvious difference lies in the spatial relationship of cause to effect. If X grows ("really" changes size), thereby becoming taller than Y, then Y becomes shorter than X. Now the only cause of this new relational property is whatever it is that causes the growth of X. It is because X grows that its size changes in relation to Y's and Y's to its. Thus whatever cause results in X's growth results also in Y's acquisition of a new relative size. But there is a striking difference between the relation of this cause to X, and its relation to Y. Let us call the total cause of X's growth 'C'. Now C is a set of conditions in or around X. For the various component-conditions of C to produce the effect in question, it is not enough that they should simply *exist*; they must exist in or in the environment of *X*. If they were cancelled from there but reproduced somewhere else, they might as well not exist at all for all they would do to assist the growth of X. But it is quite otherwise with the causal relation of C to its other "effect", namely the transition from one to another relative property in Y. Y becomes (by the same amount) smaller than X wherever Y may be; however far removed from X, and however far removed, therefore, from C which caused the growth of X. But C is also and thereby the *cause* of this "change" in Y. Yet *this* "effect" of C in no way depends on or varies with the particular spatial relationship between its subject Y and its cause C. Provided that C does result in the growth of X, it is enough that C should occur merely *in the same universe* as Y for it to be true that C "makes" Y shorter than X. This is surely a reason

[10] For a contemporary statement of the problem, see P. T. Geach, *God and the Soul*, pp. 71-2: 'The only sharp criterion for a thing's having changed is what we may call the Cambridge criterion (since it keeps occurring in Cambridge philosophers of the great days, like Russell and McTaggart): The thing called '*x*' has changed if we have 'F(x) at time t' true and 'F(x) at time t_1' false, for some interpretations of 'F', 't', and 't_1'. But this account is intuitively quite unsatisfactory. By this account, Socrates would after all change by coming to be shorter than Theaetetus . . .'. (Along with Russell and McTaggart, Geach could have included G. H. von Wright, *Norm and Action*, Ch. II, on 'The Logic of Change'.) On p. 99 Geach continues: 'These, we should wish to say, are not real changes in Socrates. But I do not know of any criterion, let alone a sharp one, that will tell us when we have a real change in Socrates, and not just a "Cambridge" change. The search for such a criterion strikes me as an urgent task of philosophy.'

for fencing 'makes', 'change', and 'effect' with double in-verted commas. If we counted these shifts in relational pro-perties as real changes or real effects, we should be attributing to the cause C a power of absolute scope and absolute im-mediacy. For its "effect" would be in no way diminished by the distance of the object "affected"; nor would it vary at all on account of changes in the contents of the space sep-arating C from that object. But it is only if we refuse to recognize this "effect" as a real change that we need not recognize a "power" to produce it.

(16) The subject of a real change of a given sort must not only be capable of changing in that way, but it must also stand in a particular relationship to a cause sufficient for producing the change. And that the subject stands in this relation does not follow from its being of a kind capable of that change. Thus if a particular cause produces a change in a given subject, that is no reason to think that it also produces a similar change in other potential subjects. On the contrary, if the cause is identified with a spatial object or a condition which stands to the subject in a given spatial relationship, it is clear that there could be in existence other suitable subjects that would be debarred by the very logic of space itself from an appropriate spatial relation to that particular cause. For the same particular cause C cannot be in contact with, or at a given distance from, every suitable subject at the same time, unless it so happens that there exist only as many suitable sub-jects as there is room for near or around or at some appropri-ate distance from C. And this, if it were the case, would be a purely contingent fact. Thus in general, the particular cause of a particular real change selects, by its situation, only some among all possible subjects to be the actual subjects of its effect on any one occasion. By contrast, the particular cause of a "change" in some relational property causes at one and the same time comparable "changes" in all possible subjects that exist. If Y "becomes" smaller than X, because of C, then every other object commensurable with X and Y *ipso facto* "undergoes" a corresponding "change" by the mere fact of being a member of the class of objects thus commensurable. We may say then that what distinguishes a real change from a

relational one is that the former owes its existence to a particular cause which does not necessarily produce a similar effect in every object of the same kind. Now although we have argued this point by reference only to physical causes which occupy space, we may extend it to cover also other causes, such as e.g. souls. For although the reasons for or against regarding these as causes have not yet been considered, we should at least make room for this in an account of Aristotle's notion of agency. Now the incorporeal causes recognized by Aristotle (*v.i.* ch. V, para. (10)) are as selective in their operation as corporeal ones. The soul of an animal, for instance, controls not every body of a given sort, but one: nor could it control any other. Even the supreme incorporeal mover immediately affects one body only, the outermost sphere of the universe.[11]

(17) We may conclude, then, that the very concept of change makes essential reference to the concept of a particular cause of change standing in a special relation to the subject. For without this reference, no distinction can be upheld between real and relational change. If we could allow ourselves to identify this notion of a cause specially related to the subject with Aristotle's notion of agent or changer, it would follow that his reformulation of the original definition of κίνησις in terms of agent and patient is entirely justified. It is true that so far as corporeal agents are concerned, Aristotle restricts the range of the special relationship more narrowly than facts now known may warrant, since he holds that it must consist in *contact* between the two bodies. In speaking vaguely as above (para. (15)) of the cause C as 'in or around' the subject of the real change, we deliberately left this question open. It is perhaps an empirical matter whether or not contact is necessary. The point of conceptual importance is that the subject should be within a given range of the cause. What the range is will vary with the circumstances, with the particular characteristics of cause and subject, and with the type of change in question. All that matters for our argument is

[11] Although in the *Physics* the prime mover is not presented as the soul of that sphere, or of the universe. *V.i.* Ch. V paras (33) ff. and Appendix pp. 257 ff.

that 'within range of C' cannot be interpreted so widely as to cover any object wheresoever located. In the same way we may extend the specification of the special relationship which Aristotle employs when describing the case of an incorporeal agent causing change in a physical object. He says of the former that it touches without in turn being touched (*De Gen. et Corr.* I.6, 323 a20-34). Commentators have usually dwelt on the negative aspect of this curious extension of the concept of touching, i.e. on the implication that the agent is not and cannot be affected in turn by the patient. But that the agent *touches* is no less significant than that it is *not touched*, for this makes the point that the agent stands to the patient in a relation in which it (numerically the same agent) does not stand to any and every possible patient. The agency of the agent presupposes that the agent has an *ubi*, although it has, in this case, no *locus*. Thus the metaphor of 'touching without being touched' is appropriate insofar as it attributes *position* to the agent even though incorporeal. It is inappropriate so far as it suggests that the literal fact from which the metaphor is taken must always involve the over-restrictive condition of contact. We can remedy this by rephrasing the metaphor as follows: the incorporeal agent 'reaches to the patient but without the patient's in turn reaching to it'.

(18) If the argument of the last four paragraphs is acceptable, will it succeed in upholding Aristotle's apparently illegitimate slide from the concept of change as such to the concept of change brought about by an agent in a patient? It certainly illuminates this slide, but would fully justify it only if 'agency' in Aristotle's scheme of concepts had no other function than to mark the logical difference between properties in respect of which real change is possible, and relational properties acquired and lost without real change. We have argued that the need for a specially related cause is what differentiates real changes. But this conclusion is only a special case of a wider conclusion attainable by the same argument. For the *having* of a "real" property, no less than the acquiring it by a "real" change, differs in just this way from the having of a relational one. If X grows (or is made to swell) to a certain size, then its *remaining* at this size depends in part upon what

happens where it is, and similarly with qualitative states. But Y's remaining shorter than X depends in part on a situation which may be as far removed as we please from Y itself, namely the environmental situation of the other term of the relation, X. If by 'agent' we were to mean no more than 'cause (or causal condition) whose causality depends on its special situation *vis-à-vis* the subject', then it is not just *change* that requires an agent. But it is evident that for Aristotle 'agent' has a narrower meaning which relates *especially to change*. He would of course say that some non-relational non-change conditions require an agent: e.g. conditions of contra-natural rest. But there is no sign of his supposing that in general rest depends on agency. By contrast, he holds that *all* changes are "sufferings", and as such are agent-dependent, No doubt one motive for this insistence is the need for a universal premiss from which to argue that the ultimate physical change of the universe depends on something other than the mere changing body itself (*v.i.* Ch. V). This aside, his grounds for maintaining a necessary connection between change in particular, and agency, remain obscure. And in view of his willingness to alter the meaning of 'agent' in order to be able to locate an agent for every change (cf. para. (11) above), we cannot but wonder whether there is any single interpretation of this concept by which he would be prepared to abide.

(19) But although we have not succeeded in pinning him down to a precise meaning of the terms 'agent' and 'changer', there are some instances of change to which it would seem reasonable to apply the notion of 'agency/patiency' if to any at all. I refer to those cases in which one individual physical substance determines the change in another. Let us now leave the question whether *all* changes have agents, and concentrate on those which most obviously do. If we can make out the conceptual features of these paradigm cases, it may be possible to decide whether the more dubious ones resemble them sufficiently to be brought under the same schema. How otherwise, for instance, can we evaluate the curious notion, propounded in Book VIII, of a 'self-changer', a single substance that somehow comprises within itself both agent and patient?

Unless the alleged changer and changed within the self-changer can be shown to bear some analogy to changer and changed in clear-cut external cases, 'self-changer' is only a metaphor, and provides no sound basis for philosophical argument. Moreover we have still to elucidate the third of the propositions listed in paragraph (4) above, namely that a changer as such does not (intransitively) change, according to Aristotle. If this cannot be shown to make sense in the obvious cases, there is little hope of defending it in connection with dubious and marginal ones.

(20) But since we are not criticizing Aristotle only on his own terms, let us begin by asking what from a philosophical point of view is *ever* gained by speaking of agency and patiency, even in those cases where this phraseology seems most obviously to apply. To say that one thing acts upon another, or does something to it, or makes something happen in it, seems to suggest that there is a concrete and particular process of causing, as concrete and particular as the change itself which is caused, and as the substances concerned in the change. Yet Hume's theory of causation, whatever its defects, has at least, one might suppose, succeeded in correcting any tendency to believe in "causing" as some kind of particular process. Such a thing is empirically unidentifiable, and the idea of it fails to explain either the events themselves or our knowledge of them. Indeed 'making', 'acting upon', etc., appear to represent nothing more than the projection on to nature of mere forms of language. These forms are the transitive verbs, active and passive, by which we so often describe causal relations. These verbs are tensed, and they connect grammatical subjects and objects which denote actual concrete particulars (called the 'agent' and 'patient'). As a result, it might be argued, it is easy to imagine that these verbs denote certain particular connecting relationships that exist at particular times and places, just as the objects connected do. But even critics of Hume are mostly agreed that he has rightly taught us to think of causation as a relation between objects and events considered not in their particularity but as members of classes of resembling ones. The main area of combat, both against Hume himself, and of his critics amongst themselves, concerns

the precise specification and grounds for asserting this general relation. But it is assumed on all sides that the general relation (which for our purposes it is sufficient simply to denominate 'law-like', however this be interpreted) cannot itself be regarded as a particular. Neither (a) the connection between antecedent and consequent of a law-like generalization, nor (b) the "falling-under" relation in which particular objects and events stand to that antecedent and consequent, is itself a particular fact pertaining to a particular region of space-time. These relations hold, if not timelessly and spacelessly, at any rate everywhere and always. Thus the transitive verb 'causes' can, on this view, be eliminated in favour of a universal hypothetical covering particular objects or events whose changes are described intransitively. The singular sentence 'X heated Y' is translated as 'X was a member of the class ϕ, and Y of the class ψ, and whenever under certain conditions (supposed to have obtained on the occasion in question) a ϕ is within a given range of a ψ, the ψ becomes hot.' In this formula, the clause following 'whenever' does not denote a particular fact or facts. Thus, if this analysis is correct, it shows that the apparent 'thisness' of what is referred to by 'heated' in 'X heated Y' is only apparent: it is nothing but a reflection of the concrete particularity of the *terms* of the relation, not of the relation itself.

(21) If all transitive causal verbs are indeed reducible in the way just outlined, it follows that the philosopher would do well to discard them altogether from his reflective vocabulary, so as to be rid of a standing source of temptation to read into real events and changes mysterious connectings: a notion which may possibly satisfy some psychological need, but which lacks all cognitive meaning. We cannot here enter fully into this issue, but raising it serves to frame two conclusions for which I shall argue in the next few pages. These will be (i) that for Aristotle, no less than for Hume, 'agency' and 'acting upon' are not to be understood as referring to any kind of extra non-empirical process beyond or behind the phenomena; but (ii) that for Aristotle by contrast with Hume, these expressions, far from being eliminable from the cognitive vocabulary, perform a cognitive function that could

not be adequately catered for by formulae in which the particular terms of particular causal relations are connected only by a covering law-like generalization.

(22) The Aristotelian passage that first concerns us is III.3, 202 a13–202 b22. Aristotle's problem here is different from the one just raised in response to the Humean theory, but his discussion contains the elements of an answer to the latter. His question (apparently a familiar one[12]) is: Is the change (κίνησις) in the patient, or in the patient *and* in the agent? And his answer is: In the patient.[13] The problem arises because Aristotle must tailor his concept of agency and patiency to accommodate the notion of a first changer in every causal series of changes. There must be a first changer, because there must be an originating determinant of change (and 'changer' here means 'determinant': *v.s.* para. (7)). But if there is an originating of change, it cannot be the case that the substance which originates itself changes (intransitive) in so doing. For then either we have a change *without* a changer; or there is a changer other than the originating substance (which would contradict its being an originator); or the originator itself causes the change in which its originating consists: but then this causing too would consist in a change (intransitive) in the originator, so that another causing is required, and so on, and there will thus be no originating by the originator, since every act of originating would require an infinite number of similar acts by the same agent. Therefore the causing of change by the originator (whether the latter be the cause of the heavens' motion, or a sublunary natural substance operating according to its own nature) must not be or entail any change in which the *originator* changes (intransitive). So whatever causing a change may be, it is not for Aristotle, any more than for Hume, an extra process of *change*.

(23) This conclusion will assume particular signifance in the context of Aristotle's later struggles with the problematic concept of 'self-change'. Meanwhile, however, he argues for

---

[12] Cf. Ross, *Aristotle's Physics*, p. 540.
[13] Cf. *Metaph.* Θ 8, 1050 a28–b1.

it in general, and takes as his only illustration the case of teaching and learning, where the agent and patient are clearly different individual substances. His argument proceeds on the following assumption: the only reason anyone could have for supposing that being a changer (an actual changer) entails change in that changer, rests on a false view of the difference between causing and suffering change. It is only through regarding these (in some given instance, such as teaching and learning) as *different concrete events*, that one could be misled into thinking that the changer as such undergoes a change. But once it is seen that these are different ways of describing the same event, the problem disappears, leaving only one change, which is to be located in the *patient*. This is the outline of Aristotle's argument, and its drift may be roughly clear, but some detailed comment is necessary.

(24) The problem as Aristotle presents it in III.3 is shaped by two assumptions. The first (i) relates to the meaning of 'κίνησις'. Aristotle here uses it as the generic term for anything corresponding to a verbal noun with the typical '-σις' ending. By this criterion, not only are comings-to-be-in-a-new-state (represented by such nouns as 'γήρανσις', 'μάθησις') changes, but so are transitive change-causing activities such as those represented by 'οἰκοδόμησις', 'δίδαξις', 'ἰάτρευσις', etc. This double use of 'κίνησις' is reflected in the passage already quoted from VIII.4 where he says that the simple bodies each contain a principle of κίνησις, 'not of causing change (τοῦ κινεῖν) nor of making it happen (τοῦ ποιεῖν), but of suffering it (τοῦ πάσχειν)' (255 b30–1). So in some places he uses 'κίνησις' to include 'causing change'. However, this usage is not the common one of the *Physics*. More often 'κίνησις' means a process of coming to be in some new state (see especially Books V and VI). The second assumption (ii) is that for every κίνησις something κινεῖται, i.e. comes to be in a new state. Now these assumptions taken together seem to yield the following: teaching (δίδαξις), no less than learning (μάθησις) is a κίνησις (by (i)). Thus teaching no less than learning involves the coming to be of a new state (by (ii)). Thus the teacher, who is the subject of the verb 'teaches', must be the subject of the coming to be. Hence the teacher (the agent) is

as much a subject of κίνησις (in the more usual sense) as is
the pupil in whom the teacher brings about a change. (So
being the agent of a change necessarily involves a change in
the agent. Thus, given that for every change there is an agent,
every change would entail an infinite regress of logically prior
changes.)

(25) But this argument is valid only on the assumption that
X's teaching is a distinct concrete event from Y's learning. If
this were the case, then indeed, since teaching is a κίνησις by
(i) above, and since by (ii) for every κίνησις there is a coming
to be, it would follow that the teacher, being the only substance involved in the distinct event of teaching, would be
the subject of this coming to be, since no other subject would
be available within that distinct event. But the point of crucial
importance which Aristotle emphasizes again and again in
this passage, is that X's teaching is not a different concrete
event from Y's learning. These are one and the same actuality
under two descriptions. In effect Aristotle's reply consists in
refining presupposition (ii) so as to read: for every *concrete*
κίνησις-*event* there is a coming to be. Now no one denies that
Y's learning involves a coming to be of which Y is the subject.
But if Y's learning is the same actual event as X's teaching,
there is no need to look for another coming to be that corresponds to that teaching: it has already been specified as Y's
learning. And this coming to be is in Y; so that it already has
a subject, and there is therefore no need to pin it on to X as
if it would otherwise float about without any subject at all.
This would be necessary only if X's teaching were a self-
contained actuality that was, as he says, 'cut off' ('ἀποτετμη-
μένη', 202 b8) from Y; but then it would not be teaching
since in it no one would be taught. Nor is there any paradox
in saying that the teaching and the learning (since they are
the same concrete event, and the learning is a coming to be in
Y) are both in Y. Some dialecticians[14] may try to twist this
into absurdity by saying that it would entail Y's learning and
also teaching the very same thing (202 b1-5). But they achieve
the appearance of paradox only by ignoring the different

[14] The Eleatics, apparently. Cf. Simplicius, ed. Diels, p. 440, 23-4.

directionality of the two descriptions (5-22). The same road runs from Thebes to Athens and from Athens to Thebes, but it does not follow that a man travelling this road is at one time travelling to Thebes and to Athens. If 'Athens' enters into the description of his journey as the name of his destination, then 'Thebes' must enter into the description in the opposite sense, as naming his terminus *a quo*. Thus if another man is travelling on the same road to Thebes, 'Athens' must enter into the description of *his* journey in the sense opposite to that in which it enters into that of the first man. Similarly, if Y is learning and X is teaching, 'teaching' applies to Y only in the opposite sense from that in which it applies to X; thus while X is teaching, Y is *being taught*. If we think of 'teaching' ('δίδαξις') as like a neutral verb-stem determinable by active and passive voices, then we may say (*a*) that 'teaching' is a predicate of Y as well as of X; and (*b*) that 'teaching' applies to Y in a determinate form (the passive) which is perfectly consistent with the statement 'Y does not teach'.

(26) It is to be remarked that in this argument Aristotle dispenses altogether with any discussion of the meaning of transitive verbs of agency, or any comparison of this with the meaning of verbs of becoming. What matters to him here is what we should call the distinction between sense and reference: he thinks that it is enough to show that 'X teaches' and 'Y learns' refer to the same concrete event, and ignores any difference in logical structure between these two senses. This is borne out by the Thebes-Athens illustration, for here the two descriptions 'the road from Thebes to Athens' and 'the road from Athens to Thebes' have senses of identical structure apart from the direction of the relation. Similarly with 'teaching' and 'learning', for all that could be gathered from III.3. Hence we are entitled to complain that III.3 is not on its own adequate to ensure Aristotle's desired conclusion that being an agent is not to be the subject of a becoming. What the chapter shows is that there is no *extra* becoming, true of the agent, beyond that which the agent brings about in the patient. It proves therefore, that *if* we have reason to locate the one and only becoming in the patient, we are left without any further becoming to locate in the agent. But the argument

does not explain why the becoming should be associated only with the patient. In arguing that there are not two distinct becomings corresponding to 'X teaches' and 'Y learns', Aristotle has not shown that these are not descriptions of a single becoming which can be assigned indifferently to X or Y, just as Thebes and Athens can be equally destinations.

(27) Thus to complete his proof Aristotle needs to be able to show that transitive agency is not as such a becoming. He offers no argument for this, but an argument can be constructed on his behalf which not only accords with his general position but bases itself specifically on the Aristotelian concept of the incompleteness of κίνησις (in the sense of coming-to-be). This notion has already come to the fore at the end of III.1, where he asserts that κίνησις is an incomplete (or imperfect) actuality. It is further developed in *Metaphysics* Θ 6, where he draws a distinction between κίνησις and what he calls 'ἐνέργεια', in terms of completeness and incompleteness. I shall now argue that his method of drawing that distinction can be applied in such a way as to show that the transitive causal activity of an agent is not incomplete in the way in which the change effected in the patient is. If this incompleteness is to be regarded as built into the notion of change, it follows that an agent's transitive activity is not only not an *extra* change (or coming to be) but not a change at all.

(28) Aristotle normally uses 'ἐνέργεια' to mean 'actuality', and in that sense a κίνησις, when actual, is an ἐνέργεια. But in *Metaphysics* Θ 6 he marks off a narrower sense of the latter term in which it is contrasted with the former.[15] He opposes the two categories by reference to the concepts of 'τέλος' (meaning both 'end' and 'complete condition') and 'πέρας' ('limit'). A κίνησις has a built-in limit, and the end or complete condition associated with the κίνησις occurs only when the limit has been reached. A κίνησις continues only so long as the limit has not been reached, and therefore while it

---

[15] For contemporary discussions of the distinction see Ackrill, Kosman, and Penner, opp. citt.; also T. C. Potts and C. C. W. Taylor, 'States, Activities and Performances', *Proc. Arist. Soc. Supp.* XXXIX, 1965, pp. 65 ff.

continues its τέλος has not been achieved, and so it is (while it exists) 'ἀτελής' and 'οὐ τελεία'. An ἐνέργεια in the narrow sense has, by contrast, no built-in limit; its end or complete condition exists already in it, at any moment of its duration. Now at first sight it may seem that this distinction is not going to show any logical difference between transitive agency and the corresponding change in the patient, since in *Metaphysics* Θ 6 Aristotle illustrates the concept of κίνησις by reference to both kinds of process indifferently. Thus 'making thin' and 'building' are offered as examples along with 'learning' and 'becoming'. This shows, I think, that Aristotle is not here fully aware of the power of his own distinction. But its scope will become evident only when we have examined the way in which he spells out the difference indicated above between κίνησις and ἐνέργεια. He does this by asserting and denying certain conceptual relationships between 'X φs' and 'X has φed', where the values of 'φ' are verbs corresponding to the two categories.

Thus for instance at the same time one sees and has seen, thinks and has thought, understands and has understood [all examples of ἐνεργέιαι]. But it is not the case that one learns and has learnt, is [being] restored to health and has been restored. At the same time one lives well and has lived well, is happy and has been happy. Otherwise it would be necessary at some point to stop, as when one makes something thin. But as it is, this is not the case: one lives and has lived. So we should call the one class 'κινήσεις', the other 'ἐνέργειαι'. For every κίνησις is incomplete (ἀτελής): making thin, learning, walking, building. These are κινήσεις, and certainly they are incomplete. For it is not the case that at the same time one walks and has walked, or builds and has built, or becomes and has become, or changes and has changed (κινεῖται καὶ κεκίνηται). If these happen at the same time the subject is different. But the same subject at the same time has seen and sees, thinks and has thought. I call the latter kind 'ἐνέργεια', the former 'κίνησις'. (1048 b23–35)

(29) Here, then, Aristotle is saying that when 'φing' designates an ἐνέργεια, 'X φs' is compatible with 'X has φed', while where it designates a κίνησις, the sentences are not compatible.[16] This point depends on a rather special sense of 'has φed', in which it means neither (*a*) that the φing is over, nor (*b*) that there has been some φing. For if (*a*) were meant,

---

[16] But see n. 20 below.

'X ϕs' would in all cases be incompatible with 'X has (just) ϕed'; while if (b) were meant, 'X ϕs' would be compatible with, since it would entail, 'X has ϕed' even where ϕing is a κίνησις. Or at any rate so Aristotle would hold, according to his doctrine of 'no first moment of κίνησις', (*Physics* VI.5, 236a13-36). Thus in the passage just quoted, 'X has ϕed' must mean something like: 'X has completely ϕed' or 'X has performed a complete act of ϕing'.[17] This sense fits well the condition for κινήσεις, namely that in their case 'ϕs' is incompatible with 'has ϕed'. But it requires an effort of interpretation to fit it to the condition for ἐνεργέιαι, since it is by no means clear what, in ordinary speech, could be meant by e.g. '"X sees" is compatible with "X has completely seen"', or '"X thinks" is compatible with "X has completely thought"'. However, it is obvious that Aristotle means that if X continues to think or to see, this does not entail that its previous thinking and seeing were *incomplete*. A κίνησις can continue only for as long as it has not reached its inherent limit, hence it can continue only so long as it is in this sense incomplete. Since ἐνέργειαι have no inherent limit, they cannot in this sense be at any point incomplete: and Aristotle chooses to say that they are therefore at every moment complete. We might prefer to say that they are neither complete nor incomplete, not being complete*able* by attainment of an inherent limit. Thus, in the sense of the perfect tense that implies completeness, we might prefer to say that when ϕing is an ἐνέργεια, 'X has ϕed' is neither true nor false. We should then have to re-phrase his distinction between κίνησις and ἐνέργεια as follows: In the case of the former, 'X ϕs' entails that X's previous ϕing was incomplete; while for the latter, 'X ϕs' does not entail that X's previous ϕing was incomplete (since it was neither complete nor incomplete). The reason why Aristotle prefers to say (by means of the special use of the perfect tense) that the present continuance of an ἐνέργεια is compatible with its earlier *completeness*, is that he wants to stress that ἐνέργειαι (or at any rate those which he lists) are ends in

---

[17] Potts, p. 68, adduces Chomsky's transformational proof that the perfect in English is not a past tense, arguing that in *Metaph.* Θ 6 Aristotle uses the Greek equivalents of 'ϕs' and 'has ϕed' not as present and past tenses but as progressive and perfective.

themselves, while κινήσεις are not. For in fact the notion of completeness embodied in the special use of the perfect shares all the ambiguity of 'τέλος', 'τέλειος', etc. A κίνησις is ἀτελής, both in the sense that so long as it continues it is incomplete (being completable) *and* in the sense of not being an end in itself. Aristotle's ἐνέργειαι are τέλειαι in the sense of being ends in themselves, so that even as they continue, the ends (i.e. themselves) for the sake of which they are engaged in have already been realized for some length of time. But in the other sense an ἐνέργεια is neither τελεία nor ἀτελής. Not distinguishing these senses, Aristotle holds that the ἐνέργειαι, while they continue, are already τέλειαι *simpliciter*.

(30) Let us return to the logical difference between the transitive causal activity of an agent, and the corresponding change in the patient. Above (para. (27)) I claimed that the former can be shown not to be incomplete like the latter. If this is true, then the transitive activity is or resembles an ἐνέργεια. Now in one respect activities such as building differ from the ἐνέργειαι of *Metaphysics* Θ 6, in that they are not ends in themselves. In one sense then they are ἀτελεῖς, since their τέλος lies beyond them, in the completed house etc. In that chapter, however, perhaps because of the conflation of senses of 'τέλος', Aristotle overlooks the fact that from one point of view housebuilding is free from the incompleteness that characterizes κινήσεις. This point of view emerges if we make a conceptual separation between the transitive activity of a particular agent, and its particular patient. By the argument of Θ 6, housebuilding counts as a κίνησις if it is tied down to a particular patient; where 'X' and 'Y' name individuals, 'X builds up Y' is incompatible with 'X has built up Y'. But instead let us particularize only with respect to the agent X, and speak not of X building Y, but of X building something, or, for short, of X building. 'X builds something' is not incompatible with 'X has built something'. 'Building something' designates an activity which the same subject could in principle continue indefinitely, or without a break.[18]

---

[18] Cf. E. McMullin, 'Four Senses of Potency', *The Concept of Matter in Greek*

What this shows is that the activity of building has no inherent limit. It is not a process of acquiring a new property.[19] If it were, then the subject (the agent) would have to lose this property before re-engaging in the process of acquiring it, and logically there would have to be an interval between successive acts of building during which the loss of the acquired property took place. By contrast, 'being built up by something' does designate a process involving a necessary break before the same subject can undergo it again even at the hands of a different agent. If Y is being built up, a limit is eventually reached, and Y must undergo some contrary change before being built up again; but X the builder does not have to get "unbuildered" before building again.[20]

and Mediaeval Philosophy (ed. E. McMullin), p. 313: '[Learning, healing and building] as they stand, . . . do not exemplify "terminating" activities, as they purpose to [*sc.* in *Metaph.* Θ 6]. One, having built, could still have the ability to build. To see them as "terminating", they must be *particularized* (building a particular house, learning a particular theorem . . .).' However, McMullin is mistaken in classifying learning along with the other two examples. The schema in para. (31) shows that learning is a κίνησις in its subject, while healing and building are not.

[19] This gives a foundation for Aristotle's statement in *De Anima* II.5, 417 b8-9: 'It is wrong to say that the thinker, when he thinks, is altered (ἀλλοιοῦσθαι), any more than the builder when he builds.' Note that Aristotle here *takes it for granted* that the builder is not altered: he is arguing for extending the same concept to the thinker. His point is that builder and thinker are not *patients*; but given the principle that every κίνησις has an agent (i.e. is a form of passivity), this entails that they are not as such subjects of κίνησις. Again, *Eth. Nic.* X.5, 1175 a34-5, where Aristotle mentions 'lovers of housebuilding', may be another passage showing tacit recognition that housebuilding is not a κίνησις like becoming a house. This interpretation would be justified if in *Eth. Nic.* X Aristotle clearly laid it down that enjoyment relates only to activities that are not κινήσεις but ἐνέργειαι in the narrow sense opposed to 'κίνησις'. In that case, what the lover of housebuilding loves would, in this context, count as an ἐνέργεια in the narrow sense. But although in *Eth. Nic.* X Aristotle states that enjoyment itself is not a κίνησις, he nowhere explicitly denies the possibility of enjoying κινήσεις. Cf. G. E. L. Owen, 'Aristotelian Pleasures', *Proceedings of the Aristotelian Society* LXXII, 1972, pp. 135 ff., esp. pp. 146-7. (However Penner, pp. 446-50, takes the view that an enjoyed activity functions logically like an ἐνέργεια in the narrow sense.)

[20] I have drawn upon the ἐνέργεια/κίνησις distinction as presented in *Metaph.* Θ 6 only in order to show that the logic of *causing change* differs in at least one important respect from the logic of (intransitive) *changing*. I have not here attempted a full treatment. Two major issues in particular have not been discussed: (*a*) the question whether for ἐνέργεια-values of 'φ', 'X φs' entails 'X has φed'; and (*b*) the 'quickly/slowly' criterion for κίνησις which Aristotle advances in *Eth. Nic.* X.3, 1173 a31-b4. As to (*a*), although in the *Metaphysics* Aristotle

[*See p. 188 for n. 20 cont.*]

(31) If the distinction of *Metaphysics* Θ 6 is extended to cover activities not tied down to particular subjects and objects, it becomes the basis for a classification of grammatically transitive verbs which will show (*a*) whether such a verb implies change at all, and (*b*) whether, if it does, the change is to be located in the subject or the object. Thus:

(i) If 'X φs Y' is compatible with 'X has (just) φed Y', then the activity of φing implies no change in either X or Y.

(ii) If 'X φs Y' is incompatible with 'X has (just) φed Y', then φing involves a change in either X or Y. This holds of e.g. 'builds', 'learns', 'makes thin'.

(iiA) For all verbs 'φ' falling under (ii): If 'X φs Y' is compatible with 'X has just φed Z' (where 'Z' names a particular object other than Y), but 'X φs Y' is incompatible with 'W has (just) φed Y' (where 'W' names a particular agent other than X), then the change indicated in a general way in (ii) is to be located specifically in Y, not X. This holds for 'builds', 'makes thin'.

(iiB) For all verbs 'φ' falling under (ii): If 'X φs Y' is compatible with 'X has (just) φed Z' (Z being other than Y), and is also compatible with 'W has

makes the distinction in terms of the *incompatibility* of 'X φs' with 'X has φed' where 'φ' denotes a κίνησις (so that it would appear that for ἐνέργεια-values, it is the *compatibility* of the two sentences that is being emphasized by contrast, rather than any entailment relation), Ackrill argues convincingly on the basis of other passages that Aristotle also holds the stronger position: that for ἐνέργειαι, 'φs' entails 'has φed'. Penner too takes this view. Now on the entailment criterion, 'building something' would not denote an ἐνέργεια. But as Ackrill points out, many apparently obvious examples of ἐνέργειαι (such as seeing a play) seem not to count as such either, by this rule. Hence I would not regard the failure of 'building' to meet the entailment criterion as telling against the view that building should be classified as an ἐνέργεια along with seeing. Potts and Penner both indicate ways in which the troublesome ἐνέργειαι noted by Ackrill could be accommodated to the entailment criterion. Penner's remarks are especially relevant since he explicitly refers to transitive causal activities such as building. As for the second point (*b*) above, it is not clear whether Aristotle means 'A κίνησις takes place quickly or slowly' as a necessary, or as a necessary and also sufficient condition for κίνησις. If the latter, then building would seem to count as a κίνησις. (But for a different interpretation, see Penner, pp. 446-8.) However, the determination of issues (*a*) and (*b*) does not affect the position for which I argue in the text, viz. that from one point of view, building etc. are to be classed as non-changes in their subjects.

(just) φed Y' (W being other than X), then the change indicated generally in (ii) is to be located specifically in X, not Y. An example would be 'comes to know', with 'X' as grammatical subject, and a phrase designating some "object of knowledge" as object. The condition holds good for different kinds of objects of knowledge (or, alternatively, different kinds of knowledge): e.g. this man (acquaintance); that today is Wednesday (propositional); the art of bookbinding (knowledge-how). The same object can both come to be known and have come to be known — by different subjects, just as the same builder can build and have built different buildings. This shows that coming to be known no more implies that the known acquires a new property which it must lose before coming to be known again (e.g. by someone else), than building confers upon the builder a property he must get rid of before he builds again.[21]

(32) It must be stressed that the concept of change or κίνησις sustaining this classification is not simply the concept of a process that *necessarily* (even in the conceptual sense of 'necessary') results in a new state of the subject. It is, rather, that of a process properly *defined* as tending to result in a certain state, and whose occurrence in a given subject is grounded on the subject's not being in that state. This distinction between *necessary results* and results *definitive of the process* solves a puzzle which would otherwise cast serious doubt on the ἐνέργεια/κίνησις distinction of *Metaphysics* Θ 6. Readers of this passage may well be left with the sense that ἐνέργειαι, since they are not changes, are somehow supposed by Aristotle to be outside time, or else to be in time in the way that static conditions are, homogeneous throughout their duration and permitting within themselves no distinction of before and after. But it is clear from his examples that Aristotle is not confining the term 'ἐνέργεια'

[21] Cf. S. Waterlow, 'Affecting and being Affected', *Mind* LXXIX, 1970, pp. 92 ff.

to conditions in which the empirically identifiable subject is in any ordinary sense static. The most obvious example is living, but the cognitive activities thinking and seeing also illustrate the point, for Aristotle does not use these terms only of fixed contemplation resting in a single object. Discursive thought is for him as much an ἐνέργεια as intuitive.[22] This may lead us to think that since the empirically identifiable subject is not static, he must mean that ἐνέργειαι, since they are not changes, really somehow pertain to timeless nonempirical subjects. This conclusion might be welcomed by some as tending to support certain of Aristotle's metaphysical doctrines (those concerning the active intellect and the God of *Metaphysics* Λ). But at the same time it renders the method of classification in Θ 6 thoroughly dubious. For that classification depends on the analysis of tense relationships holding of ordinary verbs in ordinary language,[23] and these verbs are predicated of empirical subjects in empirically verifiable propositions. Thus the analysis would appear to be self-refuting if it yields a classification one of whose divisions makes sense only in connection with timeless metaphysical subjects.

(33) But this problem arises only if we ignore the distinction stated above. There is no reason why we should not think of an ἐνέργεια as a process necessarily resulting, on each occasion, in new states of its subject, provided we do not *define* it as the acquisition of a given state, or take its occurrence to be grounded on the latter's absence. The activity of thinking, for instance, and also of seeing (if by 'seeing' we understand, as Aristotle often does, a cognitive activity, not a mere state of consciousness), might be said necessarily to leave 'traces', i.e. memories, increased understanding, etc. A man might reasonably be said *not* to have seen a play even if he sat through it awake and with his eyes open, unless for some time after he could tell others about it, saw things in the light

[22] Cf. Ackrill, pp. 132-3.

[23] However, cf. A. P. D. Mourelatos: 'The doctrine that "enjoyment is *energeia*" is a metaphysical doctrine; it does not simply record usage, ordinary or Aristotelian; it interprets it and it corrects it.' (*Philosophical Review* LXXVII, 1968, p. 516.) No doubt Mourelatos would say the same of the ἐνέργεια/κίνησις distinction itself.

of it, found it more familiar on another occasion, etc. And the fact that one may think about so and so even though one has already thought about it, is not in general due to the previous thinking's having left no trace, but to the subject's not being readily exhausted. And if a process of thinking left no trace, how could the different stages within one such process do so? But if not there could be no reasoning, as this involves reaching new stages by means of results carried forward. But although an ἐνέργεια may of necessity result in some specific state new to the subject, this does not *define what* that ἐνέργεια is. Acquiring memories of watching *The Tempest* is not what watching *The Tempest* is or consists in. If it were, then indeed specifically the same ἐνέργεια could not be immediately repeated (or indefinitely continued), since repetition of *it* would be repetition of a process defined as bringing about a state of a given kind; which entails that the instance of this state previously achieved must first have disappeared for there to be room to achieve a new instance of the same. As it is, a new instance of the same type of ἐνέργεια can take as its point of departure the state achieved through a previous instance.

(34) This discussion arose out of the comparison drawn above between the operation of an agent, e.g. a builder, and ἐνέργεια as distinct from κίνησις in *Metaphysics* Θ 6. Let us return now to the concept of the unchanging agent, and relate certain results so far reached to the questions raised in paragraphs (19)-(20). Our discussion has shown that for Aristotle no more than for Hume does the agency of the agent consist in a mysterious extra change which is the agent's exercise of its "efficacy". The *only* change, when X acts upon Y, is the change in Y: this is the same concrete event as that described as 'Y's being acted on by X', and this in turn is the same concrete event as that described as 'X's acting upon Y'. But all the same, it might be replied, granted X's acting upon Y is the same concrete event as Y's changing to some new state of its own, this change does *depend on* the agency of X — since otherwise why should we speak of agency at all? — so that X's agency must be something more than the mere change in Y. And even if this something more is not a *change*

in X, it does not follow that it is not *something* in X, some event, or process, or operation, and in showing that this cannot be a change, our discussion has not shown what it *is*. And if, as seems likely, whatever it is is not empirically identifiable, then is it something mysterious and metaphysical; or is it nothing? If the latter, what is to be gained by speaking of agency at all as if it were something; and if the former, what place can it possibly have in a scientific account of nature?

(35) On one level Aristotle can answer these questions in a way that even Hume would approve. In III.3, 202 a7-8, he says: 'Change is the actuality of the changeable, insofar as it is changeable, and this comes about through the *contact* of the changer'. A type of case that obviously fits this is heating, already mentioned in III.1, 201 a21-2. A hot body causes a body in contact with it to get hot; it thereby loses heat itself and becomes cool, so that the action is reciprocal. But the hot body's heating of the other does not *consist* in the change to coolness which the former thereby suffers, although this is an inevitable consequence. In fact, the heating by the initially hot body does not consist in any activity *in it*: for the heat to be "imparted", all that is necessary and sufficient is contact (or the appropriate proximity) between the hot body and a suitable patient. Under these conditions the latter simply gets hot. So far Aristotle hardly differs from Hume. But the advantage is all on Aristotle's side when we consider the significance of this shared position for each of the two philosophers. In Hume's eyes, it is the 'most violent of [his] paradoxes' that transitive causal activity should consist, objectively, in nothing but what has just been mentioned. His problem now is to explain why all of us, himself included, should have thought that there was more to causality than events in conjunction; and his explanation can refer only to subjective conditions, since he has eliminated the possibility of any extra objective feature of the external situation providing us with the idea of 'necessary connection'. However, the subjective impression which Hume drums up to fill the bill would be superfluous but for the gap supposedly uncovered by his analysis of the external agent-relationship. The

appearance of a gap is due to his assumption that if transitive agency were anything real and objective, it would consist in something extra, a *tertium quid* between objects. Since this is not conceivable, let alone identifiable, he must end by denying the reality of transitive agency. But the conclusion depends on the assumption, and the assumption presupposes that the objects themselves are intrinsically non-dynamic, an inevitable position for the empiricist who insists that power is not present in objects because its presence cannot be perceived. Thus agency, if it exists objectively at all, must lie outside and between what acts and is acted on; and since this is absurd, agency is a figment of mind.

(36) But within a conceptual system such as Aristotle's it is no paradox that the transitive activity of heating should consist simply in the fact that a suitable patient Y becomes hot when in contact (or whatever degree of proximity) with a hot body X. The objects are in themselves essentially dynamic. Given that it is the *nature* of fire to fly upwards, there is no need and no room for some further activity, a *tertium quid* binding the fire to its own natural movement. If this were necessary then it would be false that the fire *of itself* shoots up unless prevented. If the concept of natural change in the *self-same* natural substance is intelligible, why should it be any less intelligible that natural dynamism should issue also in changes in other subjects? If the parallel is accepted, there is no place for the idea of an extra link negotiating the efficacy of agent on external patient.[24] The potential agent would not *be* a potential agent if on encountering the potential patient under suitable conditions it needed some further metaphysical mechanism by which to administer its effect. Aristotle's system excludes a *tertium quid* between agent and patient

[24] Cf. H. Carteron, *La Notion de Force dans le Système d'Aristote*, p. 168: 'Aristote considérait l'action à expliquer comme aussi évidente que le mouvement lui-même.' Also: 'Voilà pourquoi la difficulté sur la dualité de l'acte dans l'actif et le passif (202 a21) est appelée logique, tout comme les difficultés des Eléates sur le mouvement. C'est que la communication du mouvement est aussi évidente que l'existence du mouvement et de la nature.' (Ibid., fn. 773.) In Carteron's view, Aristotle has for this reason failed to explain transitive agency or even to see the problem it poses. But I cannot find in Carteron a clear statement of what kind of explanation he holds to be lacking.

not because there is for him *no* efficacy in the world, but because efficacy is anyway present, in substances whose nature it is to have change happen in and around themselves.

(37) So far we have considered only the example of heating. But does contact suffice for the change in all cases of transitive action? In III.3 Aristotle's illustrations are teaching, building, and healing. In VIII.4, 255 a34–b2 he says:

In all cases, whenever that which is capable of acting and that which is capable of being acted on are together, that which is potentially so and so sometimes becomes actually so and so, as for instance the learner, from being potentially so and so, becomes potentially something else.

('Potentially something else' refers to the fact that the actuality which the learner acquires through learning is not the actual *exercise* of knowledge, but the (actual) power to exercise it.) The apparent discrepancy between 'in all cases' and 'sometimes' led Ross (*Aristotle's Physics*, p. 696) to prefer a less well-authenticated reading which omits the 'sometimes' ('ἐνίοτε', 255 a35). But there is no contradiction if we take 'in all cases' to mean 'in all types of case'. If this is the correct reading and interpretation, then Aristotle here shows himself reluctant to assert that contact alone between potential agent and patient is always sufficient for the change. In this he is surely right, since a further condition must be met, viz. the absence of external interference (cf. 255 b3–4). But his choice of example (teaching/learning) suggests that he may have something more in mind. Where the change in question is heating, cooling and suchlike, contact and the absence of interferences are doubtless jointly sufficient. But it would be implausible to suggest this of a change such as learning. It is not just that 'contact between agent and patient' cannot here be given a straightforward spatial meaning. There is also the fact that even when "mental contact" has been established, and nothing interferes, something more seems necessary for actual teaching and learning to occur. Or at least, they do not necessarily occur under the conditions just stated. So the question is what else does Aristotle suppose is needed to convert his 'sometimes' into an 'always'? There can be no clear answer to this until we are told how much to

include under (mental) 'contact'. Would it, for instance, involve the mutual recognition of willingness to teach and to
learn? But granted the existence of "contact" even in some
rich sense, and the absence of interference, the teacher must
surely also *do* something in order to set going the learning-
process. In short, this case is not at all like that of heating. In
heating there is no reason to postulate an extra activity
whereby the hot body propagates its heat once contact is
established under suitable circumstances. But unless the
teacher, apart from standing in the correct relation to his
pupil, also engages in a definite activity of propagating
knowledge, the pupil will not learn.[25]

(38) We may begin to wonder whether Aristotle's vagueness
on this matter is not intended to blur the awkward fact that
the teacher's teaching comprises various performances which
we should be hard put to it to describe without implying that
he himself, the agent, (intransitively) changes. The builder
gives even more cause for suspicion. Yet Aristotle must mean
his general account of agency-patiency to cover building,
since building is his paradigm of change in III.1 (where the
problem of change is treated as inseparable from that of
agency). The difficulty cannot fairly be evaded by saying (in
line with the doctrine as yet to emerge from Book VIII) that
the real cause of change is an immaterial unchanging something "within" the builder, with the builder's changing body
functioning only as a mediating or instrumental cause. In the
first place, by any ordinary standard it would seem that the
builder, while operating, changes mind-wise as well as body-
wise; so that the alleged unchanging cause would be neither
mental nor physical, or else is as likely to be either as the
other. Secondly, we are at present following Aristotle's
attempt in III to elucidate the general features of agency and
patiency, and he sets about this by referring to the most
obvious type of case, where one substance changes another
external to itself. Thus we are entitled to expect him to make
good the general claim that 'the change is in the patient'

---

[25] As Philoponus says (*ad* 202 b7, ed. Vitelli p. 381, 15 ff.): ʻεἴ γε καὶ παρόντος
τοῦ μαθητοῦ εἴπῃ μὲν ὁ διδάσκαλος μὴ δράσῃ δὲ εἰς τὸν μαθητήν, οὐ λέγεται
διδάξαι.ʼ

without reducing interaction between distinct substances to the problematic case in which the role of agent is played (or supposed to be) by something not a distinct concrete substance at all, but a factor "within" one. After all, we say that it is the man who builds, and the man is an embodied being, not an unmoved mover within a human body. It may be that even if Aristotle cannot show satisfactorily that there is no change in the *man* as agent, he will still, by some special argument, be able to arrive at the supreme Unmoved Mover of Book VIII. But he will not be justified in relying for support on any general presumption that a changer *as such* does not change, if in some cases (indeed, the most obvious) this has proved false or even absurd. To maintain this assumption intact, Aristotle would either have to deny that the empirically identifiable changes in the mind and body of the builder are changes at all, or he would have to say that they have nothing to do with the builder's activity as agent. Both alternatives seem absurd, and the second implies, in addition, that the real building activity, since it is not to be identified with any visible goings-on, must be something wholly mysterious and indescribable.

(39) So far as the second of these alternatives is concerned, Aristotle himself would surely be the first to scoff at the idea that the builder's bodily and mental processes have nothing to do with his building. On the contrary, they are what constitute it. The problem then is this: the discussion of the ἐνέργεια/κίνησις distinction showed that building is not a change in the builder, in the sense that building is not a process defined in terms of a new state to be achieved in the builder himself. Rather, it is a process defined in terms of a new state to be achieved in the external materials. However, this purely conceptual point does not save the builder from having to *stir* in order to be building. There is no concrete event that displays only the definitive features of building and no others, any more than there is in nature a form without matter. Building is not to be *defined* as moving one's limbs and calculating weights and positions, but these processes are the flesh and bones in which the form is realized, and what are these if not changes in the *agent*?

(40) It will help to approach this problem if we consider the notion of a *single* (particular) change. In V.4, 227 b20 ff. Aristotle says that a κίνησις is numerically one only if it takes place (*a*) in a single subject; (*b*) in respect of one specific type of property; (*c*) continuously throughout the time in which it occurs. Now these remarks amount to an analysis of the concept 'numerically one κίνησις'; they do not offer criteria by which to decide in practice whether some phenomenon or other *is* a numerically single change. Characteristics (*a*), (*b*) and (*c*) could function as criteria only if it were possible to identify their presence without having first employed the notion of 'one change'. That this is not in general possible will be clear if we consider actual cases. As examples of single subjects, Aristotle mentions an individual man, a particular piece of gold. His examples of changes are: walking, becoming healthy, becoming white. These cases are very different. A piece of gold is perceptibly simple and homogeneous; but it is otherwise with a man. Why do we not say that the many perceptibly heterogeneous parts of a man are different subjects? When one walks, different parts of the body move differently; why do we not say that these are many changes in many subjects, but rather (as Aristotle assumes) that there is one subject, the man, doing one thing, namely walking? Our basis for seeing the man as one subject lies in precisely such facts as that the various movements of the limbs and organs are co-ordinated to some over-all result such as that of getting to a different place. Thus our notion of the unity of the perceptibly multiple subject depends on the prior assumption that the various movements make up one change, described as 'walking'. Again, perception alone can decide whether something has become white: whiteness is simple, like gold. But what about becoming healthy? This may involve what from some points of view would be described as many specifically different changes, in temperature, in position of parts, in size and shape, etc. Again, what from one point of view may be a new change may from another be the continuation of a change that was already occurring. The bronze is melted, then it is poured into the mould, but the same process is going on all the time, the production of a statue.

(41) We have already seen (e.g. Ch. III, paras (10)–(11); cf. also Ch. V, paras (35)–(36)) how Aristotle's theory of substance necessarily favours the adoption, in particular cases, of a standpoint from which what might otherwise be regarded as a multiplicity of distinct objects and distinct changes are seen as composing one object and one change. This is not to say that the theory of substance provides a licence for indiscriminately viewing any and every phenomenon as parts of some single unit. The point is rather that since every phenomenon must be traced back in the end to some one substantial principle or nature, we are not entitled to look upon a particular phenomenon as lying 'outside' a whole composed by other phenomena unless there is reason to suppose that the former manifests a different principle from the latter. Now the empirical criteria for deciding whether a given phenomenon is to be included in one whole rather than another may be difficult to spell out, and one may well suspect that the decision-procedure will involve conceptual circularity of some sort. This is a problem of methodology rather than metaphysics. Aristotle would not, I imagine, be disposed to give up his metaphysics on account of it, just as there are latterday philosophers who remain faithful to the 'analytic'/'synthetic' distinction despite a similar difficulty. This however is a general problem, and at the moment we are concerned with the particular question of how it is that an agent can be thought of as not changing even though it is only through its changes that some other change is effected in an external object. I suggest that the 'unifying' approach just mentioned can solve this problem, whatever the *general* difficulties attending such an approach. (These are no more severe, so far as I can see, in this connection than in any other.)

(42) The material used by the builder, always referred to by Aristotle in the singular as 'τὸ οἰκοδομητόν', consists in many different things, wood, stones, etc., which are seen as one only in relation to the one end. Again, the processes undergone by these are different: hewing, planing, positioning, etc., but they all in turn constitute the one process of becoming a house, for the same principle controls them all. But are

not the builder's bodily and mental movements *also* parts of
this one process even though their subject is not one of the
materials? They are not logically distinct changes from the
change we call 'becoming a house', for their end is the same,
that there should be a house. And the *raison d'être* of the
changes in the agent is the same as that of the changes in the
materials: it is the potentiality of there being a house – a
potentiality which will be actualized in a new state of something other than the builder. If the singleness of the end
justifies us in seeing the perceptibly different changes in the
materials as parts of one process, why should it not justify
seeing the changes in the agent as parts of *that same process*?
If instead we take them as logically self-contained changes,
then we must suppose them to be completed on reaching the
end-states in which they terminate. Thus if the builder, in
building, raises his arm and this is a self-contained change, it
is complete when his arm is up. But this description is actually
self-contradictory. Insofar as he is a builder, the change of
which he is the source is only completed with the emergence
of an edifice. Thus if he is also regarded as the source of a
change that is completed by a certain position of his own
arm, it must be assumed that it is not *qua* builder that he is
the source of this change. But this is absurd, since the arm-
raising is not a *per accidens* accompaniment of the building
but is part of carrying it out. It follows that he can be taken
to raise his arm *qua* builder building only if the arm-raising is
not treated as a self-contained change. In this sense, then,
what takes place in the working agent is not *a change*, i.e. a
coming to be of some new state of him, although it is not a
condition of rest either.

(43) Since change is the coming to be of some new state in a
substance, and is grounded on the substance's not yet being
in that state, it is natural to designate this substance the 'subject of change'. But now the case of the builder presents a
problem of terminology. For here the change, which is the
coming to be of a house-structure, takes place (or certain
stages of it do) in another substance than the agent. But
movements of his are parts of the change, and these movements are in him. Yet if we said that this change is in him as

subject, this would seem to imply that the *builder* turns into a house. Some type of term is needed to convey the builder's connection with the change which does not imply that he is subject of the end-state. And this function is performed by transitive verbs of agency. 'X builds' indicates (*a*) that X is no less necessary to the one change than its genuine subject, viz. the materials; (*b*) that the one change does not have X as subject; and (*c*) that whatever does occur in X that is relevant to the one change is not a distinct and self-sufficient change in X. We can now see that Aristotle's retention of the language of agency has nothing to do with any postulation of a mystical (and mythical) transaction tying agent to patient, or to its effect in the patient. Aristotle, from all that we have seen, could have joined heartily in Hume's conclusion that *all* that happens (apart from psychological events in the observer) is (*a*) certain behaviour in one object, and (*b*) a change culminating in a new state of some other object; although Aristotle's reasons would be the reverse of Hume's (*v.s.* paras (35)–(36)). And where the agent-thing is a creature incapable of telling its purposes, he would have agreed that regular conjunction of similar events is our primary clue to the existence of a connection. 'What happens by nature happens always or for the most part' (*Physics* II.8, 198 b35–6). But what Aristotle could not allow is a Humean description of the two sides of the causal relationship as a pair of conceptually distinct and self-sufficient changes. The language of transitive agency makes it possible to register the fact that the change *has* two sides and involves two objects, without implying that there are two *changes*. Thus while 'builds' represents nothing extra going on "between" X and Y, it is not on that account eliminable from a correct, and from Aristotle's point of view, a scientific account of the situation.

(44) There is however another way of viewing the matter, one which undercuts altogether any attack on 'agency' as introducing a non-empirical relationship. Instead of identifying the change with the coming into being of some new state of the patient, let us follow Aristotle in III.3 in treating it as one concrete event of which the agency of one individual and the patiency of another are distinguishable but inseparable

aspects. Now if we were to consider this event prior to analysing it into the two aspects, could we say that two different
individuals are involved? What we call 'agent' and 'patient'
are of course perceptibly and spatially distinct. But Aristotle
would not in general take this as a sufficient criterion for
there being distinct beings or substances: e.g. the organs of an
organic creature are not different substances. And on the
supposition which we are considering, we would not be able
to distinguish one being as that in which the new state
happens, and the other as that which contributes to this
without itself suffering the new state. For this distinction
presupposes that the concrete event has already been conceptually split into the active and passive aspects. It seems
then that considered prior to analysis, this event occurs in a
single subject, which only *upon* analysis reveals different
factors, an agent and a patient. Now although Aristotle's
analogies in Book II between natural and artificial change are
intended to illustrate the former by the latter, why should we
not reverse the analogy, and regard the artifex and his material
as forming, in the change, a concrete organic unity, as if the
material were an extension of his own body?[26] What happens
in the one and what happens in the other have the same end
and are from the same principle. Such a consideration justifies
thinking of the parts of one body (in the ordinary sense of
'one body') as an organic unit; so let it justify a similar view
in this case. However, the difference between this and a real
case of natural change in a single substance, is that in the
former, the "organic unit" of artifex-material exists as a unit
only during the change. In particular, the change terminates
in the unit's dissolution into two free-standing substances,
one the house and the other a being capable of entering into
similar "organic" relations with other sets of building materials. And it would be a strange natural substance indeed
whose natural change necessarily resulted in its own dissolution! However, if we may disregard this important disanalogy
in order to finish the conceptual picture, let us say this: it is
only because there are two distinct beings before and after
the change that we assume that there were these during it

---

[26] Cf. *De Mot. An* 8, 702 a31–b11, for a comparison of a stick moved by the
hand to an extra limb.

too. Of course the two distinct beings are materially continuous, both before and after, with the one subject of the
concrete change as it actually occurs. But is this a reason for
supposing that during the change there were two actually
distinct beings involved? Surely not, any more than the fact
that different simple bodies are yielded up when an organism
decomposes would be, for Aristotle, a ground for saying that
they were actually present as their distinct selves during the
life of the creature (cf. Ch.II, paras (38) and (42)).

(45) If this view is not too far-fetched, then nor is its implication, which is that there *is* no actual agency and patiency. In
the change as a concrete unitary event there are not different
entities to *be* agent and patient. The active and passive of the
verb, from this point of view, are used of the change itself
only derivatively, on the basis of an actual distinction existing only *ante* and *post eventum*. We cannot even call the two
beings the 'potential agent and patient', since this implies
that they could be actually so. But they could be actually so
only in the actual change, and *in* the actual change they are
not distinct and therefore not agent and patient. At any rate,
on this account the question 'What *is* it that takes place when
agency takes place?' cannot arise. Since there are not two
beings to connect, there can be neither problem nor solution
about the nature and status of the connection. If we and
Aristotle find this account incredible the reason, I suggest,
does not lie with the concept of change as such, but with the
structure of the concepts we use to describe our own practical
activities. Suppose we intend to produce some change in an
object other than ourselves. Then in the event, if all goes
well, we do, and take ourselves to be doing, *what* we already
intended. If we describe what we are doing while doing it, the
description differs only in tense from the verbal expression of
the prior intention. So in seeing ourselves as executing the
intention, we see the actual happening as of the same logical
structure as the intention itself. But in the intention, which
preceded the change, the object-to-be-changed figured as
something distinct from ourselves. Thus even when the
change is actual it continues to figure as distinct. In short,
when the change is one that *we* take ourselves to bring about in

an external object, we cannot primarily view it as a concrete event undifferentiated into the aspects of agency and patiency. The point of view of the voluntary agent is one from which the "halves" already present themselves as distinct.

(46) Any further discussion of the issues that open up here would take us far from Aristotle, who never follows out the line of thought just sketched, although his remarks in III.3 about the concrete unity of change may be said to contain its germ. While the account just given brings obvious cases of mutually external agent and patient under a schema predicating a single undifferentiated development of a single unitary subject, Aristotle himself travels in the opposite direction. He looks for distinct agents and patients even in the apparently intransitive natural changes of single living organisms, beings which for him are unitary not by some stretch of the conceptual imagination, but fundamentally and paradigmatically so. To this, the topic of *self*-change, we now turn.

V

Self-Change
and the Eternal Cause

(1) If Aristotle is in general elusive on the subject of agency and its connection with change, nowhere is he more so than when treating of the mysterious concept of something's 'changing (transitive) itself', or 'being changed by itself'. The import of this concept, the grounds of its application, its point and its relation to other Aristotelian notions are all more or less obscure. But these obscurities especially demand elucidation not only because of the intrinsic interest of the idea of something's being changed *by itself*, but because of its crucial place in one of the most important arguments of the *Physics*. This is the grand course of reasoning in Book VIII by which Aristotle seeks first to show that change never was nor will be absent from the universe, and then to explain the nature of the cause on which this fact depends. These topics may, however, seem remote from a general study of the structure of Aristotelian change and its conceptual connections with substance and agency. So far, the pursuit of these central questions has not required the assumption that change either is or is not an eternal feature of the universe, and there has been no reason to investigate what follows from either supposition. Taking it for granted that change exists, which in a work on "physics" cannot even be questioned (I.2, 184 b25-185 a3; 185 a12-17; VIII.3, 253 a32-b6), we have followed Aristotle's analyses of what it involves when and where it does exist, and these analyses seem logically independent of theories concerning the actual distribution of change through time (or for that matter through space).[1] However, as will emerge from the ensuing discussion, the conclusions of Book VIII have a vital bearing on the validity of Aristotle's original notion of natural substance put forward in

[1] I say *'logically* independent' because it is a historical fact that the cosmological inquiry of VIII led Aristotle to a closer scrutiny of the general notions of 'continuity' and 'terminus'; see Ch. III, paras (57) ff.

II.1. In particular, the proposition that there never was nor will be a time without change may be regarded as underpinning the fundamental conception of the nature of a natural substance as an inner principle of change. Aristotle demonstrates and defends the aforesaid proposition in the first two chapters of VIII, and devotes the rest of the book to spelling out certain presuppositions and consequences. It is in the course of this reasoning that 'change by self' or, as I shall usually call it, 'self-change' makes its sole appearance in the *Physics*, in VIII.4–6.

(2) The concept is first introduced in a section where Aristotle means to establish that whatever changes (intransitive) is changed 'by something' (Chapter 4). 'By something' is used by him to cover two alternatives: 'by something other', and: 'by itself' (255 b33–256 a1). Now at first sight it may look as if something's being changed 'by itself' means the same as something's changing naturally or by its own nature. In speaking of natural change, we have sometimes described the object as changing 'of itself', and Aristotle speaks of the nature of a natural substance as a principle of change 'within itself'. These reflexive locutions are perhaps easily confused, but for Aristotle they represent distinct concepts.[2] He makes it clear in 4 (especially in the summarizing lines 255 b31–256 a2) that the class of self-changes is only a sub-division of

[2] Cf. O. Hamelin, *Le Système d'Aristote*, pp. 325–6, L. Robin, *Aristote*, pp. 125–6, and Ross, *Aristotle's Physics*, p. 435. By contrast, F. Solmsen speaks in vaguely general terms of 'nature as self-moving principle' ('Platonic Influences in Aristotle's Physical System' in *Aristotle and Plato in the Mid-Fourth Century*, edd. Düring and Owen, p. 227). It is true that in *Aristotle's System of the Physical World*, pp. 100–1, Solmsen says: 'To have the principle of motion in oneself is not entirely the same as to be moved by oneself', but he goes on (ibid.): 'Aristotle himself seems at times to regard the two notions as synonymous', citing 254 b14 ff. But this passage implies only that change 'by oneself' counts as natural change, without any hint that the converse is also true; hence it affords no evidence of even a temporary assumption of synonymy on Aristotle's part. (Possibly Solmsen's interest in Platonic influences misleads him here: what *Plato* calls 'self-change' corresponds, in his system, to 'natural change' in Aristotle's, in that for Plato 'self-change' denotes the type of change that is primary and presupposed by any other; *v.i.* para. (6) and n. 24.) Unfortunately, Cherniss too (*Aristotle's Criticism of Plato and the Academy*, Appendix X) uses 'self-motion' and 'moves itself' of any change not externally determined, although he is well aware that this is not Aristotle's meaning (ibid., p. 590). For similar misleading language see also Charlton, p. 92.

natural changes. Self-change he regards as belonging only to living creatures (or animals: Aristotle seems to hover between these two positions[3]). But the realm of natural substances includes also the inanimate bodies, fire, earth, etc., or, as he here terms them, the light and the heavy (255 a2 ff.). And he is no more disposed to deny natural movements to these substances in VIII than when he first introduced the concept of natural substance in II.1. Thus, for instance, the distinction between natural change and change that is enforced or contrary to nature still applies in full force to the inanimate members of the physical world. In VIII.4, 254 b21-2 he writes: '. . . some things change ($\kappa\iota\nu\epsilon\hat{\iota}\tau\alpha\iota$) by nature, others against nature. Change against nature is illustrated by earthy things moving upwards and fire downwards.' These movements could not be regarded as 'against' the natures of the substances concerned unless it were still being assumed, as it was originally in II.1, that they have natural directions of motion too. And in 4, 254 b16-17 Aristotle recalls his original definition of nature as an inner principle of change with the following remark: 'We say that whatever has the principle of change within it changes by nature'. It is almost as if he here issues a warning against the impression that the newly introduced term 'changed by itself' implies a revision of his initial concept of nature. But it would be strange indeed if in the same context he were then to put forward a doctrine entailing a radical departure from his earlier view concerning the *extension* of this concept. Yet this in effect is what Aristotle would here be doing in VIII.4 if he meant by 'self-change' the same as what he earlier meant by 'natural change'. For this equation of the terms would entail that on the theory of VIII.4 the concept of 'nature' applies now only to animate things, since these alone merit the title 'self-changers'.

(3) It is precisely because Aristotle does *not* equate natural change with self-change that he is faced here with what he regards as a particularly knotty problem, that of showing how even in their natural motions the simple bodies can be properly described as moved by something. For they are not

moved by themselves; and the absence of any external determinant to enforce the pattern of movement makes it look as
if it is wrong to speak of them as moved by anything other
than themselves. But this Aristotle cannot accept, for he
would then have to say that they are not moved by anything,
but simply move, which contradicts the conclusion towards
which he is steering, that every change is a change by something. In the end, and with considerable effort, he argues that
a simple body in its natural motion is 'moved by' those
external substances responsible for the motion either through
having produced the body in the first place or through remov-
ing hindrances (*v.s.* Ch. IV, paras (9)–(11)). Thus he is
willing to extend the phrase 'changed by something other' so
as to cover two such different dependence-relationships as (*a*)
that between an object changing against its nature and the
external object which enforces this change, and (*b*) that
between an object changing naturally and the external objects
which make or have made this change possible. We may well
suspect a doctrine that requires such a blanketing of differences, but Aristotle's deliberately indiscriminate use of
'changed by something other' puts him at a strategic advantage
vis-à-vis the question of what exactly we are to suppose
should be meant by something's being changed 'by itself'.
What relationship can a thing have with 'itself' that would
justify describing it as both agent and patient of its own
change? By using 'changed by something other' to cover such
diverse relations, Aristotle in effect establishes for 'changed
by —' a meaning so wide and abstract that the reader is in no
position to complain at its further extension to the reflexive
case, or to object if no obvious image comes to mind to illustrate this latest application.

(4) All that we have so far gathered concerning change by
self, or self-change, is that it is natural change, and occurs
only in animate beings. In what then does it differ from the
natural change of the inanimate? The term might seem to
hint that self-change is more self-sufficient. But in general
this is not so. For if it is true to say that an inanimate thing
in natural change is changed by things other than itself, on
the ground that other things are responsible for its existence

and for its free path, then it is equally true to say this about a living thing in *its* natural change, which is self-change. Aristotle does not himself bring out this point, but it follows directly from the account he has given of 'changed by something other' in connection with natural changes of the inanimate. In fact it appears from VIII.2 and 6 that the self-changes of living things are even more dependent on external conditions than are the natural movements of fire and earth. The latter presuppose only (*a*) generation of the substance in question, and (*b*) conditions that make or keep the pathway clear; but the former require not only these but also (*c*) environmental stimuli that trigger the changes although without enforcing their pattern (2, 253a9–20), and (*d*) certain physiological conditions of the living substance which it owes to earlier interactions with the environment (such as ingestion of food) (6, 259 b6–16).

(5) What distinguishes self-change for Aristotle is not superior self-sufficiency, but the logical complexity of that which has the change. A self-changer, i.e. a substance that changes (transitive), or is changed by, itself comprises in itself both agent and patient of the same change; and this agent and patient, Aristotle insists, are in some way distinct from one another. Supplementing Aristotle's account (since he himself seems resolved to say as little as possible about self-change) we can state the following analytic difference between the case of a self-change externally obstructed and then released, and that of a change that is merely natural and not self-instigated: in the latter case, what is repressed and then released is simply a change in the object; while in the former, not only is the *change* first prevented, then permitted, but something else too, namely the effective exercise of agency by the agent-element 'within' the object. When self-change is hindered, not only is something prevented from changing (intransitive), but something in some sense *else* is prevented from producing the change. That there is some difference between changer and changed within the self-changer is one of the few points on which Aristotle is quite definite. At 4, 254b28–33, he asserts that there is a difference, and at 5, 257a31–b13, he attempts to prove that there must be. The self-changer is a complex

whole, in which the agent- and the patient-element are "parts". The idea of being in which changer and changed are in no way distinct Aristotle regards as inadmissible.

(6) In this respect his concept of self-change differs radically from its Platonic forerunner. Plato had argued that every causal series of changes must have a causally first member, and that this first member is a change in which the being that changes is itself the source of its change. He described this being as 'changing (transitive: κινεῖν) itself' (*Laws* X.894 B ff.). He further argued that self-change is the defining characteristic of soul (ibid. 895 C–896 A; cf. *Phaedrus* 245 C–245 A). He regarded the soul not merely as the source of vitality in beings other than souls, but as itself enjoying the life of which it is source. Now this life he identified with motion (*Phaedrus* 245 C). On this view, then, the very same entity, namely the soul, is both source and subject of motion in itself. What is agent is also, in this case, patient: or, if the language of 'agent/patient' presupposes a distinction, then the soul must be described as in motion (alive) with a motion not due to its being passively moved by anything, even itself. To live and move is of the essence of soul, and it might be argued that it is as absurd to describe the soul as the agent of its own essential property as to speak of the number five as the agent of its own oddness.

(7) Now Aristotle may be right in holding, as against Plato, that the phrases 'X changes (transitive) itself', 'X is changed by itself', are used incoherently unless a difference is admitted between changer and changed. But this hardly entitles Aristotle to claim coherence once this condition is met. On the contrary; if changer must differ from changed, how can 'X changes itself' escape being nonsensical or self-contradictory? On any analysis, it seems, the concept of 'self-change' collapses, for identity of changer with changed conflicts with the meaning of 'changer' and 'changed', while their difference conflicts with the meaning of 'self'. How can it help to say which Aristotle is quite definite. At 4, 254 b28–33, he asserts that there is a difference, and at 5, 257 a31–b13, he attempts changed is on this view changed by something other than

itself. It seems that Aristotle's attempt to make sense of 'self-change' ends by reducing it to change by something other.[4] And if self-change is change in one part of a whole by another part, what is to prevent us predicating 'self-change' of any combination of changer and changed, e.g. craftsman and materials, the stone and whatever pushes it contrary to its natural direction? It is extraordinary that Aristotle does not raise these problems, let alone discuss them. However it is clear enough in outline what his answer to the last would have been. The craftsman and his materials may for some purposes be considered as a whole perhaps, but they do not form one substance, and Aristotle's self-changers are single substances, organisms. Thus the postulated difference between changer and changed within the self-changer is not such as to detract from the unity of its substance. Following this line, we may say that Aristotle's position is this: nothing literally changes itself in the sense that would deny any difference at all between changer and changed. But this does not erase the distinction between being changed by self and being changed by something other. For these two phrases mark two genuinely different relationships: that which holds between elements which together form a substantial unity, and that which holds between beings, themselves each a substance, which together are only a combination.

(8) On this account, then, 'being changed by something other' refers to a relation between substances, and 'being changed by self' to a relation between different elements of a single substance. But how could anyone suppose that no discussion is needed to establish that the relation of 'being changed by' should be predicable on what would appear to be two categorially different levels? Yet from Aristotle no such discussion is forthcoming, and this silence of his is so striking a feature of his whole treatment of self-change that in addition to the philosophical difficulties of this concept we are faced with an extra puzzle in its author's refusal to consider them. For the questions he leaves unsettled are basic on any view. What ontological status, for instance, would he attribute

---

[4] Cf. Solmsen, *Aristotle's System*, p. 233.

to the "something" in a self-changer which is identified with the changer, and that other "something" which is changed? How is it possible to predicate either 'changer' or 'changed' without illegitimately hypostatizing the entities of which they are predicated? With regard to the term 'changed' this difficulty is especially obvious, as the following argument will show.

(9) Every change, at least according to the definition of Book III, results in a new state of that which has undergone the change. If the change is, as Aristotle says it always must be, brought about by a changer, then the subject undergoing it must be described by the correlative term, i.e. as 'changed'. Thus the changed is identical with the subject of change. But the subject ends by being in a new condition of some kind. And in three out of the four types of change which Aristotle recognizes, the new condition is represented by a term predicable of a *substance*. The new state is a quality, a size, or a position in space, and according to the doctrine of the *Categories*, the subjects of these are substances. Thus in a change resulting in such a property the changed must be a substance. And this must be so however the change comes about: whether, for instance, it is self-change or by something other. Thus the changed, even in self-change, must be a substance. Now Aristotle says (VIII. 2, 253a14-15; 7, 261a23-5) that the self-change of organisms is only in respect of place. This view has its difficulties,[5] but at least it shows that Aristotle does not think of self-change as involving some special, mysterious and as yet uncategorized type of terminus *ad quem*. On the contrary, what changes itself moves itself from one place to another, so that *what* it moves when it moves "itself" must be the kind of thing of which place is predicated; i.e., if the doctrine of the *Categories* is retained, a substance. But if the chang*ed* is a substance, then is the chang*er* something else in addition to this substance?

---

[5] Because according to the doctrine of *De Anima* III.9 only animals among living things have the power of natural locomotion; but if plants are not self-changers, then the division of changes in *Physics* VIII.4 into (a) counter-natural, (b) self-changes, and (c) the natural changes of inanimate substances, is not exhaustive, which the argument requires it to be. See also n. 29.

And if so, how can the self-change "whole" be itself a substance, if it consists in a substance plus something else? But perhaps this ought to be dismissed as a spurious paradox generated by gratuitously introducing terms like 'in addition to' and 'plus'. In stating that changer must differ from changed, Aristotle does not state, nor does he necessarily imply, that the difference must be such that the two are *addible*. Presumably he means that in self-change the changer and changed are not numerically different individuals. Resorting to a handy word, let us say that he has in mind different aspects of the same individual. Thus the doctor is a substance and so is the patient, but not necessarily a different one. On such a view the changer in self-change is not a meaninglessly hypostatized *aspect* of a substance, "acting upon" another hypostatized aspect, but is the same *substance*, to which two different descriptions apply. This seems the most promising line of analysis, or at any rate the one least at variance with Aristotle's metaphysics, but Aristotle does not at any point steer us towards it by indicating, for instance, that changer need differ from changed only in description ($\lambda \acute{o} \gamma \omega$) and not numerically. He is as studiously vague as to the *nature* of the difference as he is positive that there is *some* difference. 'That [living things] are changed by something is clear, but what is not clear is how we ought to distinguish in them changer from changed.' (4, 254 b28–30). But if we cannot articulate the distinction, how can we be sure that it is capable of bearing the weight of the changer-changed relation? The next sentence is equally unilluminating:

For it seems that just as in the case of ships and things not constituted by nature, so in the case of animals the changer and changed are distinct ($\delta \iota \eta \rho \eta \mu \acute{e} \nu o \nu$), and in this way [i.e. only when there is a distinction] the whole changes itself. (30–3)

If the illustration points in any definite direction, it is that of the metaphysically disastrous hypostatization of changer and changed as distinct substantial entities, like boat and oarsman. But it is more reasonable to take Aristotle to be saying that just as there is some difference (whatever it may be) between an artefact and what pushes or manipulates it, so there is *some* difference between changer and changed in an animal.

For it is unlikely that he would have used the illustration to specify the type of distinction supposed to obtain in the latter case when he has only just said that it is not clear how this distinction should be made.

(10) Our unanswered questions have so far been of an abstract kind, but even on a more descriptive level he is equally unforthcoming. Even if the metaphysical status of changer and changed in the self-changer is to be left unexplained, we might expect to be told what those features or elements or aspects are to which these roles are assigned. Aristotle gives a list of empirically knowable criteria for distinguishing self-changers: they are alive, they exhibit more than one kind of self-change,[6] they have the power to stop their own changes, they are physically complex (4, 255 a5–18). But the context shows that his purpose in giving this list is not to explain what is involved in self-change but rather to establish that the simple bodies do not count as self-changers, on the ground that they possess none of the characteristics. This says nothing as to which (if any) of these is what being a self-changer consists in, and which are merely signs and symptoms. However, Aristotle could hardly have expected his immediate audience with their Platonic background not to take him as identifying the source of self-change with *soul*. Soul, then, it would be understood, is the changer-element, and body therefore the changed, and being ensouled is not a mere criterion for predicating 'self-changer', but that in virtue of which the predication would be true. That this is Aristotle's meaning in or behind the text of VIII.4 may seem to go without saying.[7] Yet it is odd that he never in the *Physics* mentions soul as the changer-element in self-change. However, we shall see how this omission, whether or not deliberate, helps to smooth the course of the main argument of VIII (*v.i.* paras (33) and (37)).

(11) Perhaps it is not surprising that Aristotle should not have spelt out the equation of soul with changer and body

---

[6] Since he holds that locomotion is the only type of self-change (see para. (9)), this must mean locomotion in different directions.

[7] Simplicius *ad* 255 b28–9 (ed. Diels 1208, 36–7): 'προφανὲς γάρ ἐστιν ὅτι ὑπὸ τῆς ψυχῆς κινεῖται τὴν ὡς ξῷων κίνησιν.'

with changed in the case of live creatures. *Given* the doctrine that these are self-changers, the equation suggests itself. What is puzzling is his willingness to take on the doctrine and its attendant problems. Having argued against Plato's interpretation of 'self-change' he cannot have been entirely unaware of the difficulties threatening his own. Why then think of organisms as self-changing at all? Why say more than that they simply *change* (intransitive)? Of course these substances are physically and psycho-physically complex in ways that set them apart from the inanimate bodies. But why try to think of the elements in the complex, however these are distinguished, as standing to one another in the relation of agent to patient? It may seem that Aristotle is compelled to treat organic creatures in natural change as changed by themselves for the reason that otherwise they would not be changed by anything; which would falsify his universal principle that whatever changes is changed by something. But the principle can be saved without the introduction of 'self-change', for in denying this predicate to the inanimate bodies in their natural motions Aristotle does not deny that they are changed by something, and the "agents" he lights on in this case are paralleled for organisms (*v.s.* paras (3)-(4)).

(12) He goes some way towards providing an answer to this problem when in 4, 254b17-20, he mentions situations in which the natural change of an organism may consist in or involve movement contrary to the natural bent of a limb or organ, or of the body's main material component. Thus it is natural to a bird to move (fly) upwards, but not to the earthy stuff of its body. And in some cases a creature may be unable to perform some function natural to it except by moving a part or organ in a manner contrary to the norm for the part. Thus a man might have to use his hands to walk with, or to grow upwards a plant might have to wind sideways first. If it is of the nature of an organism to pursue certain biological ends as best it can, then in such cases the *organism* may be said to behave naturally, although some bodily part or material is thereby subject to counter-natural change. Thus (*a*) we do differentiate between the organism and its parts, and between it and its matter; and (*b*) we describe their relation

in terms similar to those used for situations in which one external substance acts upon another. The matter moves contrariwise to its own nature as earth or whatever, and it does so *because* of the natural change of the *organism* whose matter it is. Thus there is a basis for applying the language of changer and changed to the organism and its part or to the organism and its matter.[8]

(13) If Aristotle had confined himself to such cases when speaking of the self-change of organisms, the concept would be relatively unproblematic. At least we could understand why he uses it, despite the theoretical difficulty of formulating the difference between changer and changed. A similar difficulty arises over the analysis of common English reflexive phrases such as 'X controls himself', 'X makes himself eat', where what is said to be overridden is not a purely physical propensity of some physical part or component, but a desire or inclination. But inability to give a theoretical account of how the self controlled differs from the self controlling does not debar us from the everyday use of these expressions to hit off something not conveyed by non-reflexive locutions such as either (*a*) the intransitive 'X eats', or (*b*) the transitive 'Y makes X eat' (where X is a different person from Y). In the same way we can see the point of reflexive expressions that imply the checking of a physical tendency. But these considerations do not ease the difficulty of Aristotle's theory, for the simple reason that he sees *all* cases of organic natural change as cases of self-change.

That which is changed by itself changes by nature, as for instance each of the animals. For the animal is changed by itself, and everything that has the principle of change within itself we say changes by nature. Thus the whole animal changes itself by nature, but its body *can change both by nature* and against nature. It depends on what type of change is occurring and on what type of element constitutes the body. (4, 254 b14–20)

[8] The statement that the *whole* organism is agent and its matter or bodily part the patient may appear to conflict with what in paragraph (10) we said was surely Aristotle's implied meaning in VIII.4, viz. that the *soul* is agent. But on the doctrine of *De Anima*, whereby the soul is the form constituting the bodily parts an organic whole, these are two ways of saying the same thing.

Here Aristotle shows that he would describe the animal as a whole as *changing itself* by nature even in the case where its body and bodily parts follow the natural tendencies specific to each. Thus when the man walks on his feet, and when the bird swoops downwards, this according to Aristotle is not merely natural movement of the whole, but self-movement. Now it is true that the drop of a bird as it lets itself drop is, as we say, controlled, since the bird can check and gear it to the purpose in hand. This power to check a natural motion was one of Aristotle's criteria for being a self-changer. But in ordinary discourse, the fact that the falling creature can stop itself and move upwards against the weight of its body would not license the description 'It makes itself move down'. Nor would it be correct to say of someone who indulges a strong inclination to eat, but who can all the same do what might reasonably be described as 'stopping himself from eating', that he 'makes himself eat'. Ordinary discourse, in other words, applies the language of 'self-change' to movements and actions that are actually contrary to nature or inclination, not to those which are not, even when these are in the agent's power to control.

(14) The reason, I believe, for Aristotle's failure to discuss or even acknowledge the difficulties we have been surveying is this: the concept of living things as self-changers figures in *Physics* VIII not as an item of any interest in itself, but purely as a step in an argument concerned with other issues. 'Self-change' tells us nothing about organic substance, nor about the agency of beings familiar in experience. It is intended to uphold a certain conclusion concerning the ultimate eternal source of change in the universe as a whole, and Aristotle has accordingly invested 'self-change' with no more meaning than is necessary for the discharge of this ulterior function. I shall argue below, moreover, that attempts to precisify the concept as applied to organisms can only render it unfit for the larger task; thus it is left obscure not because it is difficult, but because if clarified it would be useless for the main argument, and the main argument provides its only *raison d'être* in the *Physics*. That argument we must now consider, in order to prove this claim.

(15) Let us begin with the opening words of Book VIII:

Did change ever come into being, not having been before, and will it revert to non-being, so that then nothing will change: or is it something that always was and always will be, an immortal and unceasing property of things, like a kind of life of all beings constituted by nature? (250 b11–15)

This, if a genuine query, is a courageous one to propose at this stage, for it calls into question the fundamental starting point of many elaborate investigations already conducted. I mean the assumption that the nature of a substance is a principle of change. Possession of such principle, it was stated in II.1, is what distinguishes a natural substance from an artefact; possession of a principle for a specific type of change is what defines the specific type of a natural substance. Yet what stronger basis had Aristotle for these assumptions than everyday experience?[9] It is one thing to observe that an inner principle of change distinguishes the natural substances with which we are familiar from artefacts; another to erect this into a necessary feature of natural substance as such. Aristotle may have been justified in assuming that no one would dispute the *observation*. But some argument is required to uphold the view that the observed difference is a definitive difference. It is not, for instance, self-evidently absurd to suppose that the natural world might for a time have existed, or one day exist, without any change at all taking place in it. Certain eminent thinkers had believed themselves to be talking sense when they stated that just such a changeless state of things had occurred or would occur in the history of the natural world. And if this is even possible, let alone true, then change and principles of change cannot be what *defines* natural substance, since according to such hypotheses, the world of nature, i.e. of natural substances, could exist without change. Now Aristotle never envisaged this problem in Book II. There he simply assumed that the natural world is as *we* have always found it to be (and cannot perhaps imagine it otherwise than being). He pronounced it absurd to ask for proof that nature (in the sense of an inner principle of change) exists:

---

[9] Cf. Mansion, p. 101.

That nature exists it would be absurd to try to prove, for it is clear that many beings are like this [i.e. possessed of such principles]. And to prove what is obvious by means of what is not is the mark of someone who cannot distinguish what is knowable in itself from what is not. (II.1, 193 a3-6)

It never occurred to him that it might not be so absurd to ask for proof that nature, in this same sense, never fails to 'exist'; i.e. that the to us indisputable occurrence of change-originating substances is not just an episode in the history of the physical universe. But if it is possible that 'nature' in the sense of II.1 has application in some epochs but not in others, then 'nature' in that sense cannot be taken as the starting point for inquiries into physical reality as such. This is the threat posed by the theories to which only now, in Book VIII, Aristotle gives his attention.

(16) Empedocles, for instance, had held (or so Aristotle tells us in VIII.1, 250 b26-251 a5) that the universe as a whole alternates between periods of stasis and periods of change. Aristotle interprets Empedocles as implying that these periods belong to a single continuous history, so that when change takes over from stasis or vice versa it is not as if a totally new universe has come into being. The alternation is a single pattern, not a succession of discrete universes. So on this view, *this* world, at present undergoing an age of change, has been and will be devoid of motion and development. It makes no difference whether we are to suppose that there are special types of substance which get their chance of existence only in the epochs of stasis, or that throughout history the same types always exist, expressing their natures sometimes in change, sometimes in total non-change. Either way Aristotle's earlier starting point loses any claim to absolute status. But the alternating theory ascribed to Empedocles is only one example of a class of speculations threatening this claim. The threat is the same on any supposition that change is not continually present, whether the theory be that it alternates with non-change, or that non-change once and for all preceded or will supersede it.

(17) I shall not dwell on the question of the accuracy of Aristotle's account of Empedocles in VIII.1, nor on whether

he was fair in including the views of Anaxagoras and Plato among those which he has to combat. Nor shall I engage in a detailed account of his arguments that there never was nor will be a time without change. For the present purpose it is enough to say that by the end of VIII.2 he takes himself to have established this conclusion, thus answering the opening question of Book VIII.[10] His answer moreover, makes no overt appeal to the original conception of natural substance. He does not, for instance, formally assume this and then draw the conclusion as follows: 'Natural substance is by definition that which is possessed of an inner principle of change; there can be no natural world without natural substance; therefore change is an inherent feature of the natural world throughout its history.' It seems in short that in VIII.1-2 Aristotle proceeds as if the original conception were not available for building upon. This is the only indication that he intended the arguments of VIII.1-2 to *support* it. However, whether or not this was his intention, support is what they logically provide: not by entailing the concept's validity, but by contradicting a group of theories whose truth would undermine it.[11]

[10] In fact, the position argued for in VIII.1 comprises two logically distinct theses which Aristotle does not separate: (i) At no time is the natural universe devoid of change; (ii) Time is infinite in both directions. If we assume that the natural universe exists only in and through time, then the II.1 doctrine of natural substance depends on the truth of (i) but not on that of (ii). For the doctrine requires that the existence of change as such should not have a beginning or end *within* the history of the natural universe, i.e. a beginning or end in time. But this does not entail that there might not be a sense in which time itself, and the history of the natural world, has a beginning and/or end. And if there were the possibility of a changeless state of things "before" or "after" time, this would not conflict with the view that natural substance is essentially characterized by change, since by the initial assumption what exists "beyond" time would not be a natural substance. (Thus Aristotle's doctrine of natural substance does not require him to argue, as he does in VIII.1, against the *Timaeus* view (taking it literally) that time was created. This is fortunate, since the argument rests on a fallacious inference from the truism that time cannot have a beginning or end *in time*, to the conclusion that it cannot in any sense be said to begin or end. Cf. G. E. M. Anscombe, 'Aristotle', in *Three Philosophers*, G. E. M. Anscombe and P. T. Geach, pp. 60-1.) However in the rest of this chapter I have followed Aristotle in his amalgamation of theses (i) and (ii): thus, e.g., I use 'eternal change' to imply, as he does, a change that has no beginning or end in time *and* which is infinite because time is infinite.

[11] However, VIII.3, 253 b5-6 'ὑπόθεσις γαρ ὅτι ἡ φύσις ἀρχὴ τῆς κινήσεως', is not the remark of someone who sees any current need to defend the II.1

(18) The positive case for the everlastingness of change is made in Chapter 1, and in 2 Aristotle answers what he takes to be the main objections. These all start from the same point, namely the undeniable fact of changes that begin and cease. The first objection states temporal finitude to be a necessary characteristic of all change; for all change, says the imaginary opponent, is from contrary to contrary, one of which marks the beginning, the other the end of the change, so that no change can continue indefinitely (252b10-12). Secondly, if, as Aristotle has argued, change never comes into being not having been before, how is it that there are beings, e.g. the inanimate substances, that begin to change, not having changed before? (12-16). And thirdly, when we consider living things such as ourselves, it is even more obvious that a change can simply start, without the subject's having been already in course of change. But if this can happen with the finite organized substances within nature, why should it not also be the case with the natural world as a whole, assuming this to be an organized entity logically analogous to those familiar organized substances which we call living things? The latter put themselves into motion from a state of rest, so that their self-change has a beginning in time: what reason then have we for supposing that the universe as a whole did not begin to change, having been previously at rest? (17-28). This last objection seems irrelevant at this stage of the argument, for it assumes that Aristotle's own position entails (a) that there is a change that belongs to the universe as a whole considered as a single subject, and (b) that this change is everlasting. But neither Aristotle's arguments nor his conclusion in Chapter 1 logically commits him to either of these propositions. The logical truth-conditions of the conclusion that there never was nor will be a time without change may be presented as an inclusive disjunction: Either (a) there never was nor will be a time when it is not the case that some change or other is occurring, or (b) there is some change such that there never was nor will be a time when it is not occurring.

conception of nature. The tone of the preceding passage echoes that of II.1, 193 a3-6. But does 253b5-6 express the original unquestioned attitude of II.1; or does it rather reflect confidence newly gained through successfully defending the II.1 starting point?

And the second disjunct could be true *either* because (b_1) there is an everlasting change of which the world as a whole is the subject, *or* because (b_2) there is an everlasting change whose subject is some being within the world. But Aristotle's actual arguments in VIII.1 make no reference to the disjunct (b) nor to (b_1) or (b_2). Starting (like his presumed opponent in VIII.2) from the fact of temporally finite change, Aristotle has argued in 1 that the conditions under which finite changes begin and cease involve prior and posterior changes. Obviously this does not depend on the assumption that any particular change is of other than finite duration. He also argued that the concept of a 'time without change' is incoherent, on the ground that time has already (IV.11) been shown to be 'a sort of qualification of change' (251 b27-8). But there is no suggestion in VIII.1 that there must be some *single* everlasting change of which time is the qualification.

(19) However, the last of the objections in VIII.2 is not as inconsequential as it may seem. The connection becomes apparent in Chapter 6, where Aristotle sets forth the presuppositions of the thesis that there is always change. One of these is that there should be at least one change that is individually everlasting. A temporally infinite succession of finite changes is possible only if some one change in the universe is of infinite duration and absolutely continuous. In other words, although the proposition that there is *a* change without beginning and end does not follow by logical necessity from the proposition that there never was nor will be a time without some change or other, the truth of the former proposition is for Aristotle a metaphysical necessity, given the truth of the latter. His reason for this we shall consider presently. Meanwhile, however, he is not yet ready to assert the former proposition, since to do so would be pointless in the context of replies to objections to the doctrine that there is never a time without change. The assertion could not function as an effective premiss in an argument supporting this doctrine against the objections, for the objector would simply refuse to accept it. Experience shows us changes which begin and cease; but experience could not show that any single change goes on for ever. So in Chapter 2 Aristotle

contents himself with pointing out that the possibility of an individually everlasting change is not excluded. He answers the first objection by agreeing that change between contraries begins and ceases, but says that this is no reason why there should not also be a change (not between contraries) that is everlasting and eternally unbroken (252 b29–253 a1). He further (253 a2 ff.) states that changes that have a beginning (especially the self-locomotion of animals) depend on prior changes in the environment; which implies that if there is some entity (as for instance the whole universe, mentioned by the objector at 252 b25–8) that *has* no environment, *its* change, if it has one, must necessarily never have begun.

(20) In the context, however, this implication is not stressed, and the main burden of Aristotle's reply in 2 consists in an expanded version of the point already propounded in 1: that when a finitely changing object begins to change, this is not an absolute beginning of change in the sense that there never was, or need have been, any preceding change. A beginning of change in a particular substance necessarily implies a prior shift in external conditions, which explains why the change begins just when it does. (And this, Aristotle makes clear (253 a15–19), is as true for the self-changes of animate creatures as it is for the motions of lifeless matter.) *If* it is assumed that a particular beginning of change in a particular substance is a beginning of change as such, and not merely of change in that particular substance, then of course it would be correct to argue, as the objector does at one point (252 b12–16), that the existence of substances that begin and cease to change is inimical to the doctrine that there is never not change. But the assumption is false. With this it would seem that Aristotle has adequately defended his doctrine. Yet in his view there still remains a serious difficulty: this concerns the possibility of temporally finite changes, and therefore of substances whose natures are expressed thereby. How can it be that some things are sometimes changing and sometimes not, rather than always changing or always at rest (253 a3–7; 22–4)? Why this is a difficulty is not immediately clear, but the context shows that he sees it as a problem to be faced if one holds the view that change as such never begins

nor ceases. The objector of Chapter 2, he implies, was right to wonder how the fact of particular finite change is consistent with that view; and the puzzlement has not been eradicated by Aristotle's answers in that chapter. Thus he begins 3:

> The starting point of our enquiry is a question which also relates to the problem already mentioned: What is that on account of which some things sometimes change and sometimes revert to a state of rest? (3, 253 a22–4)

(21) The sequence of thought between Chapters 2 and 3 is obscure. Given the proof in 1 that temporally finite changes are necessarily preceded (and succeeded) by others, what more is needed than the replies to objections in 2 to reconcile the fact of temporally finite particular changes with the doctrine that change as such is not temporally finite? The problem is not one of logical consistency but of metaphysical compossibility. It is not enough, he says, to explain the beginning of a finite change by reference to prior changes in the environment, for the alteration in the environment equally stands in need of explanation.

> It is not in the least absurd that something should change which has not been previously changing, given that the external cause of change is sometimes present, sometimes not. However, we have to consider how this is possible: I mean, how it is that one and the same potential agent of change should sometimes give rise to a change and sometimes not, in the same subject. (2, 253 a2–5)

This passage shows that what Aristotle finds puzzling is not just the fact of changes that begin and cease, but variation in general. The variation of a natural substance between change and non-change is one instance of this, while another is the variation in the substance's spatial relations to those external factors whose presence converts them from potential into actual causes of its change.

(22) But *why* should Aristotle find variation problematic? To him, apparently, the difficulty was so obviously a difficulty that he does not even pause to state what it is before proceeding straight to the task of solving it. This task takes him from the beginning of 3 to the end of 6, and it is only in 6, where

a solution is finally announced (260 a11–14), that the modern reader can begin to see the nature of the puzzle. What emerges from 6 is that it is not so much the *doctrine* of everlasting change that casts doubt on the possibility of substances whose nature it is to vary between change and rest, but rather a certain *postulate* required to make sense of the truth of that doctrine. The postulate is that there exists at least one eternal and absolutely changeless cause on which the fact of everlasting change depends: and the difficulty is to see how such a cause could give rise to effects that are in any way variable. Let us consider these points in turn, first the postulate, then the resulting difficulty. Aristotle takes himself to have established not merely that there always was and will be change, but that this is necessarily so. The question now is how this necessary and everlasting fact of change is possible. To answer the question we must start from what we know beyond any doubt, and what we know is that there are temporally finite changes preceded and succeeded by other temporally finite changes. We do not at the outset *know*, prior to argument, that there is any single particular change that is individually everlasting. Hence to explain the everlastingness of change as such, we begin by assuming that what makes change as such everlasting is simply the fact that there is an everlasting succession of finite changes. We must, moreover, regard this succession as *necessarily* unbroken and everlasting, since otherwise we have no reason to accept that change as such is necessarily everlasting. But what can account for the necessary everlastingness of the succession? Not, Aristotle implies, a *succession* of causes, each responsible for one of a succession of changes, for the succession of causes must be necessarily everlasting, if this is to be true of the succession of their effects; and the former succession will stand as much in need of explanation as the latter. Nor can the cause of the succession of changes be identified with any single substance whose nature is expressed in temporally finite change, for just as change in such a substance gives way to rest, so every such substance passes away, one generation replacing another. Nor, finally, can the totality of such substances account for the infinite series, for this "totality" is an infinite multitude which does not all exist at once, so that it cannot be an actual cause even for a limited time, let alone throughout all time.

The eternity and continuity of the succession cannot be accounted for by any one of them, nor by all together. For it is eternal and neces-sary, while the totality of them is infinite and they do not all exist at one time. (258 b29-32)

The cause must be some single being, not a succession of beings, and it must be eternally present throughout the series. Thus, Aristotle concludes, even if the immediate reason why change as such is everlasting is that there is an infinite succes-sion of finitely changing and transiently existing substances, each giving rise to changes in itself and in other things, still:

. . . it is nonetheless true that there is something that comprehends (περιέχει) them, being other than any of them, and that this is the cause of some things existing while others cease to exist, and of the continuity of change (τῆς συνεχοῦς μεταβολῆς). (259 a3-5)

(23) Everlasting change then depends on an eternal cause, or causes:[12] for Aristotle's argument does not exclude the possi-bility of a plurality as such, but only of a successive plurality. In addition to being eternal, the cause or causes must, he assumes, be absolutely changeless. Aristotle does not make explicit the reason for this assumption. In VIII.5 he argues for the point which we have already considered (*v.s.* Ch. IV, paras (22) ff.), viz. that causing change is not itself a kind of change of which the cause is subject. But the fact that the eternal cause, insofar as it functions as cause, neither changes nor needs to be able to change, does not entail that it is in all respects changeless; any more than the fact that building is neither a change nor a potentiality for change in the builder entails that the man who builds is in every respect changeless. However, the vital difference between the two cases, although Aristotle does not spell it out, is that the changes effected by building are of limited duration and interruptible, so that there is no contradiction in supposing that the individual who builds might change in ways that would terminate the build-ing activity; whereas the eternal cause is postulated as the

[12] Nothing in this discussion hangs on whether the references in VIII.6 to a possible plurality of eternal changeless causes are late insertions.

cause of an *eternal* effect, which rules out its liability to any
changes that could suspend its activity as cause. And since
all that we know of this postulated cause is the function for
which it was postulated, viz. to be the cause of everlasting
change, its absolute unchangeability in the actual fulfilment
of this function implies that for our knowledge it must figure
as absolutely unchangeable *simpliciter*. Now it is this that
creates the problem for varying substances and their varying
conditions. For how can variation result from the eternally
unvarying causation of such a cause? If such a cause can be
supposed to produce *change* at all, the change must be a
process whose properties mirror its own as far as it is possible
for change to mirror the changeless. The change, then will be
an *eternal* process which is no more made up of successive
finite processes than its cause consists of successive transient
substances. Thus it would seem that the effect of the eternal
cause or causes can only be one or more than one individually
eternal changes. Now unless there is some escape from this
reasoning, Aristotle's argument up to this point could legitimately be converted into a proof that the succession of finite
changes, and of substances whose nature is expressed in finite
change, is not infinite. For if the succession can be supposed
infinite only on the assumption of an eternally unchanging
cause, and if such a cause can cause only change that is individually unbroken, then the concept of infinite succession is
self-invalidating; for the *infinity* of the succession must be
explained by an assumption which rules out the possibility of
succession. So that if there is succession of changes, which no
one can deny, the succession itself must be of finite duration;
which is as much as to say that there has been or will be a
time devoid of finite change, and therefore of natural substances as defined in II.1. But if such beings exist only in
certain temporal pockets of the world's history, it is sheer
parochialism to assign them the central position in what is
intended as a universal philosophy of nature.

(24) Aristotle's answer is skilful. He postulates a *tertium
quid* causally intermediate between the eternal changeless
cause and the varying transient effects, which participates
sufficiently in the characteristics of each to be rationally

conceivable as the effect of the former and cause of the latter. This connecting link is a process of change which resembles the changeless cause in being absolutely unvarying in its form and unbroken in its duration, while at the same time resembling variegated change in that it too is a *change*. Since there can be no change without a changing subject, and since a single unbroken change presupposes a single individual subject persisiting throughout, it follows that there must be at least one eternally existing entity other than the changeless cause, viz. the subject of the change which this cause brings about. Thus at 6, 259 b32-260 a5, Aristotle writes:

If there exists something which is always such as we have said, a cause of change which is itself changeless and eternal, that which is primarily changed by it must also be eternal. This [*sc.* the conclusion that the primary patient cannot be any transiently existing and transiently changing substance] is also clear from the fact that otherwise there would be no coming into being and passing away and variation (μετα-βολή) of other things, unless there is a cause of change which is itself a subject of change. For the changeless will always cause change in the same way, the change being [*sc.* numerically] one, since it does not itself vary in its relations to what it changes.

Whereas a *changing* entity, even if its change is single and eternal, may be supposed to stand in different relations at different times to other beings, and so to be able to affect them variously. Aristotle's next sentence, according to the generally accepted text, shows that he does not regard variation as the immediate effect of the eternal change that is due immediately to the changeless; instead he separates variation from the changeless by another intermediate eternal change. (260 a5-10) The details of the implied cosmology are not made clear in the *Physics*, nor need they be for Aristotle's present purpose, which is to work out the bare metaphysical basis of an eternal sequence of finitely changing substances. Logically, this reasoning does not commit him to identifying the eternal change whose existence has been proved *a priori* with any process known to us through observation. However, he and his audience were already disposed to regard the motions of the heavens as eternal, so that heavenly bodies were naturally cast in the role which he has shown must, as a matter of metaphysical necessity, be filled by *something or other*. Once the general role is assigned, questions concerning the number and causal order of distinct eternal (celestial) motions and moving bodies become problems for science, to be solved by whatever hypotheses best explain the astronomical data.[13]

(25) To establish the position outlined above, Aristotle needs to have reasoned his way past a serious difficulty, and it is here that his argument depends crucially on the concept of self-change. But before considering this, I want to examine what to me a spurious problem raised in connection with the position itself by Professor Solmsen. Solmsen claims to find an inconsistency between the doctrine of an eternal ultimate cause of change in the universe and the II.1 conception of natural substances as containing each within itself a principle of change. Describing the inference to the eternal ultimate cause as 'a Platonic line of thought', Solmsen writes:

Aristotle has so faithfully preserved the Platonic line of thought — and how could he help it if he wished to find the first mover? — that he does grave harm to one of his own new doctrines. As we know, Book II

---

[13] Paragraphs (22)–(24) are an exposition of VIII.6, 258 b26–259 a6 and 259 b32–260 a19. These two passages together yield the following argument (let us call it A): (i) Given that the sequence of finite changes is eternal, there must be an eternal changeless cause; (ii) given that there is an eternal changeless cause, there must be an eternal change (and an eternal subject of this change) by the mediation of which the changeless cause operates and which connects it with finite changes. However, Aristotle also argues (B): (i) Given that change as such is eternal, there must be some single unbroken eternal change; (ii) given that there is a single unbroken eternal change, there must be an eternal subject for this change and an eternal changeless cause, since otherwise it would not be unbroken (VIII.6, 259 a13–20; step B (ii) is elaborated in VIII.10, 267 a 21–b6). In B the pattern of thought neatly matches the relations between the objects, the unbroken eternal change acting as middle term in the argument just as it is causally intermediate in reality. In A, the changeless cause is the logical middle term. I have preferred to expound A rather than B, partly because Aristotle gives rather more space to the two parts of A, but mainly because B is an inferior argument, offering no plausible account of the inference in B (i) from the eternity of change as such to a single eternal change. Noting this *non sequitur*, Ross and Solmsen hold that Aristotle's 'certainty that [some single unbroken eternal] change exists arises from a reason which has never been mentioned in the argument' (Ross, *Aristotle's Physics*, pp. 91–2). According to Ross, the 'unmentioned reason' is 'observation [*sic*] of the never-ceasing rotation of the heavens' (ibid.), while in Solmsen's view (*Aristotle's System*, pp. 225–8) it is the influence of Platonic cosmology. No doubt observation and inherited outlooks play a part, but the text of VIII.6 *also* provides an explicit argument, namely A, for the alleged *non sequitur*. Both commentators overlook this, perhaps because B is more prominent than A in *Metaphysics* Λ.

defines nature as 'a source of movement' and natural objects as 'having a source of movement in themselves'. What in Plato was reserved for soul has in Aristotle become the property of all nature. Yet that which has the source of movement in itself should certainly be able to initiate its own movement and not be in need of receiving the impulse from a remote principle. Evidently in Book VIII Aristotle is developing a legacy of the Platonic world soul which conflicts with his own doctrine that all natural entities have their source and principle of movement in themselves.[14]

I do not dispute Solmsen's account of the historical development of Aristotle's position in *Physics* VIII from certain Platonic doctrines, but only question the view here expressed, that this development conflicts with Aristotle's own concept of the nature of a natural substance. The seriousness of this conflict (supposing Solmsen to be right) depends partly on the general light in which we regard Book VIII. From any point of view, the most important conclusions of VIII are by Solmsen's account inconsistent with all those earlier writings that take the II.1 concept of nature as starting point. On the other hand, Book VIII itself could be regarded as broadly speaking self-coherent if we were to interpret it as a free-standing enquiry which neither questions nor seeks to justify that earlier concept. But if, as I have suggested, VIII is to be read as an attempt to defend the latter, (a) by showing that the existence of natural substance as defined in II.1 is indeed an eternal feature of the universe (thus vindicating the title of 'substance' for objects falling under the definition), and (b) by explaining how this is possible, then if Solmsen's criticism is apt, Book VIII is not only rampantly at odds with itself but provides all the materials for a *reductio ad absurdum* of Aristotle's original concept of nature.

(26) It is for the gravity of these implications that the criticism merits attention, rather than for its plausibility. It arises partly from the author's apparent inability to see how something could coherently be said *both* to change by its own nature *and* to depend on something else for the realization of this change; and partly on his belief that in certain passages

---

[14] *Aristotle's System*, p. 232. See also pp. 233–4, 100–2, and 'Platonic Influences', pp. 228–9.

of VIII Aristotle actually does what to Solmsen is the only consistent thing for him to do, namely sets aside his earlier theory of nature. Certainly, *if* at any point Aristotle did this, his doing so would be evidence that (at moments anyway) he sensed some inconsistency between that theory and the newly established position of VIII. But in fact there is nothing in VIII to suggest that he is troubled in the way in which Solmsen thinks he ought to be. Solmsen is presumably leaning on his own assumption that at 4, 254 b 14–15, Aristotle makes 'self-change' synonymous with 'natural change' (*v.s.* para. (2), note 2). If this were so it would entail that Aristotle is no longer prepared to ascribe nature to inanimate substances. But there is nothing to support the assumption of synonymy, as we saw. Solmsen also seems to regard Aristotle's insistence on a distinction between changer and changed in the self-changer as entailing that nothing can be properly described as 'changed by itself': which on the synonymy assumption would imply that nothing can be said to 'change by its own nature'. Finally (although this is not made clear), Solmsen also seems to draw support from those passages in VIII.2 and 6 where Aristotle argues that all sublunary changes, even those of living creatures, are causally dependent on prior changes in the environment. It is true that Aristotle paid virtually no attention to this aspect of change when first expounding the doctrine of nature in Book II, and brings it now into focus only when he needs it to help support the thesis that there can never have been a time without some change or other. But there is no need to interpret this shift of interest as a withdrawal from the earlier doctrine, which, as we have stressed from the first, is entirely consistent with the view (which no sane person could deny) that natural substances are not absolutely self-sufficient sources of their natural changes. A cursory glance at 5, 260 a 1–10, where Aristotle speaks of an eternally changing body as proximate eternal changer[15] of sublunary substances, being responsible by its activity for their coming to be and passing away and other variations, might cause us to fear for the earlier doctrine

---

[15] This is not the outermost sphere, but that of the sun, which is 'moved by something which itself is in motion but owes its motion to the motionless'. Cf. *De Gen. et Corr.* II.10, 336 a 31 ff.

of nature: but only as long as we fail to note that Aristotle has already in 4 committed himself to using the active and passive of '*κινεῖν*' in a blanket sense to cover a number of types of causal dependence, some of which have nothing to do with immediate determination of the *form* of the dependent change. If a releaser from hindrance can be called a 'changer', then why not also a heavenly body such as the sun, whose eternal rotation through positions at differing distances from the earth ensures the continual passage of seasons conditioning the transiently varying lives of sublunary substances? And why should the sun, any more than the releaser, be thought to usurp the change-forming function earlier assigned to the natures of these substances, or rather, to the substances themselves considered as natured? But if natural changes are compatible with dependence on a proximate eternal cause such as the sun, there is no reason why they should not be also compatible with dependence on the ultimate changeless cause which sustains, via however many causal stages, the sun's motion and the sequence of its finite effects.[16] Solmsen, it seems, has failed to take full account of Aristotle's view of

[16] Solmsen describes Aristotle in *Physics* VIII as maintaining 'the causal dependence, by way of *chain transmission* [my italics], of all other movements and changes in the world on [the] *primum mobile*', 'Platonic Influences', p. 216; cf. *Aristotle's System*, p. 248. This suggests a universal mechanistic determination which indeed would rule out change from a thing's own nature as explained in II.1. But while Aristotle in VIII maintains universal *dependence* of all changes on the ultimate eternal rotation, he is aware that dependence takes other forms than the reception of transmitted motion. (The generator and liberator are agents of natural inanimate movement, but by making possible, not by transmitting.) Since 'transmission' literally implies that the self-same change is passed on to the patient, the theory of VIII not only does not entail but actually rules out dependence-by-transmission of all changes on the motion of the *primum mobile*, since if this eternal motion were passed on, what is passed on would be eternal, and there could result *no* finite changes. It is true that in VIII.5 Aristotle examines causal series in which the dependent changes might not unreasonably be described as 'transmitted': the man pushes the stick which pushes the stone, etc. Here the dependent changes are counter-natural to their subjects. Aristotle's point is that every such series starts with a 'self-change', of which a human voluntary movement would be an example. Thus, e.g., if a particular eternal rotation is simply the mechanical effect of the rotation of an ulterior body, still the series must originate with a 'self-rotation' (involving an unchanging agent and rotating patient). But there is no evidence that Aristotle thinks that all other changes stand to the eternal self-motion in the *same* type of dependence relation; i.e. that all, eternal and finite, are to this self-motion as its mechanically determined dependents. If he did think this, how could he take the man's voluntary movement as an example of self-change?

the ultimate changeless cause. Perhaps it is Solmsen's pre-occupation with the Platonic antecedents of this concept that causes him to overlook the way in which it actually protects the Aristotelian doctrine of nature. If, as Aristotle insists, the ultimate cause must manifest itself in an eternal change, this is because it cannot manifest itself in finite sublunary *changes*,[17] but (at most at their level) in the *fact that the series* of such changes is endless. But this means that the ultimate cause in no way competes for the role of nature in Book II. For an inner principle of change and stasis does what the ultimate cause (as demonstrated in VIII.6) could not conceivably do: namely manifest itself in transitory events; while the ultimate cause does what sublunary natures individually and collectively could not conceivably do, namely ensure the necessary eternal continuity of the series of substances in which those natures are realized.[18]

(27) The real conceptual difficulty besetting Aristotle's position is this. He has argued (*a*) that the *eternity* of the series presupposes an eternal changeless cause, and (*b*) that its *variegation* presupposes a cause in process of change. He has then (*c*) related these two presupposed entities by causally subordinating the second to the first, and this move has led him to postulate (*d*) that the change in the second entity is such as to reflect, as far as possible, the invariance of the first. Thus, as he says at 3, 253 a28–32, the sequence of beings that are sometimes changing and sometimes at rest can be explained only on the assumption that not everything is of this kind, but that something is always changing and something always unchanging. But now why should we suppose that the always unchanging and the always changing are *different* beings? Why, in other words, should we not accept the arguments (*a*) and (*b*) above, but put them together so as to draw a different conclusion from Aristotle's, viz. that the ultimate cause is a unitary being comprising within itself *both* eternal change *and* eternal changelessness, in that it ever-lastingly changes with a *changeless* change? This is in fact the true description of the entity which for Aristotle stands to

[17] Cf. Zeller, *Aristotle and the Earlier Peripatetics*, vol. I, p. 421.
[18] For further discussion see Appendix to Ch. V.

the ultimate cause as its immediate patient; and our question now is why this entity needs to be regarded as a patient at all, rather than as the ultimate cause itself. For Aristotle by his own reasoning is anyway forced to endow the *primum mobile* with eternal change and eternal unchangingness (i.e. continuity and uniformity of change); and eternal change and unchangingness are the two properties needed to account for the endless succession of transitory changes. It seems as if in postulating distinct beings as bearers of the two properties, Aristotle is pointlessly reifying the properties themselves. But if we refuse to allow him this move, he cannot get beyond the *primum mobile* itself; and since (i) its demonstrable properties account for the sequence of finite changes, and (ii) reasoning from these premises can go no further, *it* may reasonably be termed the ultimate source of all change.[19] And since, as Aristotle will argue extensively in VIII.7-9, *locomotion* is the one type of change that could continue eternally, it would follow that the ultimate cause is some kind of corporeal object moving through space.

(28) If an opponent put this point to Aristotle no doubt he would reply that even if an eternal body in eternal circular motion is adequate to account for the effects which it is postulated to explain, still it is not adequate to account for its own motion: this change like any other must depend on an agent, and this agent must be in some sense distinct from the moving body itself, so that it is the agent, not the moving body, that is the true ultimate cause. But the opponent could justly complain that so far nothing has been said to block the following move: Why should we not conceive of the primary eternal body as analogous to earth and fire? Just as the natures of these substances are natures for tracing out certain characteristic paths through space, so, let us say, it is the nature of the former to trace out (for its parts, not for its total bulk, since it rotates always about the same centre) a

---

[19] Philoponus *ad* 259 b32, ed. Vitelli 893, 6 ff., writes as if someone had indeed suggested that an eternally moving body is a sufficient cause of the unbroken succession of generated things' '. . . ἐπειδὴ τῆς ἀιδίως τῶν γενητῶν διαδο-χῆς ἀνάγκη εἶναι ἔν τι καὶ ἀίδιον αἴτιον, τοῦτο δὲ ὁ μὲν ἴσως ἂν εἴποι κινούμενον εἶναι ὁ δὲ ἀκίνητον, διὰ τοῦτο δείκνυσιν ὅτι εἴτε κινούμενον εἴη τοῦτο τὸ ἀίδιον, ἀνάγκη καὶ ἀκίνητον εἶναί τι ἀίδιον ἀφ'οῦ τὸ κινούμενον ἀιδίως κινεῖται . . .'

circular path. This in fact is precisely the position for which
Aristotle himself argues in *De Caelo* I.2-3, and he also says
in that book that there is nothing superior ('κρεῖττον') to the
eternal body that could act as agent of its change (I.9, 279
a33-4).[20] We may spell out the challenge to the *Physics* VIII
position as follows: if it is the *nature* of the primary eternal
body to rotate, then the rotation does not require an agent.[21]
For firstly, if the relation of this body to its own rotation is
comparable to that of fire to motion upward, then the
eternal body's *nature* cannot be regarded as agent of its
change. The nature of fire, as Aristotle makes clear in VIII.4,
is not the agent of fire's rising: this follows from his refusing
to class fire etc. as self-changers, and from his statement that
in such substances the inner principle is not for causing the
natural change, but "suffering" it. The only agents that he
recognizes here are external substances which have made the
motion possible. But secondly: the primary body cannot be
supposed to stand to any other substances in the relation in
which fire stands to the external agents of its natural action.
The body must be eternal, hence ungenerated, and since its
motion is not only continuous but necessarily so (for it could
not otherwise account for the *necessarily* unbroken succession
of finite changes), it is immune to any possibility of hindrance, hence owes nothing to a liberator. In short, if fire
were ungenerated and were so powerful that nothing could
hinder its natural motion, then fire too would be without an

[20] This common interpretation of the passage is disputed by Cherniss, *Aristotle's Criticism of Plato*, etc., pp. 587-8. Solmsen's rebuttal of Cherniss (*Aristotle's
System*, p. 308, n. 30) is in my view unanswerable. But even if Cherniss were right
about Aristotle's meaning, this would not affect the logical point that a distinct
agent is redundant if the eternal body is of a nature to rotate. See Appendix
to Ch. V.

[21] *De Caelo* I is remarkable for the way in which two contrary tendencies contribute to the same conclusion, viz. that there is no distinct mover of the rotating
body (although, notoriously, this is not a conclusion to which Aristotle consistently
seems to keep in *De Caelo* as a whole). Firstly, the comparison with the sublunary
simple bodies, and especially the attribution of a nature specifiable like theirs in
purely locomotory terms, makes of the heavenly rotation a thoroughly natural
fact, representable by physical concepts and no more dependent than ordinary
sublunary motions on a mysterious transnatural agency (cf. Solmsen, 'Platonic Influences', pp. 226-7). But secondly, the eternity, uniformity, and perfect circularity of the heavenly motion manifest the divinity of the moving subject, and
now it is this divinity that excludes dependence on an agent (cf. below, paras
(43) f.)

agent: which does not entail that fire would *lack* motion, but rather the opposite, i.e. that its nature to move would have absolutely free play. And so, for all that has been shown to the contrary, it may be with the eternally rotating body, or bodies.

(29) In *Physics* VIII, however, Aristotle does not hesitate to claim a distinct agent for the primary eternal motion. Indeed he proceeds as if unaware of the possibility of an account such as that just suggested or as if it needed no refutation. Presumably, then, he is viewing the topic from a conceptual basis that keeps this problem out of sight altogether, or else solves it without ado. Either way, that basis is provided by the notion of *'self-change'*, which comes to the fore in 4 and 5, i.e. between the first and last stages of the enquiry which opens in 3 with the question of how an eternity of finite change is possible, and ends in 6 by stating that it is possible only on the assumption of an eternal motion and a changeless source of that motion. To reach the latter position by rational steps, Aristotle needs a concept that meets the following requirements: (*a*) it comprises within itself the notion of something changing, and of something distinct although not physically distinct which is the cause of change; (*b*) it can be illustrated and therefore proved meaningful by instances in the sublunary world; (*c*) it can be shown to be necessarily instantiated on the level of the primary eternal motion. The notion of 'self-change' in *Physics* VIII meets all these requirements, and indeed could have been constructed purely with them in view, since it has virtually no content beyond what they demand. Our earlier discussion of self-change has already taken account of (*a*) and (*b*). Let us therefore turn to Aristotle's efforts to meet (*c*). To do this, we must follow his manoeuvres with 'self-change' in some detail.

(30) When he first introduces the concept in Chapter 4, it is in order to help sustain that chapter's conclusion, that whatever changes is changed by *something*. From this he doubtless hopes to be able to deduce that even what eternally moves is moved by something. But his ground is weak, for the range of cases on which he bases the universal proposition includes

only sublunary substances, and by what right do we extrapolate from these to the eternal case? Moreover, two of the three classes into which he divides sublunary change (enforced, natural-inorganic, and natural-organic, i.e. self-change) are irrelevant to the question whether eternal change has an agent. We have seen that the primary eternal motion, unlike the natural ones of fire and earth etc., cannot depend on a generator or a liberator of the moving substance (*v.s.* para. (28)). Nor can it be attributed to an *enforcing* agent. The enforcement would be eternal, and to Aristotle there could hardly be an idea more absurd than that of a nature eternally repressed. Thus the existence of self-changing organisms is the only sublunary fact that provides any ground for inferring to an agent for the eternal change. But as so many sublunary changes are not self-changes, the sublunary world in general provides dubious support for Aristotle's conclusion concerning the eternal case. He may be justified in asserting that *if* the eternal change is 'by something' then it is more akin to sublunary change by self than to either of the other types. But he does not succeed in making a cogent argument for the antecedent of this hypothetical.

(31) He next (VIII.5) tries to show that in every case where a thing is changed by something other than itself, the source of the change can be traced back through one or many causal stages to a self-changing agent. He puts this forward as a general thesis, but its main effect is to establish that if in particular there is such a thing as eternal change, this too either is or depends ultimately upon self-change. And the self-changer concerned can then be analysed into a changer (the Prime Mover) and a distinct changed (the *primum mobile*). In this way Aristotle blocks off in advance any attempt to merge these two entities metaphysically demonstrated in 6. He rests his case in 5 on the proposition, there taken as axiomatic, that there is a causally first changer in every causal series of changes.[22] His examples show that by 'changer' here, he means 'agent that currently determines the form of change', and not 'condition that makes possible the change', nor

[22] For an attempt to prove this, see *Physics* VII.1.

'agent that brought about a condition making possible the change'. Thus when a man moves a stick which moves something else, and when the wind pushes a stone which in turn knocks something over, the first changer is the man or the wind. The proposition that there must in this sense always be a causally first changer follows directly from the II.1 doctrine of nature, for if everything owed its behaviour to an external *determining* cause, there would be no natural change. Thus within the terms of Aristotle's system, the proposition is indisputable and legitimately functions as an axiom. But what is questionable is his identification in 5 of the causally first changer with a *self-changer*. The human agent does of course qualify for this title according to the division made in Chapter 4, but not the wind, which for Aristotle is only air in motion. Thus, as regards the eternal case, he may reasonably hold that there cannot be an infinite causal series of eternal motions; but this does not automatically entitle him to conclude that at the head of the series there stands an entity that *changes itself* in some sense analogous to that in which sublunary living things are supposed to. For it would be just as reasonable to conclude that the series starts with a naturally-changing eternal entity similar to the wind, i.e. a simple, through and through physical, substance.

(32) However, Aristotle now brings into play the conclusion of 4 that whatever changes is changed by something, either itself or something else. In the examples given, the first changer causes change only by itself changing (intransitive), and since *ex hypothesi* this change is not due to anything other, it must, he argues, be due to itself (5, 256 a19–21). By this reasoning even the wind must count as a self-changer: an unwelcome consequence,[23] not only because it contradicts

---

[23] However, at 256 a22 ff. Aristotle may be deliberately treating the wind as a self-changer for the sake of his current argument. The question turns on the meaning of the conveniently ambiguous 'αὑτῷ' in 'ἢ γὰρ αὐτῷ κινεῖ τὸ κινοῦν ἢ ἄλλῳ'. Here 'αὐτῷ κινεῖ' stands for the relation between the first changer in the series and its proximate changed. On the one hand he glosses the above sentence with 'οἷον ἄνθρωπος ἢ αὐτὸς ἢ τῇ βακτηρίᾳ, καὶ ὁ ἄνεμος κατέβαλεν αὐτὸς ἢ ὁ λίθος ὃν ἔωσεν'. On this explanation, 'αὐτῷ κινεῖ' seems only to deny an intermediate or instrumental link, hence can in this sense apply to any causally first changer whether or not this has the logical complexity that would justify calling it 'self-changer'. But on the other hand, the contrast 'ἢ αὐτῷ κινεῖ ... ἢ ἄλλῳ' suggests

the division of substances in 4, but because it so devalues the concept of self-change as to make it hardly worth arguing for an eternal self-changer as the ground of all change. For on this extension of the concept, even if the eternal ground can now be shown to be a self-changer, this would give no reason for supposing that its change is not on the same logical level as those of the sublunary simple bodies, being dictated only by the sheer corporeal nature of the changing body, and not by any principle remotely comparable with life, soul, spirit or mind. And even if Aristotle might be willing under pressure to waive (surely to the detriment of scientific investigation) his sublunary division into animate and inanimate, treating fire and earth etc. in animistic terms, this would not much strengthen his position in VIII: at least not if his motive is to uphold the dignity of the supreme cause. Souls of earth and fire would rank pretty low on any scale of psychic levels, lower perhaps even than those of plants. Thus there would not be much to choose between a theory by which the ulti-mate cause might be an inanimate body inanimately rotating, and one by which it might be something whose closest sub-lunary analogues are souls of the most rudimentary kind.[24]

(33) When in *Physics* VIII Aristotle takes the natural changes of organic creatures as his model for the ultimate eternal change, he does so for the purely negative reason that the only alternative sublunary models would be even less suitable, and not because he sees more than the vaguest resemblance between the eternal case and that of an organism. Indeed the

that the changer can be its own instrument or intermediate link, which implies logical complexity, a distinction between the changer's body *with* which it causes change in something else, and an internal agent-element whose instrument this is.

[24] The Academic audience (and possibly Aristotle himself) may have been deceived into accepting the proposition that every causal series of changes starts from a self-changer by its verbal similarity to Plato's position in *Phaedrus* 245 C ff. and *Laws* X.894 B ff. Since for Plato a self-changer is not a complex of distinct agent and patient, but an entity that changes of itself, the axiom forbidding an infinite causal regress of changes is on its own sufficient to prove the existence of a self-changer in Plato's sense — but not in Aristotle's. Whereas for Plato, self-change is the defining property of soul, in Aristotle's system the beings that most closely approximate to Platonic self-changers are, paradoxically, the simple in-animate bodies, because they (*a*) change of themselves, and (*b*) are not internally differentiable into agent and patient.

list of criteria in 4 by which he distinguishes sublunary self-changers from sublunary non-self-changers makes it doubtful whether there could be *any* resemblance. The body of the eternal self-changer is a physical sphere without internal physical diversification: this simplicity is a condition of its being absolutely indestructible. Since the eternal motion is single and simple and takes place in it as a whole, the body has no need of variegated parts with which to function. Nor can it stop and start or change in different ways.[25] Nor can it be regarded as alive or ensouled in the sense in which this characteristic is displayed in one or more levels of biological functioning.[26] It may be for this reason that in 4 Aristotle makes possession of soul a *criterion* of sublunary self-change, but stops short of laying it down as a defining characteristic, and also of explicitly identifying the soul with the internal agent. A definite commitment on either of these points might call into question his right to extend the concept of self-change to the eternal case. And in general, the less he commits himself regarding the import of 'self-change' as applied to sublunary substances, the better for his main argument. Questions about its coherence even in this connection are best ignored, for two reasons. In the first place, Aristotle cannot afford to furnish critics with grounds for querying 'self-change' as a predicate of sublunary substances, for if it is meaningless in this application what reason have we to suppose it meaningful in any other? And how could we understand it without illustration from the sublunary world that we know? Secondly, even if the conceptual problems raised earlier (*v.s.* paras (7)–(13)) can be solved, this is worse than useless for Aristotle's main argument, if, as seems likely,

[25] Aquinas (*Comm. in Phys. VIII*, Lectio VII.7) sees the inapplicability of this criterion to the eternal case, but is comforted by noting that Aristotle does not say in VIII.4 that self-changers *must* be capable of different externally undetermined changes, but only that it is unreasonable (ἄλογον) that they should not be (255 a10–11).

[26] Of course it may be suggested, and has been, that the mover of the eternal body is a type of soul not exemplified by any sublunary creature, and this may have been Aristotle's position at a certain stage. But there is no sign of this in *Physics* VIII, and in 9, 265 b32–3 he speaks of those who 'make soul the cause of change' (i.e. the Platonists) as one who does not count himself among them. Cf. Solmsen, *Aristotle's System*, pp. 242–5.

the solutions would rest on features present only in sublunary cases.

(34) For in fact there are several ways in which a case could be made for distinguishing an agent- and a patient-element in organisms along lines consistent with the unity of the organic substance. We might for instance take a cue from Aristotle's remark in Chapter 6 that the only type of change that organisms originate of themselves is locomotion. This entails that changes of quality, such as temperature, and growth insofar as it depends on qualitative change, are determined as to their character by external conditions. Such changes, then, are only indirectly due to the organism itself, arising when its externally undetermined locomotion, whether of whole or parts, brings it into contact with the external determinants of qualitative change. Thus at the moment when the actual heating, for instance, takes place, the organism or some part of it is the passive subject of this change, as much so as if it were an inanimate substance. In taking this point of view, we are identifying the change with the actual emergence of the new property (cf. Ch. III, para. (4)). But alternatively we might include under the change (the becoming hot) the process leading up to the emergence. Since this consists in an externally undetermined locomotion, the creature is not passive with respect to the change is this sense, any more than the physician who applies a poultice to his own body. Thus the organism could be described as bringing about for itself the situation in which it or some part of it is passive with respect to the immediate cause of heat, and so it may be said to change itself. Obviously no such analysis could be applied to the eternal self-change, consisting as it does in a single uniform motion.

(35) Again, the natural changes of organisms, unlike those of Aristotle's simple bodies, involve two aspects which it is not unreasonable to regard as active and passive. When fire flies upwards and earth falls, the unforced motion is what it is the nature of each to realize, and a description of the motion gives a complete specification of the nature: it is the nature of the substance to move like this whenever unobstructed.

But when a living thing displays unenforced change of a given description, this description does not exhaust the account that might be given of the nature of the substance, since there are many forms of unenforced behaviour which the same individual realizes on different occasions, and the mere fact that a given behaviour-sequence would meet with no external impediment is not sufficient for its actually coming about. Different situations trigger different types of behaviour, as does the same situation at different stages of the creature's development. It might seem that a description of the whole range of these unenforced changes might be adequate to characterize the nature of the individual, so that this case differs from that of lifeless substances only in complexity. But even assuming it possible to arrive at a complete description of everything that the organism would unenforcedly do under different circumstances, it would be wrong to say that all this is what it is the organism's nature to do, leaving the matter at that; for this statement does not exclude what for Aristotle would be the metaphysical impossibility of a substance endowed with a plurality of natures each coming into play under different circumstances (*v.s.* Ch. III, para. (10)). It is not enough to say that the substance is of a sort to do (if unhindered) A under conditions X, B under conditions Y, etc., for to say that it is of *a sort* at all already implies some underlying or overall unity of nature, which can be expressed only in a corresponding unity of behaviour, and this is not brought out by such a list of hypothetical behavings. In short, Aristotle's theory of nature presupposes that there is some single description true of each item on such a list. And if we ask what this could be, which the individual satisfies in and through all its various unenforced changes, the answer, it seems, can only refer to the maintenance of the life-form of which this individual is an instance. *This* is what it is the nature of this creature to do, being an activity that takes (as we should expect) quite different shapes under different conditions.

(36) Thus for organisms there is a conceptual gap between the description of the activity that defines their nature, and the descriptions of the specific, immediately identifiable,

unenforced changes in which they engage. The defining activity stands to these as form to matter, being realized through them. The activity can also be said to be the cause of any particular specific unenforced change that occurs. The claim that causal dependence runs in this direction rather than the opposite one may be supported by the consideration (which empirical evidence confirms) that if the creature were not living, it would not have displayed that particular specific behaviour, whereas if that behaviour had been prevented, it does not necessarily follow that the creature would have ceased to live, since it might have continued to realize its characteristic life-pattern in some different change adapted to the circumstances. In view of this distinction between the two aspects of any concrete stretch of unenforced behaviour, and of the causal relation between them, it is perhaps not unreasonable to apply the terms 'agent' and 'patient' to the same organic individual. According to this analysis, it is not the *physical matter* of the organism (e.g. the earth of which it is composed) that is the patient of self-change, but the *organism itself regarded as the subject of those unenforced changes that stand to the life-activity as behavioural matter to behavioural form*. The agent, correspondingly, is the *organism itself regarded as subject of the life-activity typical of its kind*. This agent, moreover, logically resembles such conceptually obvious external agents as the craftsman at work on his materials, in that it too, *qua* agent, is not a subject of change (κίνησις). For the activity of living out a certain life-pattern is not a κίνησις, any more than the activity of building. It is true that for organic substances living has an inbuilt terminus (since death in Aristotle's view is a natural event, not necessarily due to externally enforced interruption: cf. *Physics* V.6, 230 a25–8). But whereas a genuine κίνησις is defined in terms of the subject's present lack of the property in which the κίνησις naturally terminates, it would be absurd to regard even a necessarily finite life as the privation of the "condition" of non-existence in which it naturally ends. Where a κίνησις defines the nature of a substance, this nature can also be defined by reference to the non-kinetic end-state of the κίνησις: thus it is the nature of fire to move upwards because it is its nature to *be* in the upper region. If the enactment of a certain type of life-pattern were a κίνησις of its subject, we should similarly have to say that it is the nature of this subject to live out its life because it is its nature to not-exist or "be" dead.

(37) The analysis just suggested of 'self-change' relies only on Aristotelian concepts and distinctions, and employs them so straightforwardly that it is hardly credible that such an account would not have occurred to Aristotle himself, had he been aiming to give one. But if he was inexplicably blind to the suitability of his own conceptual apparatus to clarify 'self-change' along such lines, the blindness was perhaps a blessing in the present context. He could not, on either of the accounts just suggested, invite us to view the ultimate eternal motion as a self-change, since its absolute homogeneity excludes all distinctions of process from emergence, behavioural form from behavioural matter. In general, his vagueness on 'self-change' as applied to organisms is due, I believe, to the need to make the same concept cover a case which differs from these in every one of its deducible features. This also explains why he thinks of organisms as changing themselves even when the change of the whole goes against no natural tendency of any bodily part or material (v.s. para. (13)). 'Self-change' cannot be allowed to entail a conflict of tendencies between whole and part, for the *primum mobile* has no plurality of constituents.

(38) What account then is to be given of the agent and patient in self-change if not one anchored to features peculiar to the sublunary soul–body relationship? In VIII.5 Aristotle sets out his answer, and it is clear from the start that he will not stay to be trapped by the organic model, for his argument now rests on the most abstract concepts, those of potentiality, actuality, and the presence and absence of a property.

Let us make another start and consider the following question: If something changes itself, how does it cause change and in what way? Now every changing thing is necessarily infinitely divisible. For this has already been shown in our treatise on nature, that whatever is in motion in virtue of itself is continuous. Thus it is impossible that what changes itself should in entirety change itself. For in that case the whole would be both cause and subject of the same locomotion, if it were one and indivisible in nature: it would be being altered and would be causing alteration, so that it would both teach and learn at the same time, and would be producing and being restored to the same health. Moreover, it has been laid down that what changes [or: is changed (κινεῖται)] is the changeable. But it is through potentiality that this changes, not through actuality.[27] That which is potentially so and so passes into actuality, and the change is the incomplete actuality of the changeable. But the changer is already actually so and so; e.g. the hot heats, and in general what generates is that which possesses the form. So the same thing will at the same time be both hot and not hot in the same way. Similarly in all other cases in which the changer must possess the property in the same sense [sc. as that in which the changed eventually possesses it]. So in that which changes itself, there is something that causes change, and something else that is changed. (257 a31–b13)

(39) What more decisive difference could there be between two things than that one has a certain property which the other has not? Aristotle now needs no tool besides the Law of Non-Contradiction itself for distinguishing agent from patient (even in self-change) on grounds that presuppose no unity *in diversity* of change. Since the Law holds good even (indeed primarily) of *single* properties, it guarantees a difference even where the change is in a single simple respect. However, the guarantee can take hold only if it is certain that for every agent and patient there *is* a property possessed by one and not the other. This Aristotle ensures through the model of giving and receiving.[28] To change (intransitive) is to acquire a new property, and to acquire is to be given. Hence there must be a giver, and the giver must first possess what it gives. That which acquires does not as yet have what it acquires. Hence what gives is not at the same time acquiring what it gives, for it gives only what it has. So what gives is not being

---

[27] 'τοῦτο δ'ἐστὶν δυνάμει κινούμενον, οὐκ ἐντελεχείᾳ'. The obvious translation, 'This is potentially, not actually, changing' (adopted by Hardie and Gaye (Oxford) and Wicksteed and Cornford (Loeb)), is surely incorrect. This meaning contributes nothing to the argument, which turns on the contrast between the changing subject's potentiality *to be* in the terminal state, and the actuality of that state, which is also the actual state of the changer. Moreover on this interpretation 'τὸ δὲ δυνάμει εἰς ἐντελέχειαν βαδίζει' would refer to the subject's coming to be actually changing, and although the transition from rest to change is a sort of μεταβολή, Aristotle would hardly have described it as a 'βάδισις'. Themistius and Simplicius ad loc. support my rendering.

[28] Cf. *Cat.* 5, 4 a29–b18, where 'πάσχειν' is in effect glossed by 'πάθος δέχεσθαι'.

given what it gives, since to be given is to acquire. Thus at one stroke Aristotle achieves the prized results (*a*) that the changer is distinct from the changed, and (*b*) that the changer, while operating as such, is not itself changing or being changed in the respect in which it causes change. Moreover, since on this model the giving of the giver depends only on the fact that the giver *has* a certain property and is in contact with a patient in a suitable condition to receive the latter, it is irrelevant to the giving whether or not the giver is currently changing in any other respect (being given some other property). Thus the changer need not change or even be changeable, in any respect whatever.

(40) The changer must be supposed to have the property which it then gives. For if the changed could get this property from something not possessed of it, why should the changed not get it from itself — in which case, it would not be a chang*ed*, but something which simply of itself originates an intransitive change to the new state? On the other hand, the giving/receiving model, if interpreted literally, implies that where the change is in respect of a physical property (as in most of Aristotle's examples) both agent and patient must be physical objects, since each in turn has the physical property. This hardly assists an argument for an absolutely changeless (and therefore non-physical) first cause which stands to the body whose motion it causes in a relation not totally unlike that of a soul. Thus, as Aristotle hints in the penultimate sentence of the passage last quoted, there must be some sense in which something can be said to "have" (so that it can give) a physical property without being physically characterized by it.[29] It might be objected that if there are different senses or ways of "having", so that the same property can physically

---

[29] The condition of desiring some as yet unachieved physical condition would be a way of non-physically "having" a physical property. '. . . the thought (or image) that one has in one's mind when one knows *x* is for Aristotle as fully actual an instance of the form of *x* as an external object exemplifying this form', J. Hintikka, 'Conceivability and Realizability in Aristotle', *Time and Necessity*, p. 126. If Aristotle is identifying the subject's 'non-physical possession' of P with P's being an object of perception and/or desire for that subject, this would explain his tendency to confine self-change to animals and to equate it with the distinctively animal change of locomotion.

qualify the changed whereas it non-physically qualifies the changer, then the reasoning of the passage breaks down. For the Law of Non-Contradiction does not prevent the subject that has the property in the non-physical sense from being numerically identical with the subject that lacks it in the physical sense. However, this does not hinder the general drift of Aristotle's argument, for he needs only to show that agent and patient are in some way distinct, even if only distinct aspects of the same individual. And he is assured of at least this conclusion, for if a being is capable of the non-physical possession of properties of whose physical possession it is also capable, then it must be regarded as having two dimensions or aspects, a corporeal and (however related to this) a non-corporeal.

(41) This stage of Aristotle's First Cause argument bears heavy responsibility for the aura of pseudo-metaphysics which for many still hangs about the whole notion of 'inner principles of change'. The concept of nature in *Physics* II is not unempirical in the sense that no observation is relevant to its application in a particular case. To say that it is of the nature of fire to move upwards implies that regularly fire does so move, and that the motion is not shaped by the external environment. The first of these claims can be verified without difficulty, and the second with no more difficulty than many causal propositions in modern science. Nor does the II.1 identification of nature with form in organized substances put 'nature' beyond the scope of empirical application. Minimally, this identification entails that the regular and externally undetermined changes of the substance cannot be reduced to products of the changes natural to its elemental components. Although presumably false, the doctrine of the natural motions of the elements is to some extent supported by ordinary observation, and if the doctrine is accepted, ordinary observation leads to the conclusion that many substances behave in structured ways not derivable from elemental behaviour (*v.s.* Ch. II, paras (35) and (44). Thus to uphold the notion of form as the source of change there is no need whatever to postulate "within" the substance some kind of incorporeal counterpart of the change or of the result

thereby achieved, and in *Physics* II Aristotle showed no sign of being drawn in this direction. We have also just seen that the concept of self-changer as applied to organisms can be analysed in terms of externally undetermined behaviour together with the observable fact that this behaviour has the common property of tending to development, survival, and reproduction. These facts give grounds for conceptually isolating changer from changed, and on this level it is gratuitous to assume an incorporeal counterpart, or to identify the agent factor with such an assumed entity. I say 'on this level', because at a logically posterior stage of inquiry it may, in the case of some behaviour of some organisms, seem necessary or reasonable to postulate a state of consciousness, desire, and/or perception, as a link in the explanatory chain, and this state may be thought of as being or involving an incorporeal counterpart (mental presentation) of the object desired or perceived. However, we make this move only when the behaviour and physical characteristics are such as to suggest that it would not be absurd to attribute consciousness to the creature in question. For some cultures and outlooks the threshold of absurdity may be lower than for others; thus there have been people for whom apparently, *any* directional behaviour, even the fall of stones, indicates a spirit present. But Aristotle like ourselves sets the threshold at a level to exclude not only these cases but many far more complex organic ones; which means that he, like ourselves, is bound to base the attribution of consciousness on characteristics not universally present in all natural objects. And it is fairly certain that any attempt to specify these special characteristics, even roughly and open-endedly, will point to features which the eternally moving body lacks, and indeed must lack if its motion is to be in keeping with its metaphysical function. In the absence of empirical criteria, Aristotle's only ground for assuming a non-physical dimension to be operative in the eternal case is supplied by the empty verbal logic that pictures change as a *receiving*, and so as requiring a giver, and therefore a prior possessor, and therefore, if there is no observable prior possessor, one that is unobservable and possesses only incorporeally what it gives. But although it is perhaps only in the eternal case that Aristotle needs this reasoning to assure him of the existence of a cause distinct from the subject of the change, the reasoning itself is presented as general, being allegedly derived from the concept of change as such.[30] Thus it logically extends to all areas previously covered by the original concepts of nature and form, imposing on these an otherwise groundless[31] interpretation in terms of ghostly inner blueprints striving for physical embodiment through change.

(42) Such are the measures by which Aristotle seeks to establish an eternal source of change which itself stands outside any actual or possible change, including even the eternal motion which is its immediate effect. I end by considering why this position is so necessary for Aristotle. The answer may seem obvious: for theological and perhaps also religious reasons he could not accept that the source of all change is a corporeal object: but this is what it would have to be if the source were itself a subject of eternal change (since the only eternal change is a species of locomotion). The being on which all change depends is the being on which depend all natural substances, since their nature is to change; and the being on which all natural substances depend is God; and God must be changeless and incorporeal. The theological assumptions expressed by the last two clauses are matters for metaphysics rather than philosophy of nature, but it would be absurd to make this a reason for denying their influence on the central argument of *Physics* VIII. On the other hand, this consideration must be balanced against the fact that the argument is not on the face of it a proof of God. Nor is it simply an attempt to find a First Cause. It does of course result in this, but Aristotle's avowed aim in *Physics* VIII.3–6 is to show how there can be individually transitory changes

---

[30] Cf. M. de Corte, 'La Causalité du Premier Moteur dans la philosophie aristotélicienne', *Revue de l'Histoire de la Philosophie*, vol. V, 1931, p. 105: '. . . on ne peut pas ne pas être frappé par l'insistence que met Aristote à ramener toute l'essence de sa preuve à l'unique analyse du mouvement . . .'. See also p. 107.

[31] See Gotthelf, pp. 226 ff., for a demythologizing analysis of Aristotle's treatment of sublunary nature. Gotthelf does not however note that Aristotle is himself (by his theory of the eternal changeless cause) in a measure responsible for the 'immaterial agency' interpretation against which Gotthelf argues (especially pp. 251–2). See also Balme, 'Aristotle's Biology was not Essentialist', esp. p. 9.

even though change as such is an eternal feature of the universe. His solution invokes (*a*) an eternal source of change, and (*b*) a being that eternally changes; but it is an extra assumption that what satisfies these two postulates is not one and the same thing. It would be somewhat unsatisfactory if this assumption, for which he contends so hard without mention of God (unless we count a passing reference to Anaxagoras' Nous at 5, 256b24-7), should turn out not to answer some demand intrinsic to the problem raised in 3 and solved in 6. Hence without meaning to discount the theological aspect I shall now draw attention to another pressure at work here, one whose source lies nearer home.

(43) Instead of debating whether a body in eternal motion is fit to be assigned the position of ultimate source of all change, let us rather consider whether this motion could by the standards implicit in the definition of III.1 be properly described as a κίνησις or process at all.[32] The problem is to see how it can count as an incomplete actuality, an actuality of what is potential *qua* only potential. Changes that fall neatly under the original definition all naturally culminate in states of non-change, the change itself being actual only up to that point. But where there is no future culmination, there is no corresponding present potentiality for this, and hence, it would seem, no process. The problem for eternal motion would be avoided if we could suppose it to consist in a series of discrete movements to successive termini, but this is ruled out by its absolute continuity, a property as essential as everlastingness.[33] It is true of course that the eternal body is never, during any sub-period of its rotation, actually doing all that it can do. Thus, if A, B, and C are points on the circular path of some section S of the eternal body, while the body is

[32] Philoponus refuses to take it for granted that the III.1 definition of change is equally applicable to finite and to eternal change: see *ap.* Simplic. *Ad Phys.* VIII.1, ed. Diels 1129 ff., and Simplicius' virulent reply.

[33] For a brilliant summary of the problems of fitting the eternal circular motion to the III.1 definition of change, see Cherniss, *Aristotle's Criticism of Plato etc.*, pp. 582-3. Cf. also Robin, p. 132: 'Ainsi, avec ce mouvement [*sc.* le mouvement circulaire], qui est le mouvement par excellence, s'effondre la definition physique du mouvement'. However I argue (paras (44)-(50)) that the position of *Physics* VIII upholds the intention of III.1.

rotating so that S passes from A to B it is not as yet actually rotating so that S passes from B to C; yet it has the potentiality to be doing so.[34] But this fact hardly serves to bring the motion into line with the earlier definition. That definition avoided circularity only by analysing change in terms of a potentiality for some form of non-change; whereas if the eternal rotation can be analysed at all without prejudice to its absolute continuity, this is possible only by reference to a series of potentialities to *be in motion*.[35]

(44) Sublunary changes are incomplete actualities by contrast with the complete ones in which they naturally terminate; but there is no such contrast to justify the term 'incomplete' as applied to the eternal case. The consequence seems clear: either the eternal motion counts as a *complete actuality*, or its incompleteness derives from an entirely different type of contrast. As a natural phenomenon, the eternal circular motion is as complete as anything in nature could be.[36] Since it never started, it follows that at every moment every part of the rotating body has just completed a circle;[37] and since it will never end, there is never any falling short of a complete number of circles. Thus any actuality by comparison with which it would make sense to describe the eternal motion as incomplete would lie beyond nature and change, and would be of a perfection inconceivable in natural terms. Nor could such an actuality be brought into existence by any process. Hence it must necessarily exist for eternity, making true Aristotle's statement in *Physics* VII.3 that besides substances

---

[34] Cf. Simplicius *ad VIII.1 contra Philoponum*, ed. Diels 1131, 9-22, and Alexander *apud Simplic.*, ed. Diels 1218, 20-7.

[35] But a 'series of potentialities' casts doubt on continuity (cf. Ch. III, para. (38)). In addition, there is the absurdity of 'becoming of becoming' (ibid., para. (67)).

[36] On its energeic (as opposed to kinetic) character, cf. W. K. C. Guthrie, 'The Development of Aristotle's Theology I', *Classical Quarterly* vol. XXVII, 1933, p. 167, n. 2; J. B. Skemp, *The Theory of Motion in Plato's Later Dialogues*, p. xi, n. 3; Kosman, op. cit., pp. 59-60.

[37] In other words it is arbitrary what point we take as the defining terminus of this motion. In fact 'terminus' has been drained of meaning in this connection: not because there is no lingering at the selected point but because the latter represents no sort of culmination. (The passage of the pendulum can be said to culminate at each extreme although neither is a resting-place). Cf. Ch. III, paras (52) ff. on 'instantaneously occupied terminus'.

that begin and cease to change, there is something eternally changing, and also something eternally changeless. The point I would stress is that *without the eternally changeless to provide a term of comparison*, the eternal motion could not be classed as a change or process at all, so long as these terms retain some semblance of the meanings assigned them in *Physics* III.

(45) Perhaps when Aristotle framed the definition of III.1 he had no thought for the eternal motion. The celestial spheres and their rotations lay outside his current concern with familiar substances whose developments the scientific observer can trace.[38] By comparison with these experienced objects, eternal body and eternal change are theoretical entities known precisely to the extent that they satisfy certain explanatory requirements. It would have been no surprise, then, if in broaching the new level of discussion in Book VIII Aristotle had quietly left his old definition of change behind as a tool unsuitable for such a different type of venture. Nor would it have been generous on our part to criticize him on this score, especially since twentieth century philosophy of science provides striking illustrations of ways in which concepts of space, time, and motion viable on the level of ordinary experience collapse when applied beyond it. But Aristotle himself disallows any such concession by reverting explicitly to the old definition in VIII.1 (258 a8-10), and again in VIII.5.

(46) For instance, in the course of considering in what sense something can be said to change itself, he writes:

It has been laid down that what changes (intransitive) is the changeable. But it is through potentiality, not actuality, that it changes.[39] That

---

[38] Compare II.1, where (*a*) the examples given of a natural substance are all sublunary, and (*b*) nature is said to be a principle of change *and stasis*. However, II.7, 198 a29-31 shows that Book II does not totally ignore the eternal world. But this passage says that eternal moving things fall under a different branch of knowledge from destructible changing things: i.e. the former do not come within the scope of "physics" as conceived in II. (For a list of the numerous comments, ancient and modern, on the inapplicability of the II.1 definition of nature as a principle of change *and stasis* to eternal bodies, see P. Moraux, *Aristotle: du Ciel*, p. xlv, n. 1.)

[39] Cf. n. 27 above.

which is potentially so and so passes to being so in actuality, and change is the incomplete actuality of the changeable. But the changer already has the property in actuality: e.g. what is hot heats, and in general the generator possesses the form. (257 b6-10)

Here Aristotle firmly bases himself on the account in III, according to which the complete actuality is the terminal state. In particular, he recalls the doctrine of III.2, 202 a9–12, that the complete actuality (or another instance of it) belongs also to the agent, being what constitutes it a possible agent of this type of change. This suggests that one formal feature of complete as opposed to incomplete actuality is the power to reproduce or replicate itself in some other subject. The change in the patient is the acquiring of this replica-actuality, but the acquiring itself is not another replica of anything currently present in the agent, since otherwise the agent even when acting would be acquiring what it must already possess as a precondition for such action. Now the question is how eternal locomotion, or indeed locomotion in general, fits into this conceptual scheme. It is to be noted that Aristotle presents it as covering *all* cases of agency and patiency, those where the action is between mutually external substances, as well as the peculiar case of self-change.[40] But one body in locomotion can transmit locomotion to another: can carry another along in its own direction. Thus according to the model, *locomotion* functions logically as a complete, because self-reproducing, actuality. When a moving body A causes motion in B, the only *change* to occur in B, according to Aristotle's conception, would be *acquisition*[41] of locomotion, not the locomotion acquired. If the locomotion acquired by B were a change in Aristotle's sense, it would be an incomplete actuality. The same then would be true of the locomotion in the agent A. But it is *because* A is in locomotion

---

[40] Cf. Solmsen, *Aristotle's System*, pp. 248-9: 'As long as it is at all possible, Aristotle continues to think in physical terms; even of the self-mover he speaks as though it were a body [better: a conjunction of bodies (my insertion)] and had extension and parts.'

[41] It may seem odd to speak of the acquisition of locomotion as a change (κίνησις), since it must be instantaneous. But Aristotle's own example, becoming hot (257 b9), is also for him instantaneous; and in general there is no inconsistency in viewing the same event as an instantaneous transition and as the climax of a process (*v.s.* Ch. III).

that it is able to cause locomotion in B. Thus A *qua* agent would be in a condition of incomplete actuality: which flatly contradicts this system of concepts.

(47) But Aristotle is so mesmerized by the system and at the same time so certain that locomotion is of course to be counted a change or κίνησις (at 9, 266 a1-2, he mentions that the word 'κίνησις' is strictly applied only to locomotion) that he altogether overlooks the problem. At 5, 256 b31-257 a3, he writes as if the same absurdity attached to the proposition that a subject is both in locomotion (in a given direction etc.) and causes such locomotion in something else, as to the proposition that a subject is both learning and teaching the same lesson to another.[42] Certainly, *if* being in locomotion is an incomplete actuality (like learning), then locomotion (like learning) could only be caused by an agent not itself in locomotion (learning) but in some sense already in possession of the destination (already in possession of knowledge). Aristotle simply asserts the antecedent of this hypothetical, and therefore the consequent, without stopping to consider whether experience does not give grounds for denying the latter and hence the former.[43] If he had, he would have been faced with the necessity of abandoning either the assumption that locomotion is in all cases a κίνησις or the proposition

[42] Assuming that particular attributes (including changes) are individuated by reference to particular subjects, X cannot be both subject and cause of L in another subject, where 'L' refers to the same particular locomotion. (But it is arguable that Aristotle does not share the assumption; cf. G. E. L. Owen, 'Inherence', *Phronesis* X, 1965, pp. 97 ff.) However this cannot help Aristotle here: if locomotion is to count as κίνησις in his scheme, it must be impossible for the agent to be in and to cause *specifically* the same locomotion. For it is in this sense of 'same' that an agent's supposed possession of complete actuality entails its not undergoing the same process as it causes. This is clear in the case of teaching. Still, it might be said that on a narrow definition of 'specifically same locomotion' in terms of points traversed, different spatial objects cannot undergo specifically the same locomotion at the same time; so that Aristotle is justified in holding that with locomotion as with other types of κίνησις an agent cannot undergo what it causes. But the fact that (in some cases) the agent is as such in locomotion *at all* still shakes Aristotle's scheme; for this requires not merely that the agent not be undergoing the change which it causes, but that *qua* agent it be in a state of non-change, complete actuality.

[43] Cf. Philoponus in VIII.5, 257 b9, ed. Vitelli 835, 1-3: 'ἀλλ' οὐδε ἐπὶ τῶν κατὰ τόπον κινούντων ἀληθὴς ὁ λόγος · οὔτε γὰρ αἱ ἡμίονοι αἱ κινοῦσαι τὴν ἅμαξαν ἐνεργέια εἰσὶν ἐν τῷ τόπῳ ἔνθα δεῖ πορευθῆναι.'

that κίνησις is in all cases incomplete actuality. Now what shields Aristotle from realizing this is, I suggest, his certainty that locomotion, and in particular the primary eternal rotation, depends on an agent distinct from its subject.

(48) To explain this, let us recall the assumption behind Aristotle's argument in VIII.4 that the natural movements of the sublunary simple bodies are agent-dependent. The only agents to be found were the generator and/or liberator. Now to call these 'agents' presupposes that the simple bodies are, in their natural motions, *patients*. And Aristotle's only reason for regarding them as patients of their liberators etc. was the fact that it is a *change* or κίνησις that these alleged agents make possible. If the upward motion of fire were (*per impossibile*) a non-kinetic activity or ἐνέργεια in the narrow sense of *Metaphysics* Θ 6, then the liberator, although it might still be necessary, would not count as an agent. For ἐνέργεια is not a passivity, hence its subject not a patient. It would be absurd, for instance, to think of a living thing as passively receiving the ἐνέργεια that is its own life-activity. The assumption, then, in VIII.4 was that only κίνησις requires an agent.[44] Now the natural motions of the sublunary simple bodies are clearly incomplete actualities, so they fit the definition of κίνησις in III.1. The criterion of their incompleteness, hence of their kinetic status, is that they proceed to a culmination. And in VIII.4 their status as passivities was assumed to follow from this already established kinetic status. But to turn now to the case of the eternal rotation: here Aristotle lacks the criteria upon which he has so far been relying to divide kinetic from non-kinetic, incomplete from complete. If he takes the criterion of incompleteness to be 'proceeding to a culmination', the eternal rotation is not incomplete. If he takes the criterion for completeness to be the power of self-replication, locomotion of all kinds must often count as complete. There remains one path of escape from the obvious conclusion, and Aristotle in my view has taken it. This is to convert agent-dependence from a *necessary consequence* of kinetic status into a *criterion* for the same, where other

---

[44] *V.s.* Ch. IV, paras (12) and (13).

criteria fail. Thus it is *because* (as he never in *Physics* VIII doubts) the primary eternal rotation has a distinct agent that we can continue to class it as a κίνησις. Conversely, if we supposed it to stand in no need of an agent, with the eternal body functioning as the self-sufficient subject *and* source of its own motion, we would automatically put that motion outside the class of κινήσεις, in the absence of any other reason for calling it 'incomplete'.[45]

(49) Earlier (paras (27)-(28)) it seemed that in explaining the infinite succession of sublunary variations by reference both to an eternally changeless principle and to something in eternal change, Aristotle was under no necessity to assume that these were not one and the same being; for the eternal process is, *qua* process, entirely changeless. But what is now in question is not its invariance but, for that very reason among others, its status as a process or κίνησις, as opposed to an ἐνέργεια. And its claim to that status turns out to rest on a single assumption: that it is the effect of a distinct and absolutely changeless (because ultimate) agent. But unless the eternal rotation is indeed a κίνησις, it cannot fulfil the function for which it was postulated, which was to account for the inexhaustibility of change in the universe while allowing for seriality and transience on the sublunary level. Thus Aristotle had no choice but to make his eternal rotation intermediary rather than causally ultimate, for reasons unrelated to theology. For if eternal rotation counts only as a changeless ἐνέργεια, it is as remote, metaphysically, from the transient as is a changeless incorporeal cause. But now his argument in VIII.6 for the intermediacy of eternal rotation begins to show a distressing circularity of its own. For only a κίνησις is fit to mediate, whereas eternal rotation cannot rank as κίνησις unless its intermediate position is already established.

---

[45] However, it is doubtful whether even postulating the Unmoved Mover gives a sufficient condition for classing the eternal motion as κίνησις. The latter's homogeneity is the physical replica of the simplicity of the incorporeal agent; but by the scheme of III.2, it is not the replica in the patient, but its acquisition, that is the incomplete actuality.

(50) But this is a minor problem compared with what now comes into focus as we examine the conceptual role of the distinct eternal agent. I mean the fundamental weakness of the equation of change with incomplete actuality. Suppose that it were allowed that the primary rotation is agentless. Then it would have to be classed as complete, and it could not figure as κίνησις. But no amount of juggling with classifications can obliterate the palpable difference between this sort of complete actuality, which involves passage through space, and one that goes nowhere. And a philosopher cannot argue away the fact that for ordinary thought at least, this is the difference between change and staying the same, between motion and rest, between process and the static. But this difference is not registered in the distinction of complete versus incomplete actuality which inspires Aristotle's III.1 definition of κίνησις. On the contrary, the common-sense distinction between locomotion of whatever kind (whatever its cause) and rest, cuts across the class of possible complete actualities, bracketing at least one member (the eternal rotation, supposing this possibly agentless) with the sublunary motions classed as incomplete.

(51) Yet Aristotle, even in *Physics* VIII, continues to use the dichotomy 'complete/incomplete' to express the essential difference between non-process and process (although Book VI may be described as an abortive effort in another direction). He is only able to do so, I believe, because in the *Physics* he never admits as possible the one case that would drive a wedge between the two distinctions; this is the case of agentless eternal rotation. He need not question the synonymy of the distinctions as long as they coincide, and the coincidence seems certain as long as he is assured that any process recognized by common sense has the technical status of incomplete actuality: whether because it culminates, or because it is agent-dependent, or on both counts. Once faced with the possibility that even one locomotion (let alone that on which the whole of nature depends) lacks both these characteristics, Aristotle would have had to acknowledge the failure of III.1 as a definition of process and change. This recognition is held at bay by his assumption of an agent for the primary rotation.

In short, the definition of κίνησις in III stands and falls with
the doctrine in VIII of the incorporeal Prime Mover. That is
why Aristotle has no real basis from which to *argue* that the
primary eternal κίνησις is powered by a distinct eternal agent;
for him the very terms of this thesis presuppose its truth. If I
am right, his manoeuvres with 'self-change' in VIII.4–6
amount in the end to no such argument, but instead to a
defence, conscious or not, of the idea that κίνησις is incomplete actuality. We have seen (paras (15)–(17)) how his initial
conception of natural substance is buttressed in VIII by the
doctrine that change never ceases in the universe. Just so, the
associated theory of a supreme changeless agent now emerges
as no less necessary to sustain his original definition of change.

Appendix to Chapter V

In the text I argued as follows that the concept of self-change plays an
essential part in establishing the position reached by Aristotle in *Physics*
VIII.6: (i) He is not logically entitled to postulate an eternal cause
distinct from any eternally moving body merely on the ground that
otherwise there could be no infinite sequence of finite changes, since
this sequence could be adequately accounted for by eternal motion
alone. (ii) His ground then must be that eternal motion in turn requires
to be explained, and that this is possible only on the assumption of a
distinct and changeless ultimate cause. (iii) But such an explanation
would be unnecessary on the view that an eternally moving body is like
fire or earth, i.e. simply of a nature to move as it does, because then
there would be nothing for a distinct mover to do. (iv) Therefore (since
there must surely be some sublunary analogue to assist our understanding of the ultimate eternal motion) Aristotle compares the motion to
the natural locomotion of a living thing. (v) A living thing involves a
cause of motion (the soul) which is in some sense distinct from that
which moves (the body), and which is not itself a body, and which (*qua*
source of change) is not itself changing. (vi) If, then, the ultimate
eternal motion is analogous to soul-directed movements in an organism,
this motion too must have an in some sense distinct although not
physically external cause. (vii) Thus *provided that* Aristotle can show
that the ultimate eternal motion is the manifestation of a mover-moved
complex analogous to the complex of soul and body (i.e. that the
motion is the manifestation of a self-mover), he has the proof he needs,
but not otherwise (given his starting position in *Physics* VIII). He tries
to meet the proviso by arguing that every series of changes starts with a
self-changer, and this is where his proof breaks down, since the proposition is groundless in his system according to the Aristotelian meaning of

'self-change', although not, as we saw, according to the Platonic (*v.s.* Ch. V, paras (31) f.).

However, proposition (iii) above needs fuller discussion than there was space for in the text. As against H. von Arnim (*Die Entstehung der Gotteslehre des Aristoteles*) who maintained (iii), W. K. C. Guthrie, followed by H. Cherniss, holds that the distinct changeless cause is not redundant even if the subject of eternal rotation is endowed with a nature to rotate (Guthrie, 'The Development of Aristotle's Theology I', *Classical Quarterly* vol. XXVII, 1933, and introduction to Loeb *De Caelo*; Cherniss, *Aristotle's Criticism of Plato and the Academy*, App. X, pp. 584 ff.) Guthrie in fact claims not merely that the doctrine of eternal body as natured to rotate is consistent with that of the change-less agent, but that the former doctrine is incomplete without the latter.

These scholars were especially concerned with the *De Caelo*, but their views have implications for the argument of *Physics* VIII, and especially for any assessment of the function of 'self-change' in that argument. If Guthrie and Cherniss are right, 'self-change' is an unneces-sary complication. If it is possible to argue for the changeless eternal agent even on the assumption that the *primum mobile* is, as in *De Caelo* I, of a nature analogous to that of fire etc. then Aristotle had no need to introduce a special category of natural changes (self-changes) from which those of fire etc. were carefully excluded. Nor need he have insisted on the distinction between internal agent and patient within the so-called self-changers. His purpose of arriving at the position of VIII.6 would have been equally served if he had adhered to the II.1 conception of nature as inner principle without subdividing natural substances into self-changers and non-self-changers. (This is not to say that he would have regarded them as all alike ensouled or not ensouled; but this difference would not have mattered for the argument.) Or if, when treating of eternal things, continuity with Platonic tradition inclined him to use the Platonic term 'self-changer' in this context, he could have used it without adding the un-Platonic assumption that it implies a distinction between changer-self and changed-self. In that case, the term would have functioned as an equivalent to 'originator of change', and have applied as well to fire etc. as to organic creatures: in short, it would have been a Platonically-tinged synonym for 'natural substance' as explained in II.1.

It is Aristotle's refusal to use 'self-change' in this simple sense, and his insistence on the internal distinction, that generates the serious doubts and obscurities surveyed near the beginning of Chapter V above. Thus if Guthrie and Cherniss are right, these doubts and ob-scurities are not (as to me it seems they are) the necessary price for an otherwise coherent argument culminating in VIII.6; for the concept which generates them, 'self-change', turns out to be an unhelpful intruder. It is not incredible that Aristotle should have failed to realize this; indeed Guthrie seems to suggest that it is not until *Metaphysics* Λ (where 'self-change' does not appear) that he reaches a coherent position concerning the Unmoved Mover.

To support his claim of compatibility between the doctrine of eternal body as having a nature like that of fire, and the postulate of a distinct cause of its motion, Guthrie maintains that the concept of nature undergoes development in the *Physics*, its original meaning being supplemented by a new metaphysical refinement.

[According to] the principles of the first books of the *Physics* . . . change and motion is to be regarded as the actualization of a potency. This actualization takes place because the φύσις of things is something dynamic, an inward urge towards the realization of form. But by the time the investigations of the *Physics* were completed by the theories of books VII and VIII, A. had logical proof of what he had always believed to be true, but would not allow himself to state until the proof was ready to hand, namely that this inward urge would remain dormant unless there were actually existent some external perfection to awaken it, by instilling the desire of imitation, in so far as that was possible for each thing in its own particular mode of being. (*Classical Quarterly*, 1933, p. 171)

(Since Cherniss does not question these remarks, presumably he would not reject them.) I shall not consider whether Aristotle had 'always' held the belief attributed to him in the last few lines, but only whether he holds it in the last book of the *Physics*. For, clearly, if he does, then he holds there that a thing moves because of its nature *and* because of the eternal Unmoved Mover (the latter being what Guthrie means by 'some external perfection'). Now if in particular this is Aristotle's view concerning the *primum mobile* of *Physics* VIII, then the latter's dependence on the eternal Unmoved Mover is no reason against his retaining the *De Caelo* I analogy between the *primum mobile* and fire, earth, etc. Thus the *Physics* VIII comparison of the *primum mobile* with a self-moving organism, and the implied contrast with inanimate substances, contributes nothing to the main argument of that book.

In the passage quoted Guthrie starts with the concept of a nature as a dynamic principle (that on account of which a substance changes in a certain way unless prevented), and then distinguishes within this two metaphysical factors: one is the ground of there being any change at all, which he identifies with the urge or desire to imitate the absolute perfection of the eternal Unmoved Mover, while the other is that which determines the particular way in which the imitation of absolute perfection will be realized in the particular case. It is the second factor that Guthrie identifies with nature in the 'developed' account. Clearly, 'nature' in the latter sense (in which it refers not to an active or dynamic principle but to a *metaphysically distinguishable component of a dynamic principle*) is consistent with and indeed entails (final) causation by the Unmoved Mover. But it is doubtful whether in *Physics* VIII (whatever may be the case in the *Metaphysics*) Aristotle ever uses 'nature' in this sense. For in this sense of 'nature' the Unmoved Mover is present (as final cause or object of imitation) with equal immediacy to the natures of all physical substances — or perhaps we should say, with equal remoteness. There is nothing "between" the absolutely perfect being and the substances that try through change to imitate it, except the metaphysical gap between finite physical perfection and absolute changeless perfection; and this gap is the same for all changing substances. But in *Physics* VIII the eternal Unmoved Mover is in a special sense separated from sublunary substances, because they depend on it only at physical removes, via the eternal spheres and in particular the outermost. This fits with the analogy Body:Soul::Eternally rotating outermost sphere:Eternal changeless cause, because a soul is intimately related to one body, and to other physical substances only via this body. (For a penetrating discussion of this see M. de Corte, op. cit.)

It is therefore a reasonable conclusion that in *Physics* VIII Aristotle is not using 'nature' in Guthrie's narrow and metaphysically analytical sense. If he is not, then presumably 'nature' continues in VIII as in II to signify the dynamic principle, or that about a substance on account of which it does change in a certain way unless prevented. But a substance endowed with nature in this sense cannot depend for its change on anything other than its natural self except so far as the change can be hindered. That is, it depends on favourable conditions and on whatever is responsible for these. Thus the view that a sublunary substance changes by its own nature does not exclude the ultimate dependence of this change on some external unmoved mover; for the eternal motion caused by the latter may be supposed to keep going (by however many causal stages) the seasonal conditions for sublunary natural changes. However, in such cases, the natural change depends on the eternal agent only because it depends more immediately on physically external conditions. Where there are no conditions or possible hindrances, as in the case of the primary eternal change, there cannot be an agent whose responsibility consists entirely in its ensuring favourable conditions. Either there is no agent or the agent does more than create the possibility of change. So if the primary eternal motion has a distinct eternal agent, this can only be because the agent *determines the form* of motion, not because (as with sublunary substances) it *makes possible* the motion *already determined as to its form* by the substance's nature. If then the *primum mobile* were *by nature* determined to move as it does, there would be no function for a distinct agent. Nature (in the sense of dynamic principle) is not in general incompatible with dependence on the eternal Unmoved Mover, but it is so in the case of the first eternal body because of this body's unique independence of physically external conditions.

In *Physics* VIII Aristotle goes to great lengths to prove that there is at least one eternal change and that it is circular locomotion. Yet (by contrast with *De Caelo* I) he never says that this change stems from its subject's *nature*. The eternally moving body is never said to have a nature at all. This is evidence (*pace* Guthrie) that Aristotle in VIII uses 'nature' as meaning 'dynamic principle', and that he is now aware of inconsistency in attributing nature in this sense to an object immediately kept in necessary motion by the ultimate cause.

It might be argued as follows that even on the scheme of *Physics* VIII the object could be said to have a nature: this object is to its changeless cause as ·body to soul in sublunary self-movers, and the bodily matter of an organism is said in VIII.4 to have a natural tendency which may or may not coincide with that of the body-soul concrete as a whole. But would we be entitled to attribute to the bodily matter its own nature were it not that sometimes the natural change of the whole goes against this by a kind of constraint? If the tendency of the matter were always in harmony with that of the whole, the former could be said to have its own nature only on the grounds that when it decomposes it will yield simple stuffs whose actual natural motions differ from those of the living organism (cf. Ch. II, para. (35)). Since an eternal body cannot decompose, the *primum mobile* has no nature of its own in this sense, nor in the sense of requiring to be constrained to move.

It may seem unduly paradoxical that this body, which is after all a physical object, should not possess a nature (in the sense of II.1) and hence fail to qualify for the category of natural substance. Yet *Physics* VIII entails this, just as *Physics* IV entails the paradox, which Aristotle openly accepts, that the *primum mobile* has no place (IV.5, 212 b8–10). We may recall too the *De Philosophia* (see Cicero, *De Natura Deorum*, ii. 16, 44), according to which the motion of the heavens is voluntary, and voluntary change is neither natural nor enforced, but forms a third category. A being whose *only* motion is *always* voluntary must be presumed not to possess a nature in the sense of principle of natural change; thus the concept of a nature-less physical substance was not at every stage alien to Aristotle. This is not to say that his position in *Physics* VIII requires him to hold that the *primum mobile*'s motion is voluntary; the triple division of *De Philosophia* is of interest here not on account of its positive characterization of the third type of change, but because it recognizes that 'natural' and 'enforced' do not exhaust the possibilities, and are equally unsuitable to describe the primary motion.

It may be disturbing to have to admit the existence of a moving physical object that stands in causal relation to other physical (and natural) substances, yet is natureless itself; but this is the lesser of two conceptual evils. For in denying a nature 4o the *primum mobile*, we are safe at least from being compelled at the same time to assert one; whereas in asserting one, we should also have to deny it. If the *primum mobile* is of a nature to rotate, then (given that this excludes a distinct agent) the rotation is not a change or κίνησις in Aristotle's sense of 'incomplete actuality' (so I argued in the text); but then since 'nature is an inner principle of change or κίνησις', the 'nature' expressed in the rotation would not be a *nature* after all. Moreover, if the *primum mobile* is natureless, there is none of the difficulty that many have felt in reconciling the eternity of its motion with the II.1 doctrine of nature as principle of change *and stasis*.

List of Works Cited

(Translators of Aristotle and commentators appear under their own names.)

Ackrill, J. L., 'Aristotle's Distinction between ENERGEIA and KINESIS', in *New Essays on Plato and Aristotle*, ed. R. Bambrough, London, 1965, pp. 121 ff.

Allan, D. J., *The Philosophy of Aristotle* (2nd ed.), Oxford, 1970.

Anscombe, G. E. M., 'Aristotle', in *Three Philosophers*, G. E. M. Anscombe and P. T. Geach, Oxford, 1961.

Aquinas, St. Thomas, *Commentaria in Octo Libros Physicorum Aristotelis*, Rome, 1884.

Aristotle, *Opera*, ed. I. Bekker, Berlin, 1831.

Balme, D. M., 'Greek Science and Mechanism I and II', *Classical Quarterly* XXXIII, 1939, pp. 129 ff. and XXXV, 1941, pp. 23 ff.

—, *Aristotle's De Partibus Animalium I and De Generatione Animalium I*, Oxford, 1972.

—, 'Aristotle's Biology was not Essentialist', *Archiv für Geschichte der Philosophie* 62, 1980, pp. 1 ff.

Bonitz, H., *Index Aristotelicus*, Berlin, 1870.

Burnet, J., *Early Greek Philosophy* (4th ed.), London, 1930.

Carteron, H., *La Notion de Force dans le Système d'Aristote*, Paris, 1924.

Charlton, W., *Aristotle's Physics, I and II*, Oxford, 1970.

Chen, C.-H., 'The Relation between the terms ἐνέργεια and ἐντελέχεια in the Philosophy of Aristotle', *Classical Quarterly* N.S. VIII, 1958, pp. 12 ff.

Cherniss, H. F., *Aristotle's Criticism of Presocratic Philosophy*, Baltimore, 1935.

—, *Aristotle's Criticism of Plato and the Academy*, New York, 1962.

Cicero, *De Natura Deorum*, ed. A. S. Pease, Cambridge, Mass., 1955.

de Corte, M., 'La Causalité du Premier Moteur dans la Philosophie Aristotélicienne', *Revue de l'histoire de la philosophie* V, 1931, pp. 105 ff.

Dijksterhuis, E. J., *The Mechanization of the World Picture*, tr. C. Dikshoorn, Oxford, 1961.

Duhem, P., *Le Système du Monde*, Paris, 1913.

Düring, I., 'Aristotle on Ultimate Principles from "Nature and Reality": Protrepticus fr. 13', in *Aristotle and Plato in the Mid-Fourth Century*, edd. I. Düring and G. E. L. Owen, Göteborg, 1960, pp. 35 ff.

Geach, P. T., *God and the Soul*, London, 1969.

Gomperz, T., *The Greek Thinkers*, tr. L. Magnus and G. G. Berry, London, 1901-12.

Gotthelf, A., 'Aristotle's Conception of Final Causality', *Review of Metaphysics* XXX, 1976, pp. 226 ff.

Grene, M., 'Aristotle and Modern Biology', in *Topics in the Philosophy of Biology*, edd. M. Grene and E. Mendelsohn, Dordrecht, 1976, pp. 3 ff. (first printed in *Journal of the History of Ideas* XXX).

Guthrie, W. K. C., 'The Development of Aristotle's Theology I', *Classical Quarterly* XXVII, 1933, pp. 162 ff.

—, *Aristotle on the Heavens* (Loeb ed.), Cambridge, Mass., 1939.

—, *A History of Greek Philosophy*, Cambridge, 1965.

Hamelin, O., *Le Système d'Aristote*, Paris, 1920.

Hardie, R. P. and Gaye, R. K., *Physica, The Works of Aristotle Translated into English*, ed. W. D. Ross, vol. II, Oxford, 1930.

Heath, D. D., 'On Some Misconceptions of Aristotle's Doctrine of Causation and τό αύτόματον', *Journal of Philology* VII, 1877.

Hein, H., 'Molecular Biology vs. Organicism', *Synthese* XX, 1969, pp. 238 ff.

Hintikka, J., *Time and Necessity*, Oxford, 1973.

Hume, D., *A Treatise of Human Nature*, Oxford, 1888.

Joachim, H. H., 'Aristotle's Conception of Chemical Combination', *Journal of Philology* XXIX, 1903-4, pp. 72 ff.

—, *Aristotle On Coming-To-Be and Passing-Away, a Revised Text with Introduction and Commentary*, Oxford, 1922.

Jones, B., 'Aristotle's Introduction of Matter', *Philosophical Review* LXXXIII, 1974, pp. 474 ff.

Jowett, B., *Aristotle's Politics* (translation), Oxford, 1905.

Kosman, L. A., 'Aristotle's Definition of Motion', *Phronesis* XIV, 1969, pp. 40 ff.

Logan, J. D., 'The Aristotelian Concept of ΦΥΣΙΣ', *Philosophical Review* VI, 1899, pp. 18 ff.

—, 'The Aristotelian Teleology', ibid. p. 386 ff.

Lyons, J., *Introduction to Theoretical Linguistics*, Cambridge, 1968.

Mackie, J. L., *The Cement of the Universe*, Oxford, 1974.

Manicas, P. T., 'Aristotle, Dispositions and Occult Powers', *Review of Metaphysics* XVIII, 1964-5, pp. 678 ff.

Mansion, A., *Introduction à la Physique Aristotélicienne* (2nd ed.), Louvain-Paris, 1946.

McMullin, E., 'Four Senses of Potency', in *The Concept of Matter in Greek and Mediaeval Philosophy*, ed. E. McMullin, Notre Dame, 1963.

Moraux, P., *Aristote: du Ciel*, Paris, 1965.

Mourelatos, A. P. D., 'Aristotle's "Powers" and Modern Empiricism', *Ratio* IX, 1967, pp. 97 ff.

—, Review of *New Essays on Plato and Aristotle*, ed. R. Bambrough, *Philosophical Review* LXXVII, 1968, pp. 512 ff.

Northrop, F. S. C., *Science and First Principles*, Cambridge, 1931.

Owen, G. E. L., 'Inherence', *Phronesis* X, 1965, pp. 97 ff.

Owen, G. E. L., 'The Platonism of Aristotle', *Proceedings of the British Academy* L, 1965, pp. 125 ff.

—, 'τιθέναι τὰ φαινόμενα', in *Aristotle*, ed. J. M. E. Moravcsik, New York, 1967, pp. 167 ff. (first appeared in *Aristote et les Problèmes de la Méthode*, ed. S. Mansion, Louvain, 1961, pp. 83 ff.).

—, 'Aristotelian Pleasures', *Proceedings of the Aristotelian Society*, 1972, pp. 135 ff.

—, 'Aristotle on Time', *Motion and Time, Space and Matter*, edd. P. K. Machamer and R. G. Turnbull, Columbus, 1976, pp. 3 ff.

Peacocke, A. R., 'The Molecular Organisation of Life', in *Biology and Personality*, ed. I. T. Ramsey, Oxford, 1965, pp. 17 ff.

Penner, T., 'Verbs and the Identity of Actions', in *Ryle*, edd. O. P. Wood and G. Pitcher, London, 1971, pp. 393 ff.

Philoponus, J., *In Aristotelis Physicorum libros octo Commentaria*, ed. H. Vitelli, Berlin 1887-8.

Plato, *Opera*, ed. J. Burnet, Oxford, 1899-1906.

Polanyi, M., 'Life's Irreducible Structure', in *Topics in the Philosophy of Biology*, edd. M. Grene and E. Mendelsohn, Dordrecht, 1976, pp. 128 ff. (first printed in *Science* 160).

Potts, T. C., 'States, Activities and Performances', *Proceedings of the Aristotelian Society Supplement* XXXIX, 1965, pp. 65 ff.

Robin, L., *Aristote*, Paris, 1944.

Ross, W. D., *Aristotle's Metaphysics, A Revised Text with Introduction and Commentary*, Oxford, 1924.

—, *Aristotle's Physics, A Revised Text with Introduction and Commentary*, Oxford, 1936.

Sambursky, S., *The Physical World of the Greeks*, tr. M. Dagut, London, 1963.

Simplicius, *In Aristotelis Physicorum libros octo Commentaria*, ed. H. Diels, Berlin, 1882-5.

Skemp, J. B., *The Theory of Motion in Plato's Later Dialogues*, Cambridge, 1942.

Solmsen, F., 'Platonic Influences in the Formation of Aristotle's Physical System', in *Aristotle and Plato in the Mid-Fourth Century*, edd. I. Düring and G. E. L. Owen, Göteborg, 1960, pp. 213 ff.

—, *Aristotle's System of the Physical World*, Ithaca, 1960.

Sorabji, R., 'Aristotle on the Instant of Change', *Articles on Aristotle*, edd. J. Barnes, M. Schofield and R. Sorabji, vol. III, London, 1979, pp. 159 ff.

—, *Necessity, Cause and Blame, Perspectives on Aristotle's Theory*, London, 1980.

Stocks, J. L., *De Caelo, The Works of Aristotle Translated into English*, ed. W. D. Ross, vol. II, Oxford, 1930.

Taylor, A. E., *A Commentary on Plato's Timaeus*, Oxford, 1928.

Taylor, C. C. W., 'States, Activities and Performances', *Proceedings of the Aristotelian Society Supplement* XXXIX, 1965, pp. 85 ff.

Themistius, *In Aristotelis Physica Paraphrasis*, ed. H. Schenkl, Berlin, 1900.

Vlastos, G., 'Zeno's Race Course', in *Studies in Presocratic Philosophy*, edd. R. E. Allen and D. J. Furley, London, 1975, vol. II, pp. 201 ff. (first printed in *Journal of the History of Philosophy* IV, 1966, pp. 95 ff.).

von Arnim, H., *Die Entstehung der Gotteslehre des Aristoteles*, Vienna, 1931.

von Wright, G. H., *Norm and Action*, London, 1963.

Waterlow, S., 'Affecting and Being Affected', *Mind* LXXIX, 1970, pp. 92 ff.

—, *Passage and Possibility, A Study of Aristotle's Modal Concepts*, Oxford, 1982.

Wicksteed, P. H. and Cornford, F. M., *Aristotle, The Physics* (Loeb ed.), London–New York, 1929.

Wieland, W., 'Das Problem des Prinzipienforschung und die aristotelische Physik', *Kant-Studien* LII, 1960-1, pp. 206 ff., translated in *Articles on Aristotle*, edd. J. Barnes, M. Schofield, and R. Sorabji, vol. I, London, 1975, pp. 127 ff.

—, *Die aristotelische Physik*, Göttingen, 1962. (Ch. 16 on teleology is translated in *Articles on Aristotle*, vol. I, pp. 141 ff. (full reference above).)

Zeller, E., *Aristotle and the Earlier Peripatetics*, tr. B. F. C. Costelloe and J. H. Muirhead, New York, 1962.

Index